The Political Economy of Greek Growth up to 2030

Series Editor
Panagiotis E. Petrakis
Department of Economics
National and Kapodistrian University of Athens
Athens, Greece

This book series analyzes the medium to long-term prospects of Greece's political economy by studying concepts such as sustainability, sustainable governance and political functioning, economic inclusivity, cultural behaviors, and economic dynamic growth through an evolutionary approach. This series also publishes policy-oriented books outlining steps for increased economic growth and a sustainable future for the Greek economy. This series stands out in that the books depict the conditions that must prevail for the Greek economy to escape the economic stagnation that has lingered from persistent economic recession.

Using Greece as a lens to discuss pressing questions, this series will be of interest to economists interested in Eurozone policies, economic growth, evolutionary economics, and more.

More information about this series at
http://www.palgrave.com/gp/series/16496

Panagiotis E. Petrakis · Pantelis C. Kostis

The Evolution of the Greek Economy

Past Challenges and Future Approaches

palgrave
macmillan

Panagiotis E. Petrakis
Department of Economics
National and Kapodistrian University
of Athens
Athens, Greece

Pantelis C. Kostis
Department of Economics
National and Kapodistrian University
of Athens
Athens, Greece

ISSN 2662-7248 ISSN 2662-7256 (electronic)
The Political Economy of Greek Growth up to 2030
ISBN 978-3-030-47209-2 ISBN 978-3-030-47210-8 (eBook)
https://doi.org/10.1007/978-3-030-47210-8

This Palgrave Macmillan imprint is published by the registered company Springer Nature Switzerland AG
The registered company address is: Gewerbestrasse 11, 6330 Cham, Switzerland

Preface

The series of books with the general title of *The Political Economy of Greek Growth Up to 2030* analyze the medium to long-term prospects of the Greek reality—including the Covid-19 pandemic—in view of the political economy. They combine the notions of sustainability, sustainable governance and political operation, the inclusivity of the economic system, and cultural behavior, with the requirements of economic dynamic growth. The concurrent influence from those five areas, through suitable structural reforms, is a necessary prerequisite to change the production prototype of the Greek economy, which will ensure a medium and long-term economic development and growth. This viewpoint has an evolutionary foundation. The view supported is that conditions can be created for the Greek economy, after the 2008 depression, to avoid losing another decade due to Covid-19 and to create the necessary conditions for a great growth transformation up to 2030.

The target of this book series, presented in successive volumes, is to assess the current situation of the Greek economy and detect future potential for development and growth, particularly on a medium to long-term horizon. It represents the next step in a series of books: *The Greek Economy and the Crisis, Challenges and Responses*, Panagiotis E. Petrakis (2011), New York and Heidelberg, Springer; and *A New Growth Model for the Greek Economy, Requirements for the Long-Term Sustainability*, Panagiotis E. Petrakis (2016), New York, Palgrave Macmillan. These books marked the conditions in which the Greek economy entered Great Depression

(2008–2018) and put forth initial thoughts on exiting the crisis. In this current book series, conditions for the exit of the economy from the crisis are analyzed, along with its entry into a new period of development and growth.

The first book, in the series, under the title *The New Political Economy of Greece Up to 2030*, New York, Palgrave Macmillan (forthcoming) examined the possibility of application and findings of developmental theory and policy in the Greek economy and thus set the theoretical framework of empirical analysis. This book *The Evolution of the Greek Economy: Past Challenges and Future Approaches* addresses successively the issues of what we call "normality" in the Greek economy by the beginning of 2020 when the Covid-19 great recession occurred and how to exceed this "normality," which has now incorporated two major recessions: those of 2010 and 2020. The emphasis is on structural reforms and fiscal management, on the cultural background on how people and society make their decisions. Attention is also paid to analyzing the productive organization of the economy on the basis of its technological structure and the use of input-output tables, the role of power centers, power pooling and oligopolistic organization of the economy, etc. The analyses, as well as the accompanying projections, extend up to 2030.

In the third book of the series, under the title *Policies for a Stronger Greek Economy: Actions for the Next Decade*, the conditions for the implementation of policies (fiscal, monetary, but mainly reforms) that are necessary for the Greek economy to enter—after the Covid-19 crisis—in a decade of economic growth are presented. To do this, as has been pointed out in the previous two volumes, policies must be developed in six areas: Policies for immediate action, mainly monetary and fiscal policies aimed at meeting the production gap in the short and medium term. In the medium—and the long-term, policies are developed on five issues: sustainability policies, sustainable governance policies, enhanced inclusivity policies, pro-growth social behavior policies and policies for dynamic economic growth with medium and long-term horizon. Moreover, a simulation of the policy implementation is provided, as well as a risk assessment and a scenario analysis presenting five different scenarios for the Greek economy (normal, optimal, European growth I, European growth II and downside), and the possibility for the Greek economy to join after 2021 and by 2030 a third wave of growth.

Athens, Greece

Panagiotis E. Petrakis
Pantelis C. Kostis

Acknowledgments This book is based on the scientific contribution of Dr. K. Kafka and Mr. D. Valsamis (Researcher), with the help of Mr. G. Vasilis and Mr. M. Skotoris. The book also contains the valuable contributions of Dr. K. Loizos for Chapters 1 and 2 and Dr. A. Efstratoglou for Chapter 10, which we would like to thank. The main collaborator Mrs. E. Giouli, as well as the other collaborators in the office, offered us the opportunity to deal with the completion of our research. NKUA offered its support. Our families offered us their patience.

Introduction

The analysis of Greek political economy up to 2030, starting at the time of the creation of the Greek State, covers the abovementioned five key areas of action of human economic and social activity, since development is of a human and interdisciplinary nature.

This specific structure of thought also serves to prioritize the economic policy objectives which is extremely useful for the next book in the series, presenting policies aimed at economic development and growth in the Greek economy under the title *Policies for a Stronger Greek Economy. Actions for the Next Decade*, New York, Palgrave Macmillan (forthcoming).

Obviously, the rate of growth in the future as in the past and in all economies will result from the influence of four factors: the contribution of innovation and technology, the labor factor, capital factor (whether internal or external), and the Total Factor Productivity, including the impact of all other factors, such as the institutional framework, behaviors and all other factors. But all these "other" factors obtain values from primary sources, i.e., at the pace of change in economic reforms.

The central issue of this book is to organize a medium—to long-term projection of the forecasts for the growth of the Greek economy under two different circumstances: Business as Usual (the so-called normal scenario used in the book which we contains both 2010 and 2020 recessions up to April 2020) and under "ideal conditions" (the so-called optimum scenario). This is the scenario in which growth in Greece is following a development which can be described as a target for GDP growth up to 2030.

It is therefore a central issue in this book to demonstrate the realism of the optimum scenario. In other words, to demonstrate the link between reforms and the growth rate indicated, since reforms are an external variable and its regulation is subject to policy (policies and society) setting it so that the economy can return to an upward trend.

The rate of growth achieved is affected by the evolution of society and the economy to date, including, of course, the Covid-19 crisis. As in the first volume, we consider this crisis to be very serious, but with a short-term impact, which repositions the scenarios of the future. This is also reflected in our forecasts.

This book, following the evolution of the Greek economy, includes three sectors of detection developed in the three parts of the book: The evolution of economic history, Institutions and Cultural Background from the existence of the new Greek State to date as it develops in Part 1, Evolution of Sustainability, Governance Inclusivity, Culture and Economic growth developed in Part 2 and finally the Long term Evolution presented in Part 3. The first part consists of four chapters, the second part of six chapter and the third part consists of two chapters.

Chapter 1 presents the four defaults that make Greece a dependent state throughout its recent history, since the history of modern Greece can be described as an economic history of defaults episodes closely related to its external indebtedness: (1) The default of 1826, in the midst of the Greek Independence War. (2) The defaults of the periods 1837–38 and 1843–44. (3) The default of 1893, which coincided with the current crisis which plagued the poorly diversified Greek economy. (4) The default of 1932 just a few months after the wake of the 1931 banking crisis. On these events the (unacknowledged) default of 2010–2012, again in the aftermath of the US 2007–2008 subprime crisis could be added.

Chapter 2 presents the institutional evolution in the Greek economy. The Greek economy has been a small open economy since the formation of the Greek state in the 1830s. Hence, the external political and economic relationships have always been a significant part of its history. The Great Powers and their role in Greek political affairs did not just lay the foundations of a dependent state. They also defined, to some degree, the alternative paths and the future course of the Greek state towards modernization. Thus, this chapter presents the attend to modernize the Greek economy during the nineteenth and the twentieth century. The development of hierarchies in historical perspective is presented as well as the non-diversification of investment and production.

Chapter 3 aims to present the Greek economy in the context of geostrategic developments in the wider region of Southeastern Europe. The production system of the Greek economy operates in an international environment. In this context the concept of National Power has an important priority, because it ultimately determines the terms of the game at the global level and in the background the terms of international exchange. At the same time, it is particularly useful to detect the systemic risks that the Greek economy faces over time and which have determined to a significant extent the productive model of the economy and the behavior of Greek society. Finally, some facts regarding the pandemic of Covid-19 are presented and the global and domestic consequences are discussed.

Chapter 4 presents the idiosyncratic institutions and cultural traits and the formation of a stagnated growth prototype in the Greek economy. Optimal growth requires pro-growth institutions and culture. In an optimal growth pattern, institutions and culture facilitate entrepreneurship and innovation. In contrast, if the development and coevolution of institutions and culture are distorted, growth can become permanently stagnant, with a distorted creative destruction process causing weak entrepreneurship and innovation activity. Policymakers should, therefore, plan and implement pro-growth structural changes to institutions and culture that account for their coevolution process. Otherwise, imported growth (i.e., incoming capital flows or innovation) must be relied upon to form an exogenous pro-growth prototype that promotes growth, entrepreneurship, and innovation.

In Chapter 5 the focus is on matters concerning the environment, renewable energy sources, natural resources and formerly on population evolution, recognizing the role of epidemics/pandemics as black swans in the operation of the economic system. So, the chapter presents the above factors for Greece, thereby highlighting opportunities and threats. Sustainable Development is not only aimed at solving pre-existing problems but also at reshaping the economic and social system. Specifically, Sustainable Development seeks to meet the needs of modern (and future) generations without jeopardizing the ability of future generations to meet their own needs. Obviously, the Covid-19 crisis has come to change the priorities of human society by putting health issues first.

Moreover, the changes in the international economic system and in geopolitical power relations over the last decades have had a decisive impact on the ways in which states are now involved in shaping the economy. The globalization of markets, special competitions, the Covid-19 pandemic, new environmental and regional challenges, as well as the divisions emerging at socio-economic and cultural level, redefine the role of the state. Chapter 6 aims to present the quality and sustainability of governance in Greece, highlighting many of the weaknesses that characterize it. A good effort to measure the quality of governance is the World Governance Indicators formulated by the World Bank. The quality of political institutions has a significant impact on economic growth.

Chapter 7 presents issues related to the issue of inclusivity in Greek society, in particular compared to the EU-28 average, which relate to labor market conditions, issues related to income distribution and observed inequalities, the level of poverty and the quality of education. Lastly, the way the Covid-19 pandemic affects some aspects of inclusivity is presented. Despite the increase in prosperity and wealth for most economies, there have been a number of problems that prevent inclusivity in terms of exploiting opportunities by all. In most developed economies there are issues related to high income disparities, to reduction of the size of the middle class, to non-equal opportunities between men and women, to access to education, etc. The Covid-19 crisis has intensified several of these trends.

In Chapter 8 the cultural evolution of the Greek society is presented, as one of the most critical factors that have affected the responses to the crisis, but not adequately enough emphasized in the economic policy that was undertaken to confront the crisis. The key developments that are observed and related to the Greek social environment and related to the quality of life of Greeks are presented, as well as the political trends and the economic behavior of Greek society, and the trend towards loss-aversion behaviors. Lastly, the effects of Covid-19 pandemic on human behaviors are presented.

Chapter 9 seeks to present a clear picture of how the Greek economy has been developed up to 2019. The analysis includes critical issues that have severely affected the Greek economy, such as the internal and external balances, the evolution of structural reforms, the competitiveness, the investments, the banking system, the credit system, the entrepreneurship development, the issue of the debt, and the overburden of taxation. These developments are expected to significantly change the image of growth in the Greek economy and the image of growth accounting up to 2030. Moreover, the channels through which the Covid-19 pandemic affects the Greek economic system in the short- and the long-term are presented.

Chapter 10 attempts an initial investigation into whether and how the country's productive model changed during the economic crisis (2008–2018). The chapter also attempts to highlight the problem related to the productive structure of the Greek economy and the fact that no significant differentiation in production is achieved, with the result that there is a need to change the production model. This was highlighted by the emergence of the Covid-19 pandemic and its impact on economic production Lastly, the chapter presents short-run effects of the Covid-19 pandemic on the gross value added of the economic sectors of the economy.

The purpose of Chapter 11 is to set the background to capture the estimations concerning the Greek economy in the period from 2020 to 2030. Thus, the chapter presents the need for institutional and cultural changes in order for an economy to transform an idiosyncratic, interrelated with stagnated characteristics, model into an optimal pro-growth model, with direct reference to the Greek economy. Moreover, the relationship between TFP and structural reforms in the case of the Greek economy until 2019 and the effect of the reforms on the country's GDP are presented. Besides, the Normal Scenario (business as usual) and an Optimal Pro-Growth Scenario for the Greek economy for the period from 2020 to 2030 are described.

Finally, Chapter 12 provides an overview of the expected development for a number of macroeconomic figures up to 2030. For this purpose, the relevant developments for two scenarios are described: The Normal Scenario (business as usual) and the Optimal Scenario (pro-growth scenario). In addition, the aim of the chapter is to highlight the role of structural reforms in the implementation of a pro-growth scenario. Besides, the expected developments in the Greek economy until 2030 for the two scenarios are presented for variables such as GDP and other basic macroeconomic variables, potential output and output gap, public debt, competitiveness, investments and inclusive growth.

Contents

Abbreviations

EastMed	Eastern Mediterranean
EC	European Commission
ECB	European Central Bank
EPI	Environmental Performance Index
ESM	European Stability Mechanism
FDIs	Foreign Direct Investments
GEM	Global Economic Model
GVA	Gross Value Added
HBID	Hellenic Bank for Industrial Development
IFC	International Financial Control
IMF	International Monetary Fund
IOBE	The Foundation of Economic and Industrial Research
ITGI	Interconnector Turkey–Greece–Italy
KEPE	Centre of Planning and Economic Research
MDGs	Millennium Development Goals
MoU	Memorandum of Understanding
NAIRU	Non-Accelerating Inflation Rate of Unemployment
NATO	North Atlantic Treaty Organization
NBG	National Bank of Greece
NIIP	Net International Investment position
NPEs	Non-Performing Exposures
NPLs	Non-Performing Loans
OECD	Organization for Economic Cooperation and Development
OFED	Organization for the Financing of Economic Development
OID	Organization for Industrial Development
OTE	Hellenic Telecommunications Organization

PSI	Private Sector Involvement
REER	Real Effective Exchange Rate Index
SEV	Hellenic Federation of Enterprises
TAP	Trans Adriatic Pipeline
TFP	Total Factor Productivity
UN	United Nations

List of Figures

List of Tables

PART I

The Evolution of Economic History, Institutions and Cultural Background

CHAPTER 1

A Brief Economic History of Repeated Defaults

1.1 Introduction

Our era is characterized by a globalized economic environment. The concept of debt (public or private) reflects the promise of payment on the part of the debtor and the risk that the lender undertakes this promise not to be realized. Debt means interdependence, often one-sided, either to one or the other part. On the one hand, the credit risk assumed by the lender is directly related to both the economic conditions of a country and its institutional environment as it has been formed historically. This risk, together with the risk of strategic bankruptcy of the debtor, constitute a form of dependence of the lender on the debtor. On the other hand, the loan agreement contains the element of the debtor's dependence on the lender to the extent that it specifies the way of imposing its terms and implicitly includes the threat of non-renewal of financing in the event of an inability to repay. This dependence takes a more dramatic form when it comes to the debt of sovereign states. In any case, the enforcement of the terms of a contract and the protection of both parties is associated with

The authors would like to thank Dr. Konstantinos Loizos for his contribution to this chapter.

P. E. Petrakis and P. C. Kostis, *The Evolution of the Greek Economy*,
The Political Economy of Greek Growth up to 2030,
https://doi.org/10.1007/978-3-030-47210-8_1

the existence or the deficiency of the necessary institutional environment to ensure compliance.

In this sense, the credit risk for the lender and the risk of non-access to future financing for the debtor, become an institutional risk that affects both parties and reflects the characteristics of the political economy of the development of a particular country. This risk is not static but it is a concept with primarily historical characteristics as it is subject to changes and fluctuations during time.

From the emergence of the Greek national movement, which in 1821 led to the revolution of the Greeks against the Ottoman Empire in order to establish an independent state which was recognized in 1830, until today, Greece faces a history of repeated defaults. A key feature of the modern history of Greece is the conclusion of loans of large amounts on strict terms that have resulted for all these years into a state of high dependence of the Greek economy from its lenders.

In this chapter, the repeated defaults episodes of the Greek economy from 1827 to the present are initially presented (Section 1.2), while in sect. 1.3 the fact of the high dependence of the Greek economy on the large economies that lend it over time is presented.

1.2 The Defaults

One could, in many ways, describe the history of modern Greece as an economic history of repeated episodes of defaults which are, in fact, closely linked to its external debt. In the development of the Greek economy, at least five of the most important defaults of the modern Greek state (Reinhart & Trebesch, 2015; Dertilis, 2014, p. 37) stand out: (1) The default of 1827 which took place during the national liberation struggle and only four years before the modern Greek state was recognized by The Great Powers of the time. (2) The default of 1837–1838 and 1843–1844. (3) The default of 1893 which coincided with the raisin crisis. (4) The announcement of suspension of payments of 1932 which took place in the aftermath of the Great Depression of 1929 and the banking crisis of 1931 and just a few months after the British pound abandoned the gold standard. (5) Finally, the recent (not officially recognized) default of 2010–2012, which once again took place immediately after an event with significant international implications such as the crisis that began with subprime mortgages in the USA and developed in the financial crisis of 2007–2008.

The default of the 1820s concerned two major loans contracted by the provisional revolutionary government to finance the Greek War of Independence. These loans were concluded on particularly onerous terms. Specifically, out of loans totaling 2.8 million English pounds, only 1.3 million eventually reached the hands of the Greek side and this was because these loans were issued at less than 60% of their nominal value while the various brokerage costs and commissions were particularly high (Reinhart & Trebesch, 2015). This, however, was not a Greek distinctiveness, but seems to have been a common practice in the City of London for loans to foreign governments inasmuch as the temporary revolutionary government was recognized as such by foreigners. Indeed, all loans of this kind contracted in the London Stock Exchange between the years 1822 and 1825 were issued at high rates of discount as the rates of issue ranged from 58% the lowest to 91.5% the highest. The former concerned a loan to Mexico while the latter was a loan received from the state of Naples. The discount rate of the Greek loan was, in fact, the second highest (Andreadis, 1904, p. 16). These Greek loans were of absolute necessity given the desperate situation in which the finances of the Provisional Revolutionary Government were. The regular revenues of the government were extremely uncertain, covering only a third of the regular expenditures. It should be noted that half of this revenue came from Crete, which was quite far from the main theater of operations of the War of Independence. Unfortunately, however, the conclusion of the loans coincided with the outbreak of an internal political conflict which eventually resulted to the first civil war (1824–1826) (Andreadis, 1904, pp. 14–15). The terms of the first loan included a capital of 800 thousand English pounds, a repayment period of 36 years and an interest rate of 5%. The Greek provisional government offered the lenders its revenues as collateral for the repayment of the interest on the loan and national land as collateral against the principal of the loan. However, due to the issue price at 59%, the actual borrowed capital was only 348.8 thousand English pounds after deducting advances on principal repayment and interest plus commissions. The second loan had a face value of two million English pounds, and the contract was signed in 1825. However, the loan's 200,000 bonds were issued at a price of 55.5% of their nominal value. The final amount of the loan was reduced to 816 thousand English pounds after deduction of advances and commissions (Andreadis, 1904, pp. 15–24). However, unfortunately neither of these two loans was used as effectively as expected to finance the conduct of the war. Part of the funds of the second loan never arrived in Greece because it was used to repurchase bonds of the first loan. The portion of the loan allocated to build warships had not the expected results. What remained of the two loans was eventually used to finance the civil wars of the revolution (Andreadis, 1904, p. 19, 49–50).

Eventually the revolutionary government declared suspension of payments in 1826 which lasted until 1878, while the country regained access to capital markets again in 1879 (Reinhart & Trebesch, 2015; Petrakis 1992, pp. 38–39). Meanwhile, various negotiations have taken place in order the two sides to reach an agreement on debt settlement, which were, however, interrupted by periods of political instability and disagreement. However, the newly established, which inherited a destroyed production base due to the war of Independence, desperately needed a new loan to cover its current expenses (Andreadis, 1904, pp. 75–76). Finally, for political reasons, the three Great Powers (France, Great Britain, and Russia) who agreed to Greek Independence, accepted to guarantee a new loan of 60 million francs. This loan would be drawn from the international capital markets but the agreed amount would be paid to Greece under specific conditions, among which was for the country to put its public finances in order (Reinhart & Trebesch, 2015; Andreadis, 1904, pp. 78–80). The agreed interest rate of the loan was 5% and the repayment would have to be within 36 years. Only one-third of the loan was finally used to cover the financing needs of the Greek state, while the remaining two-thirds were devoted to the repayment of principal and interest on previous loans as well as to cover other expenses. Additionally, of this one-third, about half were paid by the Greek state to Turkey for the purchase of the province of Fthiotis, while the rest financed the expenses of the army and the Bavarian Regency (Andreadis, 1904, pp. 83–86). The loan was concluded in 1833 but the Bavarian administration declared suspension of payments in 1838 and 1843. (Reinhart & Trebesch, 2015).

Before gaining access to international markets again, the Greek state attempted, as early as 1862, to take advantage of its special relationship with the largest Greek bank, the National Bank of Greece, in order to obtain a series of loans. The supposed uses of the loan funds varied, including the financing of the government's foreign policy, especially regarding Crete, the repayment of past loans and to cover budget expenditure (Pantelakis, 1995, pp. 41–42). It is important to state that the public finances had gone to various phases throughout the period from the suspension of payments in 1843 to 1869. The first period of 1844–1849 was marked by the anxious attempt of the Greek government to balance its budget, but without much success due to the international crisis of 1847 and the political unrest in Europe in 1848. During the second period 1850–1860 the attempt to achieve fiscal surpluses was more successful. These surpluses were used to finance public constructions, such as the construction of roads, and the purchase of steamships. On the contrary, in the next period 1861–1865, the political developments that followed Otto's eviction reflected to a regression between budget deficits and surpluses. Finally, the period 1866–1869 was marked by the Cretan revolution, which had, as a budgetary effect, the permanent deficits in the budget of the modern Greek state (Petrakis, 1985, pp. 41–48)

However, by 1879, Greece could again turn to the international capital markets for financing, as an agreement had been reached with its creditors regarding the independence loans (Pantelakis, 1995, pp. 47–48). Then the Greek state seized the opportunity to borrow significant amounts in order to repay its old debt and to lift the forced circulation of the currency (Reinhart & Trebesch, 2015; Pantelakis, 1995, p. 49). Thus, on 2 April 1879 a loan agreement was signed with the French bank Comptoir d'escompte de Paris which provided for a loan of 60 million gold francs, at an interest rate of 6% and securing the income from stamp duty (Pantelakis, 1995, pp. 48–49). In June 1887 the Greek government concluded a new loan with the Comptoir d'escompte de Paris. The nominal value of the loan was 135 million gold francs and supposed to be used for the purchase of warships and firearms. To cover the loan, the Greek government offered its revenues from the state monopolies of salt, oil, playing cards, cigarette paper, and Naxos emery. The contractual interest rate was 4% and the repayment period extended to 75 years. In addition, four new loans were agreed upon in March and May, 1889, as well as in May, 1892 and 1893. The first of these loans was signed with the House of Hambro and Son and had a nominal value of 30 million gold francs. The second was issued with a nominal value of 125 million gold francs and was agreed with the Antony Gibbs and Sons banks of London, Bleichroder of Berlin, and the Bank of Constantinople. The interest rate on both of these loans was 4% and the total amount was used to repay old debts. The loans of 1892 and 1893 had a nominal value of 16.5 million gold francs and 100 million francs, respectively, while the sponsors were both Greek and foreign banks including the Bank of Constantinople and Hambro (Pantelakis, 1995, pp. 54–57).

Despite the high level of debt, the Greek government maintained large budget deficits at the same time that the country was facing a deep crisis in its export sector. Indeed, in the early 1890s, the exports of raisins, which made up two-thirds of Greek exports, fell by more than 50%. As the drachma sharply depreciated, the country was unable to service its huge external debt and declared bankruptcy. Thus the second significant episode of default took place in 1893. The situation became even worse after the unfortunate Greek-Turkish War of 1897. The country regained access to international markets in 1902 but, effectively, until the defeat of 1897 negotiations between the Greek government and its creditors were slow (Reinhart & Trebesch, 2015).

One would say that the suspension of payments of 1893 was a milestone in Greek economic and political history. Indeed, this default and the consequences of the defeat in the Greek-Turkish War of 1897 led to the imposition of International Financial Control in 1898, which is considered a leading moment of foreign intervention in the administration of public finances.

In fact, in 1898 Greece signed a peace agreement with Turkey, including the obligation of Greece to pay Turkey 4 million pounds for war reparations. The Greek state could not save the necessary funds, hence had to turn again to borrowing from abroad. This, however, required the settlement of old debts (Pantelakis, 1995, p. 58). Austria-Hungary, France, Germany, Great Britain, Italy, and Russia took part in the negotiations. However, only France, Great Britain, and Russia granted a rescue loan in 1898. This loan was accompanied by the imposition of an International Financial Control Commission which aimed to ensure its regular repayment. The proceeds of the loan were used by the Greek government to pay war reparations in Turkey, and to service old debts. In addition, foreign creditors demanded the repayment of the loan of 1833. It is noteworthy that all these loan obligations had been repaid almost completely until the next default of the Greek state in 1932. What was left was paid to private creditors by France and Great Britain. France recovered a portion of its own contribution in 1965 (Reinhart & Trebesch, 2015).

The positive effects of the imposition of International Economic Control were already obvious at the dawn of the twentieth century. The government was given the opportunity to secure a number of loans with the participation of both local and foreign banks. In 1907, the Greek government concluded a loan of 20 million gold francs nominal value with the National Bank of Greece. However, the necessary funds came from a group of banks among which were the Ionian Bank, the Bank of Athens, the Banque D' Orient, and the foreign banks Comptoir Nationale d' Escompte de Paris and Hambro. The borrowed funds were used for national defense purposes (Pantelakis, 1995, p. 61). In 1910 a new loan agreement was signed between the Greek government and the banks: National Bank of Greece, Bank of Athens, Bank of the East, Hambro, Erlanger, Comptoir Nationale d' Escompte de Paris and Société Générale. The agreement provided for an advance of 40 million francs in the form of a loan with a repayment term of 4 years and an interest rate of 5%. In addition, a new loan of 150 million francs with a repayment period of 50 years and an interest rate of 4% would be granted. However, the original contract was amended in April 1911, and the loan amount was reduced to 110 million francs. Part of the payments of this loan were used to repay the advance of 40 million francs along with other expenses. The main part of the loan was to be used for the financing of infrastructure projects such as railways, flood control and drainage projects and the development of ports. In fact, however, the loan was used to purchase military equipment and to prepare the country for the Balkan wars (Pantelakis, 1995, pp. 62–63). At the beginning of 1914 the Greek government signed a new contract with the same banks that had granted the loan of 1911. These banks agreed to cover financing with a nominal value of 250 million francs and which would be served under the supervision of the committee of International Financial Control. This loan was covered with French funds by 70%, and English and Greek funds by 30% and was used to repay old government obligations from the time of the Balkan wars (Pantelakis, 1995, p. 65).

During World War I, the Greek government tried to cover its expenses by using the act of 1910 ("ΓΧΜΒ"). This law provided for the issuance of banknotes by the National Bank of Greece which would have as a counter value foreign currency that would be granted by the Allies in the name of the Greek government (Pantelakis, 1995, pp. 68–71). According to a saying of Eleftherios Venizelos himself, the National Bank at that time had transformed to "treasurer of the state" (Pantelakis, 1988, p. 33). However, at a later time, the Great Powers belonging to the Entente warned the Greek government that they would cut off any financial aid to the country if the result of the referendum result was in favor of King Constantine (Pantelakis, 1988, p. 163). Thus, the Allies, after December

8, 1920, canceled the original agreement and the National Bank of Greece found itself in the difficult position of issuing notes without any ability to be exchanged for gold. Although the expansive interpretation of the law in defiance of its basic principles had already begun as early as 1915, and the increase in prices since 1914, the result was a growing inflation ranged to 8.7% between the years 1919–1920, increasing to 13.4% in 1920–1921, reaching 59.8% in 1921–1922 (Tsotsoros, 1993, pp. 58–59; Kostelenos, 1995, p. 332). On March 25, 1922 the Greek government proceeded with forced internal borrowing, by splitting the banknotes in circulation. Half of each banknote would replace a new banknote, while the other half would be converted into a government bond (Pantelakis, 1995, pp. 72–73). The result of the forced loan was the expansion of the money in circulation and the doubling of inflation rates between March and December 1922 contrary to the government's expectations to hold inflation in check (Tsotsoros, 1993, p. 59).

During the period 1923–1927, Greek economic and political life is characterized by great instability and uncertainty. From April 13, 1924, when the proclamation of the Republic took place, until August 19, 1928, when Venizelos formed his last government, 9 governments had been sworn in, while 6 coups had taken place. Public finances were in a very poor condition with extraordinary expenditures exceeding 35% of total expenditures between the years 1924–1926. At the same time, the state budget revenues were not enough to cover expenses, despite the fact that indirect taxation had increased. Given the urgency of the situation created by the refugee problem and the country's desperate need for infrastructure projects, borrowing seemed a one-way street (Tsotsoros, 1993, p. 61).

Thus, after the failed military campaign in Asia Minor and the ensuing national tragedy, the government contracted a series of loans including, in 1924, a loan of 12.3 million British pounds with the Hambro, Speyer and Co banks of New York, and the National Bank of Greece. The loan was issued with a price at 88%, interest rate of 7% and a repayment term of 40 years. The loan was managed by the Refugee Rehabilitation Committee (Pantelakis, 1995, p. 73). Also, a new forced internal loan of 1.2 billion drachmas was imposed on January 23, 1926. In addition, the public debt swelled, reaching at the beginning of 1928, 100% of the national income of 1927 (Tsotsoros, 1993, p. 61).

On December 7, 1927, the Bank of Greece was established as a precondition to enable the Greek government to secure a new international loan which was necessary to finance infrastructure projects in the country (Loizos, 2012). The loan agreement was signed with Hambro's Bank and Erlanger. The agreed amount of the loan was 4 million British pounds with an interest rate of 6%, issuance price of not less than 89% and a maturity period of 40 years. Finally, a new 4.6 million pounds international loan was agreed with a group of banks including Hambros, Erlanger, Mendelssohn and Co, Amsterdam, Nederlandsche Handel-Maatschappiz NV, Crédit Suisse, Stockholms Enskilda Bank, Banca Commerciale Italiana, and the National Bank of Greece. The interest rate was agreed at 6% and the loan repayment period at 37 years (Pantelakis, 1995, pp. 75–76). This loan was arranged under the auspices of the League of Nations with three objectives: to cover budget deficits, to complete the rehabilitation of refugees and to create an exchange reserve sufficient to support the stabilization of the drachma (Tsotsoros, 1993, pp. 63–64).

The Wall Street Crash of 24 and 29 October and the Great Depression that spread almost around the world, seriously affected the Greek economy. Government revenues plummeted, prices fell and exports reduced. In addition, the country's foreign exchange reserves were depleted as the Bank of Greece fought the "battle of the drachma" after the banking crisis of 1931 and the abandonment of the gold standard by the English pound in September 1931 (Mazower, 1991, p. 208; Pantelakis, 1995, p. 77; Reinhart & Trebesch, 2015). Finally, in April 1932, Greece, too, abandoned the gold standard while the drachma depreciated by 50% leading to a doubling of the cost of servicing the foreign debt. At the same time Greece declared a unilateral suspension of payments, opening the stage of a default that lasted 32 years, until 1964, while the country was able to regain access to international capital markets a year ago. In the meantime, negotiations took place between the Greek government and its creditors and were accompanied by partial debt servicing from 1932–1939 (Reinhart & Trebesch, 2015). The negotiation process was effectively terminated in 1941 due to the German Occupation (Pantelakis, 1995, pp. 77–78) and was repeated in 1954 until a final agreement on debt restructuring was reached in 1964 (Reinhart & Trebesch, 2015).

The period from 1944 to the early 1970s was marked by the Bretton Woods international monetary system which ensured monetary stability based on the stable exchange rate between the US dollar and gold. Monetary stability was accompanied by economic reconstruction and growth that in the case of Greece began after the devaluation of 1953 (Asdrachas 2011, pp. 446–454). The oil crises of the 1970s and the global phenomenon of stagnation led the Greek economy to conditions of persistent budget deficits and rising debt as early as the early 1970s (Reinhart & Trebesch, 2015). Despite persistent inflation in the 1980s, Greece managed to control it in 1990s to enter the European Monetary Union in 2001. However, the international financial crisis of 2007–2008 revealed the existence of a state budget deficit of more than 10% of GDP while at the same time the crisis stopped the inflows of foreign capital. The situation worsened in 2010 when the country faced a sharp rise in its bond yields and could not borrow from international capital markets since then. Greece's participation in the Eurozone meant that a potential bankruptcy of the country would be rather a complicated legal situation. In fact, there was not a disclosed bankruptcy but a debt restructuring which was completed in April 2012. The debt restructuring was accompanied by unprecedented bailout loans from Eurozone countries and the International Monetary Fund. These borrowed funds touched 215 million euros between the years 2010–2013 (Reinhart & Trebesch, 2015).

1.3 The Dependent State

According to Acemoglu and Robinson (2012, p. 65) the extractive political and economic institutions interact to strengthen each other in the direction of a stable path-dependent outcome In fact, a heterogeneous combination of extractive institutions on the one hand and inclusive on the other, cannot survive for very long. In the Greek case, democratic integration institutions such as the parliament or the right to vote (for men only) were introduced quite early in the post-revolution period, namely in 1844 and 1864, respectively (Psalidopoulos, 2010). Nevertheless, the Greek political system was far from being a system of integration of different social groups and was subject to constant political instability. Examples of this instability were the confrontations between the king and the respective prime minister, the interventions of the foreign ambassadors and the fact that the country experienced the formation of 54 governments in a period of only 45 years (1865–1910), i.e., an average of a new government every 10 months (Psalidopoulos, 2010). Therefore, it is not surprising why this political system had not been able to pursue a consistent economic and institutional policy, market-friendly and with integration features as described above.

The external relations of the newly established Greek state were broadly defined by the Treaty of London of April 25/May 7, 1832. This treaty gave the Great Powers the right to intervene in the internal affairs of the new state in any case that they assumed it deviated from the course they had predetermined (Kostis, 2013, p. 264). Thus, the political atmosphere and its institutional remnants were, most of the time, influenced by external interventions that often reached or even exceeded the limits of dependence. This situation was, in general, the result of the failure of the Greek state to honor its debts. An early example was the loan concluded in the 1830s between Greece and the three Great European powers, Great Britain, Russia, and France. This agreement provided for the intervention of Powers in the finances of the state in the event of its default. Indeed, in 1843 the Powers pointed to the need for fiscal adjustment, despite the fact that the Greek people were already exhausted by the heavy taxation imposed by the Bavarian administration. The King succumbed to the external pressure and made serious budget cuts thereby causing rebellion and new default in 1843 (Reinhart & Trebesch, 2015).

Another example of the external interference was the imposition of International Financial Control in 1898 in an effort to ensure that the country would repay the debts to its creditors along with paying war reparations to Turkey. Representatives from Austria-Hungary, France, Germany, Great Britain, Italy, and Russia took part in the Committee, having the power to exercise thorough control over the Greek public finances. It is worth noting that the government that most zealously supported the imposition of international control over Greek economic affairs was the German (Reinhart & Trebesch, 2015).

A form of international economic control had also been imposed on other underdeveloped countries such as Tunisia, Morocco, Egypt, and Turkey. However, it is assumed that the control imposed on Greece was more stringent. The committee of the International Financial Control had under its control the main sources of revenue of the state and aimed to regulate public finances to ensure the regular repayment of interest payments to foreign bondholders. In addition, fiscal adjustment in the spirit of "cheap management" resulted to a gradual reduction in government funding through an increase in banknotes in circulation. In this sense, both foreign bondholders, as well as the idea of a sound management of public finances, were served (Tsotsoros, 1993, pp. 49–50).

It is true that the period covering the period from 1898 to 1909 is characterized as a period of high expectations for the country due to the stabilization of public finances and the appreciation of the drachma (Tsotsoros, 1993, p. 50). Besides, the impact of the presence of International Financial Control (IFC) in the country seems to have been beneficial in the long term as it increased confidence in the prospects of the Greek economy while there was an influx of foreign capital and remittances from migrants In any case, the existence of the IFC was a proof of the failure of the Greek state to conduct a successful economic policy without foreign aid (Mazower, 1991, p. 65, 96). However, tax reform remained the responsibility of the Greek government, which proved unable to carry it out before 1909, when the tax on net income was first introduced by Athanasios Eutaxias (Psalidopoulos, 2010). In the end, the mission of the IFC succeeded in producing primary surpluses in the Greek budget and contributed to the formation of the country's finances until the German Occupation, which ended its action (Reinhart & Trebesch, 2015). However, to the negatives of this period one can include the so-called "monetary tightness" that was the result of anti-inflationary policy. According to Xenophon Zolotas, the appreciation of the currency resulted in the discouragement of entrepreneurship (Tsotsoros, 1993, p. 51).

The suspension of payments of 1932 did not result in some form of international involvement in economic affairs of Greece this was probably due to the fragmented international monetary and political order and the shock caused by the Great Depression at the international level. However, there was an episode of international intervention which preceded the default.

As mentioned earlier, Greece was in urgent need for new loans from abroad, first to address the problem of refugee rehabilitation in 1923 and secondly to finance infrastructure projects since 1927. In both cases the League of Nations played an important role in the negotiations. First of all, the 1924 loan was granted under the strict condition that it would be used exclusively for the rehabilitation of refugees and that it would be managed by a committee which would be established specifically for this purpose, the Refugee Rehabilitation Committee (Pantelakis, 1995, p. 73; Loizos, 1994, p. 25). After all, the second loan of 1927 was granted under specific conditions imposed by the League of Nations and included the reform of the Greek banking system and the establishment of an independent central bank, the Bank of Greece. The latter was considered necessary for monetary stabilization in the country. Until then, the National Bank of Greece, which also held the privilege of issuing banknotes, operated as a commercial bank alongside its role as an issuing institution. The confusion between these two functions could compromise economic stability and make monetary management more difficult (Psalidopoulos, 2012). Therefore, the League of Nations had significant influence on Greek economic affairs during the period 1923–1931 as this was a necessary condition for loans received under its auspices. The aim of the League of Nations was to control inflation, improve tax collection and reduce public spending, including military spending. It should be noted that the League of Nations was under the influence of the British treasury and the Bank of England and therefore, British politics played a key role in shaping the economic policies of the interwar period in Greece (Reinhart & Trebesch, 2015).

The post-war period until the early 1970s was not marked by an episode of Greek default, but was certainly marked by the constant presence of Western powers (Great Britain, at first, and then the United States) in Greek economic and political affairs. In the period 1950–1974, Greece was a Cold War-era state that had joined the anti-communist side. It is noteworthy that military spending in the period 1962–1974 rose sharply, placing the country very high in the corresponding international ranking. For a Cold War state, the army was an absolute priority along with expenditure dedicated to the creation of a welfare state, in the logic of competition with the alternative paradigm of social organization of the era (Kostis, 2013, p. 784, 786–787).

It can be said that this situation changed during the period that began in the late 1970s and early 1980s and lasted until the dawn of the Greek debt crisis of 2010. This was the period when the vision of Greece's participation in the European experiment became a reality. Karamanlis government, during the post-war period, redefined the orientation of Greek foreign policy toward the European Economic Community as a prerequisite for the stabilization of democratic institutions. In addition, Karamanlis attempted to escape from the close embrace with NATO and to establish friendly relations with the socialist countries as well as with the countries that did not follow the Western or the communist side (Kostis, 2013, pp. 802–803). The next governments followed his example. Despite various policies, Greek foreign policy attempted to become even more independent, when Andreas Papandreou participated in the so-called Group of Six (Greece, Sweden, Argentina, Mexico, India, and Tanzania), but at the same time more European-centered. This was especially the case from the mid-1990s onward, when participation in the forthcoming monetary union was a national goal toward modernization (Kostis, 2013, p. 820, 829–830).

However, the unprecedented in size bailout loans provided to the country at the end of the first decade of the twenty-first century from the International Monetary Fund and the Eurozone, marked the beginning of a new period of foreign policy intervention. After all, the payment of the installments of these loans, had, as a condition, the prudent management of the public finances. The country's three creditor-institutions (the European Central Bank, the European Commission, and the International Monetary Fund) imposed structural adjustment programs, aiming to the improvement of the country's international competitiveness, as well as reforms aiming to cut public spending and create primary fiscal surpluses (Reinhart & Trebesch, 2015).

References

Acemoglu, D., & Robinson, J. A. (2012). *Why Nations Fail: The Origins of Power, Prosperity and Poverty.* New York, NY: Crown Publishers.

Andreadis, A. (1904). *History of National Lands. Part A: The Independence Loans (1824–1825)—The Public Debt Under the Bavarian Dynasty.* Athens: Hestia. (in Greek).

Asdrachas, S. (2011). *Economic History of the Greek State: The Formation of the National Economy* (Vol. II). Athens: Piraeus Bank Group Cultural Foundation. (in Greek).

Dertilis, G. (2014). *History of the Greek state 1830–1920.* Athens: Polis Publications. (in Greek).

Kostelenos, G. (1995). *Money and Output in Modern Greece: 1858–1938.* Athens: KEPE.

Kostis, K. (2013). *The Spoiled Children of History: The Formation of the Modern GREEK State 18th–21st century.* Athens: Polis Publications. (in Greek).

Loizos, D. (1994). *The Great Powers, the Asia Minor Catastrophe and the Rehabilitation of Refugees in Greece (1920–1930).* Athens: Self-published. (in Greek).

Loizos, K. (2012). The Bank of Greece and the management of inter-war crises, 1929–1940: Changing the Central Banking Paradigm. In M. Psalidopoulos (Ed.), *The Great Depression in Europe: Economic Thought and Policy in a National Context* (pp. 169–196). Athens: The Alpha Bank Historical Archives.

Mazower, M. (1991). *Greece and the Inter-War Economic crisis.* Oxford: Clarendon Press.

Pantelakis, N. (1988). *Allied credits, state and National Bank (1917–1928)*. Athens: MIET. (in Greek).

Pantelakis, N. (1995). *Public loans*. Athens: MIET. (in Greek).

Petrakis, P. E. (1985). *The Banking Financing of the Public and Private Sector in Greece (1844–1869)*. Athens: National Bank of Greece Cultural Foundation. (in Greek).

Petrakis, P. E. (1992). *Points of Change in the Activity of the Greek Economy (1840–1913)*. Athens: National Bank of Greece Cultural Foundation. (in Greek).

Psalidopoulos, M. (2010). Economic Thought and Policies in 19th Century Greece. In M. Psalidopoulos (Ed.), *Economists and Economic Policy in Modern Greece*. Athens: Midnight Editions. (in Greek).

Psalidopoulos, M. (Ed.). (2012). *The Great Depression in Europe: Economic Thought and Policy in a National Context*. Athens: The Alpha Bank Historical Archives.

Reinhart, C., & Trebesch, C. (2015). *The Pitfalls of External Dependence: Greece, 1829–2015*. Brookings Papers of Economic Activity, BPEA Conference Draft.

Tsotsoros, S. N. (1993). *The Formation of Industrial Capital in Greece (1898–1939): The Slow Industrialization* (Vol. I). Athens: National Bank of Greece Cultural Foundation.

CHAPTER 2

The Institutional Evolution and the Failed Modernizing Attempts

2.1 Introduction

Political and economic institutions shape the path of nations and possibly determine their choices in the near future. In this context, concepts such as inclusive institutions versus extractive institutions (Acemoglu & Robinson, 2012), markets versus hierarchies (Williamson, 1985, 1996), and diversification of production at national level, may be perceived as factors that influence the institutional risk that characterizes this country and the lopsided creditor-debtor relationship.

In fact, the above concepts can become the organizational ideas with the help of which the path of economic and institutional development of a country that makes up the political economy of its development can be described. From here arises the question that a researcher of economic phenomena who has in his quiver the history as a method of approach would pose: How is the institutional risk formed over time in the Greek economy through the dominance of extractive structures, of different types of hierarchies that they don't always save costs and the lack of differentiation of production?

The authors would like to thank Dr. Konstantinos Loizos for his contribution to this chapter.

P. E. Petrakis and P. C. Kostis, *The Evolution of the Greek Economy*, The Political Economy of Greek Growth up to 2030,
https://doi.org/10.1007/978-3-030-47210-8_2

However, according to North (1991) the economic story is the narrative of institutional evolution and change. Eventually, institutional change is the result of the interaction between the institutional infrastructure of a society and the intended action of its subjects given their perceptions and beliefs (North, 2005, p. 26, 59). Hence, the second and more difficult question arises: is institutional change possible toward a Greek society and economy characterized by more inclusive institutions too extractive and exclusion?

The structure of capital is as follows: the second Section (Sect. 2.2) presents the way in which extracting institutions have been structured in the Greek economy and the role played by the Ottoman past in their formation. The next part (Sect. 2.3) describes the evolution of the hierarchies prevailing in the Greek economy in a historical perspective, and finally the Section 2.4 the non-diversification of investment and production in historical perspective.

2.2 The Ottoman, the Central European Heritage and the Initial Formation of Extracting Institutions

The beginning of the creation of extractive institutions could be traced back to the Ottoman and Byzantine past and linked to the peculiar formation of the ruling classes of modern Greek society. The Ottoman administrative apparatus was structured in communities, while the authority and responsibilities of the communal authority were entrusted to merchants. These merchants, members of an early bourgeoisie, had acquired within the Orthodox communities political power and social position. However, their political power was also accompanied by economic power which, however, was due to their close relationship with the Ottoman state. Their economic activities included the lease by the Ottoman state of the right to collect taxes, the management of state monopolies and other activities that were included in the privileges granted to them by the Ottomans. In stark contrast to the Western European states which faced an already formed bourgeoisie, the Ottoman state itself created a new ruling class which included Jews and Christians, mainly Armenians, Syrians and Greeks. On the other hand, however, the relationship between these upper social classes in the Ottoman regime and the state was governed rather by economic and political uncertainty and a web of corruption, bribes and intrigues (Dertilis, 2014, pp. 164–165), something not uncommon in history. These conditions that characterize the formation of the early Greek ruling class, are indicative of the reasons why liberalism and the market economy, with all their connotations, did not form the core of the ideology of the modern Greek state.

The authoritarian style of government of Kapodistrias and then the cameralistic conception of the Bavarian Regency initially and Otto afterward, did not allow liberal ideas to thrive. One of the most important institutional advances such as the recognition of property rights to landless farmers did not take place at that time (Psalidopoulos, 2010) and the economy lost a great opportunity for its commercialization and monetization. Instead, steps have been taken toward building exploitative institutions rather than creating institutional frameworks for social and economic integration. One of the distinctive features of cameralistic views is that the center of economic policy is dominated by serving the monarch's interest at the expense of his subjects, let alone civil society which was not yet formed in the Greek society of the first half of the nineteenth century. A typical example was the imposition of heavy taxation on the agricultural sector of the economy which included the tax of tithe on the value of the gross product (Kostis, 2013, p. 296) and the rent tax which was calculated on the value of production on national land (Psalidopoulos, 2010). This last tax was higher in the early years of the modern Greek state and reached the level of 30% of gross production and later fell to 25% of it (Kostis, 2013, p. 297).

Indeed, it seems that the tax system adopted by the new Greek state was a continuation of the Ottoman reality. The Ottoman tax system was the model for the gradual shaping how the Greek authorities would collect their own taxes. Of course, the most burdensome Ottoman taxes such as the poll tax, the emergency military taxes and others whose collection had been entrusted to the local authorities (Petmezas, 2003, pp. 58–59; Kostis, 2006, p. 308) had no continuity in the modern Greek state. However, the logic of the organization and management of the tax system of the new Greek state was the same as that of the Ottoman past (Kostis, 2013, p. 296).

The philosophy that pervaded the Ottoman law, and which recognized a kind of usufruct rather than property on land, was to extract income in the form of tax. There were attempts in the modern Greek state as early as 1833 to transcend customary law and to draw up a civil code that would safeguard the right to private property. The problem was traced to the necessary transition from Ottoman to Roman law (Kostis, 2013, pp. 243–244). The Civil Code finally came into force as late as 1946 (Karouzou, 2006). This longstanding ambivalence around property rights was closely tied to an exploitative tax system. The tithe tax was an exploitative taxation not only in terms of the absolute size of the tax but also in terms of the manner of collection. The collection of the tax in each municipality had been entrusted to business men who, by this means, had acquired considerable power over the peasants. The latter were obliged to have ensured the permission of these private tax collectors in order to perform whatever agricultural work they considered necessary. Moreover, the way in which the tax collectors estimated the quantity of the product that should be withheld as tax was arbitrary, while the villagers were burdened with significant transport costs in order to transfer the tax in kind from the farms to the capital of the municipality. For the most part, during the post-revolutionary era, the private tenants of taxes retained the power they had been given under the Ottoman regime, while the collection of taxes took place in conditions of tension and sometimes with the help of the army (Kostis, 2013, pp. 297–298; Asdrahas, 2011a, p. 99; Agriantoni et al., 2002, p. 57).

The tax system as an extractive institution was maintained in the years that followed after the eviction of King Otto. Soutsos, who was an eminent professor of economics at that time, observed that the governments of the second half of the nineteenth century imposed heavy taxes on agricultural production while leaving other social groups out of the tax system. The tithe was abolished in 1880 by the government of Trikoupis and replaced by the "tax on ploughing animals". However, widespread tax evasion combined with the incompetence of state mechanisms made this tax ineffective. Remarkably, the villagers deliberately reduced the number of animals they used on their farms so as to avoid paying the relevant tax. Moreover, this was a tax on capital and not on net income, which was even frantically criticized in the parliamentary debates of the time. It seems that maintaining an exploitative-oriented tax system had the unintended consequence of creating in taxpayers a culture related to the ways in which they could avoid paying their taxes rather than the opposite.

In the context of the exploitative concept, even modernizing ideas such as the distribution of national land to landless farmers were not implemented as a planned policy with a long-term horizon but instead as a measure of revenue collection. The national lands concerned arable, uncultivated and wooded areas which, before the Independence Struggle, belonged to the Ottoman state (arazi-I miriye), served the expenses of the Ottoman charitable foundations (arazi-I mevkufiye) or were part of the land (çiftlik) that "belonged" to the Ottoman Aga. This land, after independence became the property of the Greek state while its Christian cultivators maintained their bond with it (Petmezas, 2003, pp. 23–24). The first attempts to distribute this land by Kapodistrias failed for reasons related to the Governor's relationship with Russian politics and the corresponding reaction of the British government which feared the rise of Russian influence on the Greek people (Asdrahas, 2011a, p. 97). The long-standing problem of the distribution of national land was linked to two other issues, one of a political and the other of an economic nature. The political dimension was that the Bavarian administration in the first period of the free Greek state did not want the formation of a social stratum of large landowners under the fear that the latter would they could gain strength enough to challenge Otto's autocratic rule. Instead, Otto's vision was to create a centralized monarchy that would be supported by independent small farmers. The economic dimension was closely related to politics and led to the underdevelopment of the real estate market. Moreover, the uncertainty surrounding the proprietary rights on land rendered any commercial use of the land and the development of the agricultural faith particularly difficult (Gardika, Kechriotis, Loukos, Lyritzis, & Maronitis, 2008, p. 76; Petmezas, 2003, p. 27). The guarantee of property rights is an essential element in the creation of institutions of social and economic integration. However, George Finlay, a British historian who lived at that time, noted in 1844 that in Greece there was no clear and specific idea of the sacred right of land ownership. None of Greeks, either socially powerful or humble, could understand the meaning of the absolute right to property (Petmezas, 2003, p. 28). The attitude of the Greek state contributed to the perpetuation of the problem as the part of the national land that was sold, had been sold at very high prices. In fact, the sale prices had been set in an auction process rather than through a clear estimation of the value of the land. Therefore, farmers were not able to bid at high prices while people in the environment of the political elite were able to buy land as they were never going to pay such high prices because of their political connections (Petmezas, 2003, pp. 29, 32).

The distribution of national land to private individuals from 1835 to 1871 did not exceed 10% of the total arable land (Fragiadis, 2007, p. 29). The Koumoundouros government contributed to the increase of private ownership of farms when in 1871 distributed to growers 43% of the arable National Land (Sakellaropoulos, 2003, pp. 282–283). However, the land reform of 1871 remained unfinished to the extent that it was not accompanied by the creation of a cadastre. The paradox is that the latter gathered broad consensus regarding its importance in establishing an objective way of calculating farm income and collecting taxes. The high cost of such a project was probably the alibi for not implementing it. The real reason must be sought in the role that many politicians had assumed as intermediaries between the government and taxpayers. In any case, agricultural taxation has been blamed for its nearsighted perception as a collection agent of the government regardless of any developmental effects, as taxes on the agricultural product were a trammel for the production and the increase of labor productivity (Petmezas, 2003, p. 57, 82). However, the distribution of national lands, which began in 1871 by the Government of Koumoundouros and was completed in the 1930s by the Government of Venizelos, was a gradual reform process with a consensual character, which determined the course of Greek society in the long term (Gardika et al., 2008, p. 76).

Another example of a tax with characteristics of an institution of exploitation /extraction was the tax on ploughing animals of 1880 under the Government of Trikoupis. This was, in fact, a tax on capital and means of production. Moreover, it was an unjust tax as, like the tithe, it did not levied on net income. For these reasons, this tax was blamed as responsible for the stagnation in agricultural production in the period 1880–1912. Moreover, contrary to the expectations of its initiators, the owners of ploughing animals were not motivated to use their means of production more intensively and productively but preferred to reduce the number of their animals so as to reduce their tax burden (Petmezas, 2003, p. 87). Although the logic of the tax system at the end of the nineteenth century and the beginning of the twentieth century was clearly different from the Ottoman past and the period of Otto's reign, the tax system itself remains a patchwork of provisions that reproduce inequalities and injustices and are often contradictory to each other. The tax authority's focus on urban populations and emphasis on indirect taxation meant that the lower and middle classes of cities were disproportionately burdened while higher incomes were taxed only opportunistically (Kostis, 2013, pp. 481–482). The trend of reducing the taxation of farmers with a simultaneous increase in the urban population of small and middle income was related to the introduction of the general right to vote for all male adults, the majority of whom lived in the countryside (Dertilis, 2014, pp. 785–786, 789; Kostis, 2013, p. 485). On the other hand, the tax system evolved in the long term to benefit both farmers and wealthy urban strata, as the tax burden for the latter was zero or minimal and remained extremely low until 1933 (Dertilis, 2014, p. 791). Nevertheless, there was a development dimension in the effort to reduce the taxation of farmers as the latter were already burdened with paying debts, paying rents and municipal taxes, while agricultural production played a crucial role in the economic development of Greece at that time (Kostis, 2013, pp. 485–486).

Another form of extractive institutions with revenue-grabbing features is found in the financial sector and is directly related to the long-term oligopolistic structure of the Greek banking system. These structures are historically linked to the complex usury system that dominated agricultural production toward the end of the Ottoman era. The local merchant was, in fact, the only potential buyer of the production of the farmers of his district, and, at the same time, the only one who had enough capital available to lend the farmer. Over a wider area, these local merchants formed an oligopoly. This structure was maintained during the first period of the modern Greek state with the addition of another new factor: the National Bank of Greece (NBG). NBG became the main player in this oligopolistic structure as it was able to unite the individual markets and dominate the local financiers-lenders, but without radically changing the status of high interest rates and profits (Dertilis, 2014, pp. 246–247).

An interesting consequence of the formation of such institutions of exploitation /extraction has been the attempt, to a lower or a higher degree, to avoid them by smuggling. One can distinguish at that time four types of this illegal trade: first, the import and export of goods without payment of the corresponding duties which in the era of the Trikoupis governments were particularly high. The existence of many unguarded paths in the nineteenth century that crossed the border made it quite easy to carry out this kind of illegal trade. A second form was to declare at customs a lower price than the actual one in order to impose a lower duty. Third, it was common to import goods under the pretext of temporality for the purpose of transit again abroad (transit status) but they were circumvented and eventually the product was sold domestically. Finally, the state monopoly imposed on oil, playing cards, matches, cigarette paper and tobacco in order to combat smuggling was itself a cause of the development of illegal trade in these products (Dertilis, 2014, pp. 279–282). In general, one would say that from the first steps of the modern

Greek state, the smuggling, tax evasion, and the shadow economy were closely associated with fear and suspicion toward the state (Dertilis, 2014, p. 305).

The economic and political institutions of exploitation/extraction and exclusion of large social groups meant at the same time the creation of a network of nepotism, favoritism, and clientelism that permeated the public administration with the aim of influencing decisions for the benefit of specific interests. At the same time, the state did not adhere to elementary constitutional norms. It is remarkable that for a long period from 1830 to 1933 none of the state accounts for the past year were submitted for ratification by the Parliament. The system as a whole was based on a political transaction between political figures and voters. Politicians appointed their voters to the civil service in exchange for their vote in elections, thus contributing to the staffing of the public with incompetent staff (Dertilis, 2014, pp. 405–408). However, the sources of this system are probably to be sought in the Ottoman and Otto's heritage. Many local governors of the late Ottoman period redeemed their participation in the Independence Struggle by restoring contacts with the environment of King Otto, which enabled them to gain their own share of power under the new authoritarian regime. Even after the constitutional change of 1864 these families became part of the new political elite. However, the new parliamentary regime was accompanied by a network of client relationships based on solicitation of votes through promises to occupy a position in the state (Dertilis, 2014, p. 421). In a sense, these structures were also associated with corporatist practices that implied the existence of interest groups as they were gradually formed from the 1860s. They were essentially an indication of the gradual rise of civil society especially after 1909 (Lavdas, 2006). However, these developments were also linked to the problem of hierarchies versus markets in modern Greek reality.

2.3 The Development of Hierarchies in Historical Perspective

The young Greek state of the nineteenth century inherited an Orthodox Church with view over the practical problems of everyday economic and social life. The Greek Orthodox Church, which was essentially a state institution in the Byzantine era, expressed its preference for community life without rejecting private property and trade. Nevertheless, profit and individual benefit were not accepted as incentives for economic action and the state had to intervene in the formation and control of prices for the benefit of the community (Psalidopoulos, 2010). These ideas survived the Ottoman conquest and shaped the economic and social ideology of the liberated nation under the garb of the Greek-Christian culture or the ideology of Romanticism (Psalidopoulos, 2010). This was in stark contrast to the more liberal and democratic intellectual atmosphere which existed in the Ionian Islands despite the existence of the aristocracy there. It is noteworthy that the Ionian Academy, which was founded in 1824, adopted the Demotic Greek language instead of the Katharevousa language which prevailed at the University of Athens in 1837. However, when the Ionian Islands became a part of the Greek state, these liberal ideas were extinguished as they were sacrificed to a, state-led, romanticism (Gardika, et al., 2008, p. 28).

After all, the ideas of the Enlightenment in Greece were not associated with a rising industrial bourgeoisie but with the issue of national independence under conditions of economic and social backwardness. Therefore, the government in the modern Greek state was perceived as an administrative factor in the economic situation (Psalidopoulos, 2010) based, more or less, on the same hierarchical mentality that prevailed in the medieval era. This led to a contradictory state attitude to the economy: the rhetorical defense of markets alongside a daily practice that was rather arbitrary and indifferent to economic theories. This attitude is described as an "administrative perception" of the economy and is characterized by the coincidence of the government approach to economic policy with the expectations of wider strata of the Greek population of the nineteenth century (Psalidopoulos, 2010). These expectations stemmed from the Ottoman past. The economic structure of the Ottoman Empire favored a corporatist and communal concept of the economy which was based on large socioeconomic groups such as guilds of masons (esnafia, rufetia), merchants (kompaniai), breeders (cheligata), and ship owners (syntrofonaftai). The market as the dominant organizer of social relations and economic activities makes the existence and role of communities precarious (Adrahas, 2011a, p. 53).

It should be said that during the period of the Regency and that of Otto (1833–1862) an attempt took place to form an institutional framework of European—and mainly Bavarian-German—type which in many aspects had incorporated the French legal and administrative paradigm (Kostis, 2013, p. 183). In this context in 1835 the Council of State as the Supreme Administrative Court was established, the legal system was based on Byzantine-Roman law and the Napoleonic Commercial Code was adopted (Kostis, 2013, pp. 182, 242–244). A remarkable institutional development was the foundation of the University of Athens in 1837, which took place in parallel with the first efforts, already in 1834 and 1836, to lay the foundations of elementary and Secondary Education (Kostis, 2013, pp. 235, 237–238). These efforts contributed to strengthening the degree of integration of the various socioeconomic groups in the Greek society and economy.

The discussion in the literature on the difference between countries with civil law-based legal systems and those based on common law, or between countries that adopt the legal tradition of continental Europe versus that of Anglo-Saxon countries, emphasizes either the legal framework or the balance of power between conflicting interests that influence the formation of this legal framework (Pagano & Volpin, 2001; La Porta, Lopez-de-Silanes, Shleifer & Vishny, 1997, 1998). According to this literature, common law countries are building institutional structures that are more market-friendly than civil code countries in which law enforcement and investor protection are not as strong. Greece, to the extent that it abandons the old customary law of rural societies, joins the countries of the Civil Code (formally since 1946) due to the choices of the ruling elite in the nineteenth century. Thus, one could blame this choice for so many incidents in Greek economic history concerning the government's preference for hierarchies rather than markets. Another question that calls for its answer is to what extent the German style of hierarchical administration as such could be crowned with success when it was transplanted into a new state in which the concepts of loyalty and loyalty did not have the same weight as they had in Bavaria.

The "administrative concept" that prevailed in Otto's time had the additional consequence of strengthening the bureaucracy over the trading parties. The bureaucrats, however their good intentions in terms of planning industrial development and establishing model industrial units (Psalidopoulos, 2010), in fact, with their centralized mentality strengthened the hierarchies at the expense of the markets. Businesses could only survive if they were able to secure a commercial privilege or monopoly in return for their loyalty and allegiance to the authority of the monarch, especially after 1843 (Psalidopoulos, 2010). This looks like an early version of clientelism and favoritism in direct contrast to a market economy with features of integration of wider strata of the population.

The movement in favor of free trade and against tariff barriers found its expression in the "Society of the Liberties of Trade" which was active in Syros between 1865 and 1867 under the leadership of Eumorfopoulos. However, the Society failed to fulfill its goal despite the fact that its members were important figures in trade, intellectual elite and politics. Paradoxically, some of these politicians such as Koumoundouros and Trikoupis were also prominent figures of the "administrative concept" of economic policy (Psalidopoulos, 2010).

The conflict between hierarchies and markets in the financial system is closely linked to oligopolistic structures. In March 1841, the National Bank of Greece (NBG) was established as a private bank with issuing privilege. This privilege was renewed by the Government of Trikoupis. However, the economic operators of the time complained that the NBG had essentially become a government agent in the market while a network of mutual economic and political services had been formed between the bank and the political elite. Besides, it was no coincidence that the tax burden of the NBG was very low and the issuing privilege was granted at no cost for the bank.

The following year, NBG was also criticized for its unwillingness to take risks, but at the same time it was credited for its success in imposing the drachma as the dominant payment instrument within the Greek state. Its role as a state banker until the founding of the Bank of Greece in 1928 implied the existence of some form of political relationship between the state and the bank. It is for this reason that many economists of the time argued for the need for greater competition in the banking system. Finally, the special relationship that was formed between the NBG and the Greek state raises the question of the choice between markets and hierarchies in the banking sector and its possible relationship with political extractive institutions, especially in the following years when banking institutions increased in number.

Indeed, in the period 1844–1864 the Greek banking system included only one bank, the NBG. Immediately after the annexation of the Ionian Islands on May 21, 1864, the Ionian bank was granted issuing privilege which it maintained until 1920. However, the Ionian bank did not challenge the sovereignty of the NBG as until 1869 its activity was limited to the Ionian Islands. There were also some small local banks that financed maritime trade such as the "Hellenic Naval Bank", the "Commercial Bank the Argonaut", the Eastern Commercial Bank and others (Petrakis, 1985, pp. 104–105). The Bank of Epirus-Thessaly, which was identified with

Andreas Syggros, also acquired issuing privilege while during the late nineteenth century and the early twentieth century a number of banks were established without the possession of issuing privilege such as the Bank of Athens (established in 1893), the Banque D' Orient (established in 1904), Popular (Laiki) Bank (established in 1905) and the Commercial Bank (established in 1907). In 1899, Currant Bank and the Bank of Crete were founded, which later (in 1919) was absorbed by the NBG. Earlier, in 1899, NBG had absorbed the Bank of Epirus-Thessaly. Finally, the establishment of the Industrial Credit Bank in 1873 (Kostis & Tsokopoulos, 1988, pp. 37–57, 98, 108). Thus, it appears that NBG has acquired a significant share in the credit market, thereby reducing competition despite the existence of a significant number of banks in a small economy such as Greece. These characteristics were preserved in the twentieth century as the NBG took advantage of its special relationship with the Greek state in order to prevent any attempt toward a more competitive banking sector or even any attempt to modernize and streamline its organization. A typical example was the total opposition of the NBG to the establishment of a special Agricultural Bank in the 1920s (Kostis, 1987, pp. 296–297).

However, oligopolistic and hierarchical structures prevailed in other sectors of the Greek economy in the late nineteenth and early twentieth century, such as the import trade in wheat and coal and the exports of raisins, olive oil, wine, and lead from Lavrio. In Lavrio there were two companies, the French company founded by Giovanni Battista Serpieri and the company owned by Syggros. The two companies had a competitive—and at the same time, complementary—relationship, while Serpieri participated as a partner in both companies. Lavrio's case was an example of interconnected networks that included members of the Greek diaspora and the local bourgeoisie as both participated in the administrative councils of major commercial, insurance, banking, maritime, and industrial enterprises. These people were connected with each other by family, friendly, and business ties. In fact, they were members of a wider network which was closely intertwined with the political elite and which had access to the main centers of political and economic decision-making. In this mega-network, bankers and individual financiers controlled the granting of credit while the state was their biggest client, thus increasing its debt (Dertilis, 2014, pp. 631–634).

A milestone of the economic policy of the Trikoupis government was the tariff system introduced in 1884. It is characteristic that the new tariff system had as its avowed aim the increase of the state revenues regardless of the effect this would have on foreign trade. Nevertheless, the result of this system was a significant boost in protective policies toward domestic industry. The tariff regime was amended twice, one in 1886 and one in 1887 and codified in 1892 by the BPKA' act. The system provided for two types of customs duties, general and conventional, on metal and paper drachmas whereas 1 Gold drachma was equal to 1.32 paper drachmas. The duties would be levied in gold drachmas, thus ensuring the stability of the public revenues. However, Prime Minister Charilaos Trikoupis himself admitted to Parliament that the new tariff system could not be justified on the basis of the protection of local industry as "simply, there is no industry in Greece...." Finally, the tariff of 1892 continued to be the framework for the conduct of foreign trade until 1923 (Tsotsoros, 1993, p. 153).

On December 22, 1923, a new tariff was introduced which came into force from January 1, 1926. The main feature of the new system was its greater specialization in an effort to highlight its orientation in favor of the protection of local production. This direction was his main difference with the old tariff of 1893 (Tsotsoros, 1993, pp. 191–192). The 1926 system was amended twice. Law 3826 of January 1929 established three general categories of goods solely for protection purposes while law 5312 of 31 December 1931 increased customs duties ten times above their previous levels. It was obvious that the new tariff regime had a significant impact on the domestic industry through the deterioration of the final prices of goods. One can get an idea of the bureaucracy introduced under the new system by simply enumerating the paragraphs of the relevant legislation. The old tariff was described in 774 paragraphs and sub-paragraphs while the 1923 system covered 1214 paragraphs and 29 product classes. These paragraphs increased to 1326 in 1926 and to 1540 in 1933. Duties as a percentage of the value of imports ranged between 25.2% and 28.8% in the first decade of the twentieth century. As part of the measures taken for monetary stabilization in 1928, duties reached 36.87% of the value but in 1931 they went even higher reaching 45.83%. Increasing tariffs, along with their orientation toward specific industrial products such as those in the metal, chemical and textile industries, have limited the choice between goods from a consumer perspective (Tsotsoros, 1993, pp. 204–205).

A typical example of how hierarchical structures, which do not intend to save transactional costs, can create a network between government and private interests, is the way in which the new tariff system was imposed and implemented. From 1917 and throughout the 1920s there were various tariff committees operating in an advisory nature. The upshot of these committees was the Permanent Tariff Committee of May 1, 1930 with the participation of state officials, three university professors, as well as representatives of the chambers of Commerce and industry and the Association of Greek Industrialists and Craftsmen. The commission expressed its opinion on the tariff issues bearing in mind the state's needs in tax revenues that coincided with the vested interests of the most powerful strata of Greek entrepreneurs. Indeed, an increase in import duties had a direct positive impact on the profitability of the local industry of products competing with imported products. In the same spirit, law 5426 of April 29, 1932 provided for the Prohibition of imports of machinery "intended to increase production by expanding industries or establishing new ones for goods manufactured in the country" (Tsotsoros, 1993, pp. 210–211).

A typical example of a hierarchical structure in the financial sector was the organization of the Greek financial system in the post-war period. At the heart of this system was the credit policy pursued, which was related both to development objectives and to maintaining stability. The latter was achieved by using percentage controls on loans granted by banks and by maintaining special liquid reserves of commercial banks in the central bank. Credit quotas were widely used as a means of limiting credit expansion whenever price stability was threatened by excessive liquidity in the banking system. Because of this policy, there was no need to raise interest rates in order to limit the growth of the money supply (Pagoulatos, 2003, pp. 32–33).

The structured hierarchical financial system was later characterized as a version of "financial repression" (McKinnon, 1973; Shaw, 1973) was justified as a means of promoting economic development in underdeveloped countries. Banks had to reconcile the criteria of profitability with those of socioeconomic prosperity in the context of an effective manipulation of private entrepreneurship (Zolotas, 1964, p. 69). In practice, they had to serve specific objectives of government policy under a system that later led to distortions in the financial sector.

Of particular importance for the functioning of this system was the Monetary Committee which was established in January 1946 with the power to take decisions on monetary, credit, and exchange rate policy

(Pagoulatos, 2003, p. 48). Initially, the idea was to create a short-term committee to control credit growth and to channel financial aid to productive uses (Kostis, 1997, p. 90). Nevertheless, the Committee became an all-powerful mechanism for detailed scrutiny of the credit system until its abolition in 1982 (Garganas & Tavlas, 2001, p. 48). The Monetary Committee consisted of ministers with financial portfolios, the governor of the Bank of Greece and two foreigners, an American and a British citizen. However, since 1951 and then its composition has changed, and only Greek citizens participated in the Committee. These included the ministers of coordination, Finance, Agriculture, Trade, Industry, and the governor of the Bank of Greece. The Committee decided on the purposes for which bank loans could be granted, the sectors of the economy which would receive preferential financing at predetermined rates per sector, the loan rates, the terms of the loans, the procedures to be followed by the banks, and the collateral to be requested from their clients according to the type of loan (Halikias, 1978, pp. 27–29).

The credit policy had four pillars: (1) ensuring the credit of the crucial sectors of the economy, even if it meant budget deficits; (2) supervisory control of credit for those sectors of the economy that had low productivity and specialized in consumer goods; (3) reducing the cost of money in general but also by credit category; and (4) special care for long-term financing (Zolotas, 1964, p. 87). Finally, in a country with an underdeveloped capital market, where open market operations were not possible, the only way to pursue a credit policy was special qualitative and credit checks aimed at promoting both economic growth and monetary stability (Zolotas, 1964, p. 89).

The quality controls were based on an officially formulated distinction between 'productive' and 'non-productive' sectors and activities. As a result, preferential financing had to be given to activities such as export trade, agriculture, industry, mining and tourism while imports, internal trade and construction faced credit constraints. Thus, quality controls were intended to influence the composition of the loan portfolios of credit institutions while quantitative controls were aimed at regulating the size of credit expansion for specific loan categories. Given the high liquidity of commercial banks and the underdevelopment of money and capital markets, ordinary monetary policy tools such as discount rate or open market operations could not be effective. For this reason, minimum cash requirements and qualitative and quantitative controls were used as monetary policy tools (Halikias, 1978, pp. 39–40, 171, 207–208).

However, channeling credit to selected sectors of the economy combined with limiting it to others has led to a double paradox. First of all, the coexistence of a few large oligopolies along with numerous small businesses (Ellis, Psilos, Westebbe, & Nicolaou, 1964, pp. 173–175) of which the former represented the "official" subsidized part of the economy while the latter consisted more or less of the "unofficial" part that relied on its profitability and its own funds or on the "unofficial" credit markets for its financing. These economic conditions favored the oligopolistic profits of large enterprises which were essentially subsidized by the government not only through preferential financing but also through various forms of protection against external competition but also without regard to their economic efficiency. Secondly, the over-indebtedness of the favored enterprises which were receiving loans at preferential terms and interest rates and which were themselves lending back to firms facing credit constraints. The new loans were granted at higher interest rates, while the large oligopolistic companies themselves became "unofficial" financial intermediaries (Katseli, 1990).

Moreover, the dominant feature of the Greek financial system of the time was the oligopolistic structure of the banking system, in which two large commercial banks dominated, the National Bank of Greece and the Commercial Bank of Greece (Psilos, 1964, p. 186; Kostis, 1997, p. 91), and the weak capital market. Following the stabilization of the period 1953–1955 which restored public confidence in the currency, a period of both monetary stability and an increase in savings in the form of bank deposits began (Ellis et al., 1964, p. 50; Pagoulatos, 2003, pp. 48–49).

In the mid-1960s, Psilos (1964, p. 17) noted that the problem of the Greek financial system was not the inadequacy of savings but the inefficient mechanism of channeling excess liquidity into productive investments. This inefficiency was linked to the reluctance of large family businesses to seek financing on the capital market or the inability of smaller companies to do so, the inadequacies of Greek company law in terms of protecting the interests of shareholders and the lack of competition in the banking sector. All this led to the paradox of the existence of an excess supply of savings along with a high cost of capital (Psilos, 1964, pp. 246–251). The high cost of capital took the form of increased banking commissions which were added to the official interest rates charged by commercial banks. As a result, the final loan rates charged to small craft enterprises were higher than the official rates (Halikias, 1978, pp. 230–231).

These characteristics linked to the underdevelopment of the capital market also provided the justification for state intervention to channel these funds into uses that would aid economic growth through a complex system of rules and controls. Besides, as Pagoulatos points out (2003, p. 11), in developing economies with oligopolistic structures in the banking sector, the allocation of credit if determined by the market would favor import trade at the expense of economic activities with a more productive and growth character due to higher profit rates in the first case.

Courakis (1981) mentions that there were two main means of state intervention in the mediation between surplus and deficit units: (1) Controls on commercial banks with regard to the rates of their required cash (liquidity) at the central bank, reserve/rebate ratios on lending and credit rates on banks' obligations to finance specific sectors of the economy, lending limits for specific ineligible sectors of the economy, the ceilings on interest rates on loans and deposits, and the conditions laid down for loans and deposits. (2) Controls on special credit institutions—such as the Postal Savings Bank, Popular (Laiki) Bank, development banks, mortgage credit institutions and the Deposit and Loan Fund—as to the permissible scope of their operations and the structure of their balance sheets.

On the other hand, the system of administrative setting of interest rates at low levels had the undesirable effect of being a disincentive for both government and businesses to seek financing on the capital market. The direct result was the lack of financial securities offered by these entities as alternative positions for savings alongside bank deposits, resulting in the excess liquidity of the banks and the underdevelopment of the capital market (Harisopoulos Committee, 1979, p. 6; Karatza Committee, 1987, pp. 22, 66).

In addition, we should note the negative impact of the official interest rate policy on the profitability of banks which have made qualitative and quantitative controls ineffective both in terms of strengthening investment and in terms of monetary policy. The structure of interest rates—at least until 1966 when a system of equalizing bank profits from various types of loans was introduced—made long-term lending unprofitable for banks. Moreover, banks were allowed to bear the cost to the borrower of short-term loans with various commissions in addition to the official interest rates, resulting in an increase in real return from the granting of such loans (Halikias, 1978, pp. 52, 168, 185, 187). Moreover, the high costs of managing relatively small loans, the lower official interest rates for loans to craft enterprises as opposed to those for industrial units and the lower creditworthiness of the first type of enterprises were disincentives for the assignment of loans to small enterprises (Halikias, 1978, pp. 191–192). Therefore, the incompatibility between the official interest rate policy and the maximization of the profits of commercial banks provided a disincentive for the latter to cooperate with the monetary authorities in order to achieve the credit system to selected sectors. The quality controls concerning the allocation of credit to high-priority sectors for economic development failed due to indirect financing of imports and trade since the industries had themselves become lenders of commercial enterprises (Halikias, 1978, pp. 232, 212). Moreover, both qualitative and quantitative controls proved ineffective due to the excessive liquidity of banks, their unwillingness to cooperate with the authorities in terms of their preference for short-term lending and insufficient demand for long-term loans from industrial enterprises. The agreement of commercial banks to the credit regulations would be tantamount to their consent to the retention of surplus untapped funds and therefore to the acceptance of lost profits (Halikias, 1978, pp. 220–221). Finally, the success of a system of extensive controls required the operation of an effective mechanism for supervision of banking operations along with that over the uses of their customers' borrowed funds. However, such a detailed supervisory mechanism was unlikely to work effectively in terms of the separation between "socially desirable" and "not desirable" lending (Halikias, 1978, pp. 221–222).

Another result of this hierarchical financial system was the ultimate failure of the policy to provide cheap credit to specific sectors, which led to the over-indebtedness of enterprises, increased risk, the drain of business profits on unproductive activities such as real estate and the less tendency to reinvest profits in more competitive production structures. The debt of these enterprises and the risk-taking by them and the lending banks increased due to the favorable access of large industrial units to bank lending combined with indirect financing of trade by them. In addition, Greek entrepreneurs had little propensity to save as they reinvested in their businesses only a small percentage of their profits. The most popular placement of business profits was the real estate market as it provided a sense of security—as opposed to riskier industrial investments—and guaranteed high capital gains due to rising prices and growing volume of purchases in the real estate market. For these reasons, industrial enterprises in Greece operated in smaller sizes than optimal despite the intentions of official financial policies to boost investment in industry (Halikias, 1978, pp. 195–204).

Courakis (1981) points out another unfavorable consequence of the system of administrative interest rates and credit control. This system was based on the calculation of nominal returns for different categories of loans and did not take into account the current expected returns and the cost–benefit calculation behind the banks' financing decisions. The expected returns on the different types of loans did not account for the risk of default of debtors. However, the expected returns on the loans decreased as the risk of bankruptcy of the borrower increased even if the official interest rates for this type of loan remained stable. In addition, the imposition of caps on loan rates led banks to place greater emphasis on the collateral required by firms to provide them in order to reduce their risk exposure. But this has discouraged small and young firms with limited ability to provide such collateral from taking investment initiatives. More importantly, it discouraged those companies that sought higher-risk investment projects but which were socially desirable. In this way government policy has failed to promote exactly the kind of business which it is supposed to promote.

2.4 The Non-Diversification of Investment and Production in Historical Perspective

The raisin economy and its history constituted a typical example of limited diversification of production and risk in the early years of the Greek economic development, which deserves further consideration as a legacy to the subsequent development of agricultural and industrial production.

Corinthian currant was a product intended exclusively for export abroad. Especially since currants were at that time the main export product of the country which ensured the presence of the Greek economy in international markets. In this sense it was the product that determined the amount of the total value of Greek exports to the world market (Pizanias, 1988, p. 29).

The cultivation of currants had begun a few years before the outbreak of the Greek Revolution and for the next two decades it was limited to certain areas of the northern Peloponnese and the Ionian Islands. Production was gradually increasing from 1830 onward through the expansion of the arable land intended for it. Despite the destruction of raisin vines during the Struggle, the northern and western coast of the Peloponnese became the center of this production (Pizanias, 1988, pp. 30–33).

Nevertheless, the golden period of the raisin economy is observed from the mid-1870s to 1892. During this period Greek production came to fill the gap in international demand due to the phylloxera that hit the French vineyards. In fact, the Greek raisins exported to France were of rather low quality and used by the French in the production of cheap wine. The historical fact that currants was par excellence an exportable product is recorded in the statistics of the time. During the period 1851–1864 the percentage of not exported production did not exceed, on an average, 32% of the total production with the exception of 1853. Moreover, from 1865 to 1892 raisin exports increased further, thus creating the golden period of the raisin economy. Global demand was so high that it quickly absorbed the stocks of raisins that had been left unsold from the previous periods (Pizanias, 1988, pp. 39–42).

However, from 1893 onward the price of raisins fell sharply. The average annual price of raisins in the international market has fallen from 300 francs per 1000 Venetian lires in 1890 to 44 francs in 1893 and 42 francs in 1894. The corresponding average prices in the Patras market were 193.87 Greek drachmas in 1890, 129.43 in 1893, and 127.37 in 1895. The non-diversification of the economy in terms of both product and risk led to the collapse of the raisin economy and the first major wave of immigration to the United States at the dawn of the twentieth century (Vergopoulos, 1978, p. 102, 106–108). From 1893 to 1899 the quantities of raisins that were not exported ranged from 9% to 23%, while from 1901 to 1912 the same variable recorded values between 9% and 33%. The fact that prices were very low during these two periods motivated these surpluses of raisins to be converted into raw material for distilleries and wineries (Pizanias, 1988, p. 42). Indeed, a further significant impact of the raisin crisis was the resulting government intervention to get the producers out of the difficult situation. The government bought a percentage ranging between 10% and 24% of the production as a withholding, which could then be used in distilleries and wineries (Vergopoulos, 1978, p. 107). However, this measure had the opposition of landholders and traders who considered it as unconstitutional and against private property (Asdrahas, 2011a, p. 188).

The importance of the raisin crisis is related to the specific weight raisin had as an exportable product in relation to the total value of exports. In the second half of the nineteenth century, raisins represented on average more than 50% of the value of all Greek exports. In particular, in the two decades that followed after 1871 and up to 1891 this percentage increased to 60% on average. From this point onward this percentage fell to 43% in the period 1891–1900 and even lower to 34% in the first decade of the twentieth century (Pizanias, 1988, pp. 43–44). At the same time, the production of raisins accounted for only 6.5% of the arable land. The other exportable products which accounted for the rest of percentage of the total value of exports included olive oil, wine, processed leather, cocoons, acorns, figs, and cereals. In this sense, raisins in the nineteenth century was the product that connected the Greek market with the international market and at the same time gave Greek exports an undifferentiated character that manifested itself just after the outbreak of the crisis. The drop in raisin exports reduced the total value of Greek exports by 15 to 25 million drachmas compared to previous years. However, from the beginning of the twentieth century Greek exports followed a more diversified path (Pizanias, 1988, pp. 48–49). Nevertheless, until 1922 raisins remained the main export product of the Greek economy. From then on, tobacco took the first place in exports (Asdrahas, 2011b, p. 59).

The raisin problem began be solved in January 1903 when English financiers offered to buy the raisin production by using future contracts for the next twenty years. However, not all problems were resolved. On April 14, 1905, the Parliament discussed the raisin issue and especially the significant debts that had been accumulated by farmers in the Raisin Bank, which had been established in 1899 with the participation of all raisin producers. In fact, the withholding vouchers held by each farmer had been converted into shares of the Raisin Bank. Moreover, as early as 1903 the Raisin Bank absorbed the surplus production by undertaking the relative risk, which eventually led to its bankruptcy at the beginning of 1904 (Pizanias, 1988, pp. 25–27). However, the Privileged Company to Protect Production and Trade in Currants, established with the participation of Greek and French funds, provided a way out of the problem of redistribution of surplus production to industrial production, which contributed to its stabilization and improvement of the situation of the market (Kostis, 2013, p. 503).

The non-differentiated structure of the Greek economy was evident in other sectors as well. It is characteristic that the surplus over the cost created in the agricultural sector, particularly from the production of raisins in the second half of the nineteenth century, was not invested in processing or infrastructure projects in the agricultural sector in order to increase productivity. On the contrary, it was used either to increase agricultural production in the old extensive way, or for hoarding, speculation, and consumption (Petrakis, 1992, pp. 37–38). This trend was further reinforced by the attitude of the Greek diaspora. Owners of capital belonging to the diaspora used to invest in commercial activities and to act as brokers in transactions involving, inter alia, public loans, and government bonds. The global crisis of the 1870s affected the funds of the Greek diaspora that had been invested in European markets but also in the Ottoman Empire. Therefore, the prospect of investing in the modern Greek state was an outlet for Greek diaspora funds at that time. However, as they used to do, these financiers avoided investing in industry and preferred the less binding and more speculative activities of trade and brokerage (Petrakis, 1992, pp. 39–40). An additional investment way out for diaspora funds was the purchase of land. Indeed, after 1880, diaspora capitalists bought land in Thessaly and Arta from their Ottoman owners. However, these land buyers were not interested in investing in new methods of increasing land productivity. They treated these estates simply as another form of placing their money the same as any other alternative (Petrakis, 1992, p. 42; Svoronos, 1985, p. 15).

Both of these cases demonstrated the lack of any initiative for productive investment in sectors that would act as cutting-edge industries (Rostow, 1960) and boost economic growth. On the contrary, what one observes is the preference by entrepreneurs of the time for short-term investments that could relatively quickly turn into cash and for investments in land. These choices had a political purpose that was closely related to the corresponding economic one as these investments gave the opportunity to diaspora capitalists to influence the finances of the Greek state which was permanently on the brink of bankruptcy (Svoronos, 1985, p. 15).

The history of Greek industry is instructive of an economy so averse to danger as to avoid any serious attempt for industrialization except in cases where government protection was afforded. However, when protection was lifted, these industries did not have the capacity to cope with their competitors in the international arena. A relationship of dependence between industrialists and government was present as early as the first steps of industry in the country. In Otto's time, every initiative in manufacturing was necessarily accompanied by a call to place it under the protection of the king and to endow it with specific facilities, privileges and even direct funding from the state. In any case, these efforts were unsuccessful due to the underdevelopment of the Greek economy and society, which was characterized by a limited division of labor and fragmented markets (Agriantoni, 1986, pp. 16–17).

An example linking conditions of non-diversification in agricultural production and industry is that relating to cocoon production and the silk industry. Sericulture in France was attacked by an epidemic in the early 1850s. This led to a sharp increase in demand for cocoons and a corresponding soaring of their prices. Greek producers reacted quickly to these developments by turning to the production of cocoons as an exportable raw material, putting their processing in second place. In a few years cocoon exports replaced silk exports. The part of the production that was not exported was absorbed by the domestic silk industry. At the end of the 1850s there were five silk factories operating in Greece, employing about 450–500 workers and having a production capacity of 17,000 to 19,000 oke of silk. In fact, this was the first industry in Greece in the sense of systematic processing which was housed in concentrated production units according to the factory system model. However, this phenomenon was rather limited in scope without causing substantial changes in the economic and social structure. After all, these factories were under the control of traders who treated this production as complementary to their main activity. Cocoon exports reached their peak in 1868 and began to fall since then while their prices followed a downward course. Therefore, the surplus of cocoon production had to be absorbed by the domestic silk industry, but without success due to the consequent decline in the activity of the silk industry internationally at the end of the nineteenth century (Agriantoni, 1986, pp. 53–56, 59–62). This is yet another example of dependence of domestic production on international demand without any attempt to diversify local production as a strategy of protection against fluctuations in international demand.

The reaction of Greek entrepreneurs to the failure of the silk industry in the late nineteenth century was to turn toward the domestic market. The domestic market would be both a source of strength and weakness for the Greek industry (Agriantoni, 1986, p. 129). As for the composition of industrial units, about half were active in the food industry, and about 30% were textiles. Tanneries, metallurgies, and chemical plants did not exceed, all together, 15% of the units (Agriantoni, 1986, p. 209). In 1867, 22 factories were in operation with 296 steam power machines. In 1875 the factories increased to 85 with a total power of 1887 hp (Riginos, 1987, pp. 82–83). The above characteristics indicate a small-to-medium-sized industry with poor infrastructure which bought its mechanical equipment from abroad and which had been limited to the production of consumer goods (Agriantoni, 1986, p. 348). This industry went through a phase of slowdown which reached the limits of stagnation from 1875 to 1890 and finally attempted to recover during the last decade of the nineteenth century (Agriantoni, 1986, pp. 111, 113). However, due to the limits of the local market and its inadequate expansion along with the problems related to the underdevelopment of the labor market and the limited availability of capital, Greek industry was not able to take the big step forward and become the leader of economic development through industrialization in the late nineteenth century (Agriantoni, 1986, p. 349). Probably, therefore, the non-diversification model that was followed both in agricultural production and in industry, was the result of a certain mentality of modern Greek society. According to Agriantoni (1986, p. 35) this way of thinking promoted the conjuncture rather than the long-term perception and never really believed in the industrial phenomenon and its prospects. For the same reason, these entrepreneurs did not accept the necessary adjustments required by industrialization which included the long-term undertaking of capital instead of short-term profits through speculation or the security of placing in government bonds (Agriantoni, 1986, pp. 349–350).

The period from 1898 to 1914 was marked by a wave of protectionism which was a collateral consequence of the government's policy of collecting taxes. The new tariff system introduced by the Trikoupis government in 1892 significantly affected the balance between imports and exports. The situation improved during the period 1906–1908 but deteriorated again in 1909 as a result of a crisis that hit the exportable goods. The economic situation improved again in 1910 due to the success of the GXMB Act, which managed to restore monetary stability, and due to favorable international conditions. The period from 1910 to 1912 was marked by a significant rise in exports which reached 88% of imports. However, this increase in export volumes was not accompanied by a similar change in their composition. Agricultural products constituted 75% of the total value of exports for the period 1898–1914 (Tsotsoros, 1993, pp. 153–173). In any case, the Balkan wars provided a favorable opportunity for the development of industry, especially in sectors such as the flour and textile industry (Riginos, 1987, pp. 83–84).

The conditions created by the World War I (1914–1918) did not favor the development of foreign trade. The lack of sufficient foreign exchange reserves faced by the Greek government from 1920 onward led to the decisive intervention of the state in the conduct of foreign trade. This meant the continued presence of tariffs which developed into a protectionist policy tool that characterized most European countries in the 1920s. The new tariff system which was put in place from the first of January 1926 had the declared objective of protecting domestic production (Tsotsoros, 1993, pp. 190–192).

International treaties immediately after World War I (WW I) were not such as to help diversify production and investment in international markets. In particular, in economically backward countries, protectionist policies were aimed at ensuring domestic employment and improving balance of payments, while the doctrine of import substitution dominated the economic policies pursued. These national industries would be developed in an economic environment characterized by minimal infrastructure, insufficient capital, low-skilled labor, and inadequate institutional infrastructure. Industrial units were directed to the production of consumer goods or semi-final products, which in most cases were of low quality and limited competitiveness. The above also characterized the case of Greece in the WW I due to the collapse of international trade and the naval blockade of Athens and Piraeus in the period 1916–1917 (Tsotsoros, 1993, pp. 102–104; Riginos, 1987, pp. 84–85). As noted above, the Greek economy and the Greek industry in particular operated from 1884 and especially from 1892 to 1932 under the protection of the trikoupis tariff system. Although this system was not originally introduced as a means of protecting embryonic industries, it nevertheless provided an opportunity for some industrial plants to import raw materials duty-free (Tsotsoros, 1993, p. 153).

According to the first industrial census of 1917 (subject to its shortcomings and the fact that it did not include the smaller industrial units), there were 2213 industrial units in operation with a total power of 40,000 stream hp and employing 36,124 workers. The food industry dominated both small and medium-sized enterprises. Indeed, 66.76% of small enterprises and 49.4% of medium-sized enterprises were food industries. In contrast, in large companies employing more than 25 workers, textile industries took the lead with 31.21% of total industrial units (Riginos, 1987, pp. 85–87). Between 1921 and 1939, the textile and food industries increased their share in the total value of production from 37.7%

to 45.2%. The chemical industry also dropped its share from 15% to 22.1%. However, 53.9% of the total production value in chemicals was related to traditional agricultural productssuch as soap, pomace oil, and others—glass and fertilizers. In short, the types of products produced by the chemical industry indicate its delay. Even more disappointing are the figures for the units engaged in mechanical products. These products ranged between 3.3% of the total value of industrial production in 1927 and 4.8% in 1938. This is a second example of a backwardness of the country which attempts to meet its needs by importing mechanical equipment from abroad (Tsotsoros, 1993, pp. 123–130). It was also an indication of the country's limited ability to create industries that are able to diversify and become competitive.

However, to purchase "unproductive" assets as a form of investment, such as real estate, can sometimes be the rational choice. Indeed, in times of uncertainty and rising inflation, such as the period immediately after the Asia Minor Disaster, the rising prices in real estate reflected the shift of economic subjects toward the security they had (Tsotsoros, 1993, p. 59). On the other hand, industries were the first victims of those difficult times, as they found themselves at a disadvantage against short-term stock market speculation. Most of these industrial units were heavily indebted, which led to an increase in bankruptcy by 58.8% between 1927 and 1928 (Tsotsoros, 1993, p. 62).

After all, Greek industry has failed to restore a mutually beneficial relationship with the domestic agricultural sector of the economy. Agricultural production could not meet the needs of domestic industry in raw materials such as silk, cocoon wool, cotton, wood, and leather. The industrialists were obliged to import these goods as in the case of Ermoupolis in Syros where local tanners imported raw material and exported processed leather. Important exceptions were the cotton industry, which had a stable and close relationship with local production until the end of the nineteenth century, and of course the alcohol export industry which depended largely on the availability of cheap and low quality raisins. On the other hand, until the interwar period, the domestic fertilizer industry, which was founded in 1910, was oriented toward exports of its products to meet the needs of local farmers (Petmezas, 2006).

From 1928 onward there was an attempt to push economic growth on the basis of monetary stabilization with the help of the League of Nations. The development program of the Venizelos government provided for a protective-interventionist industrial policy which, over the long horizon, had negative consequences for the embryonic-state Greek industry. The main characteristics of the Greek industrial units during the 1930s were their small size, their limited modernization combined with the use of obsolete mechanical equipment, the preoccupation of most enterprises with the early stages of the production process, the small concentration of capital and their orientation toward the internal consumer market (Tsotsoros, 1993, pp. 64–65).

The above is also reflected in the composition of Greek exports during the 1920s and 1930s. During the period 1923–1933 the percentage of food and beverage value in relation to the total value of exports was 38.06% while the percentage of raw and semi-final raw materials was 58.16% on average. These two together made up a total of 96.22% compared to 3.52% which was the average percentage of exported industrial products. During the following period from 1933 to 1939 the percentage of exports of food and beverages reached 38.62% and of raw materials 57.26% on average or in total 95.88% against a weak 4.09% for industrial products (Tsotsoros, 1993, pp. 216, 223).

Another aspect of government policy which contributed to the development of an insufficiently diversified and uncompetitive industry during the interwar period was Article 16 of law 2948 of July 28, 1922. This article provided for preferential treatment of domestic industries as potential government suppliers over foreign ones if the price offered by domestic units did not exceed the foreign price by up to 5%. The legislative decree of 6/10 November 1925 in Article 9 adjusted this threshold upward to 20% while law 4536 of 12 April 1930 allowed the ceiling to be raised to 30%. In the 1930s the government made its orders with a preference limit to domestic industries of between 25% and 40% and in some cases with exclusive suppliers such as the Hellenic Wool Industry or the PYRKAL ammunition industry which supplied the Greek army (Tsotsoros, 1993, pp. 240–242). It is true that industrial production doubled in the period from 1921 to 1930. However, there was also a doubling of industrial units of medium and large size. This means that economic growth has a quantitative character while maintaining a minimum amount of investment in fixed capital as well as stagnant labor productivity (Riginos, 1987, pp. 108–111).

During the Occupation of the country by the Axis powers, the majority of industries ceased to function while money funds evaporated due to inflation. This situation changed in the post-war period and the country went through an unprecedented process of industrialization in the 30 years from 1950 to 1980, especially in sectors such as electricity, telecommunications, and transport, but with direct involvement of the state (Asdrahas, 2011b, pp. 186, 191–192). The Hellenic Telecommunications Organization (OTE) was founded in 1949, the Public Power Corporation (PPC) in 1950 and the Public Gas Company in 1952. In addition, two government agencies for the purpose of financing industry were established in the 1950s: the Organization for the Financing of Economic Development (OFED) in 1954 and the Organization for Industrial Development (OID) in 1959, which merged into the Hellenic Bank for Industrial Development (HBID) in 1964 (Asdrahas, 2011b, pp. 431–432). However, the problematic nature of this industrialization becomes obvious if one takes into account the main source of demand that led to this process. So this source was in domestic consumption rather than demand from abroad which would have given impetus to an extroverted and export-oriented economy. Domestic industrial production barely exceeded domestic demand for consumer goods, creating an index of domestic production adequacy of 103.27 in 1958 and 106.00 in 1977. The corresponding index for intermediate goods lags behind domestic consumption as it is in the order of 82.94 in 1958 and 86.51 in 1977. Finally, the adequacy ratio for capital goods and mechanical equipment was only 59.00 in 1958 and 69.27 in 1977 (Asdrahas, 2011b, pp. 212–213). In any case, the secondary sector lost ground against the tertiary sector as its share fell from 25.8% between 1963 and 1973 to 14.7% between 1974 and 1979, while the share of the tertiary sector increased from 50.1% to 77.1%. The lack of competitiveness of Greek industry found its reflection in not being able to adapt to the adverse economic conditions of the 1970s with high energy prices, high interest rates, fluctuating exchange rates and high labor costs. The result was the over-indebtedness of the industrial units and the decline of many of them in the following decades (Asdrahas, 2011b, p. 639).

References

Acemoglu, D., & Robinson, J. A. (2012). *Why Nations Fail: The Origins of Power, Prosperity and Poverty*. New York, NY: Crown Publishers.

Agriantoni, Ch. (1986). *The Beginnings of Industrialization in Greece in the 19th Century*. Athens: Historical Archive of the Commercial Bank of Greece. (in Greek).

Agriantoni, Ch., Bournova, E., Papathanassopoulos, K., Progoulakis, G., Riginos, M., Charlaftis, Tz, et al. (2002). *Introduction to Modern Greek Economic History (18th–20th Century)*. Athens: Typothito / Dardanos. (in Greek).

Asdrachas, S. (2011a). *Economic History of the Greek State: The Formation of the National Economy* (Vol. I). Athens: Piraeus Bank Group Cultural Foundation. (in Greek).

Asdrachas, S. (2011b). *Economic History of the Greek State: Economic Functions and Performance* (Vol. II). Athens: Piraeus Bank Group Cultural Foundation. (in Greek).

Courakis, A. S. (1981). Financial Structure and Policy in Greece: Retrospect and Prospect. *Greek Economic Review, 3*, 205–244.

Dertilis, G. (2014). *History of the Greek state 1830–1920*. Heraklion: Crete University Press. (in Greek).

Ellis, H. S., Psilos, D. D., Westebbe, R. M., & Nicolaou, C. (1964). *Industrial Capital in Greek Development*. Center for Economic Research, Research Monograph Series, No 8, Athens.

Fragiadis, A. (2007). *Greek Economy 19th–20th Century: From the Struggle for Independence to the Economic and Monetary Union of Europe*. Athens: Nefeli Publications. (in Greek).

Gardika, K., Kechriotis, V., Loukos, C. Lyritzis, Ch., & Maronitis, N. (2008). *The Establishment of the Greek State: International Context, Power and Politics in the 19th Century*. Athens: Nefeli Publications. (in Greek).

Garganas, N. C., & Tavlas, G. S. (2001). Monetary Regimes and Inflation Performance: The Case of Greece. In R. C. Bryant, N. C. Garganas, & G. S. Tavlas (Eds.), *Greece's Economic Performance and Prospects*. Athens: Bank of Greece and The Brookings Institution.

Halikias, D. J. (1978). *Money and Credit in a Developing Economy: The Greek Case*. New York, NY: New York University Press. Retrieved from: http://www.brookings.edu/about/projects/bpea/papers/2015/reinhart-trebesch-greek-debt-crisis.

Harisopoulos Committee. (1979). *On the Study of the Banking System*. Athens: Bank of Greece. (in Greek).

Katseli, L. (1990). *Structural Adjustment of the Greek Economy* (CEPR Discussion Paper, No 374). London: Centre for Economic Policy Research.

Karatza Committee. (1987). *The Report of the Committee for the Reform and Modernization of the Greek Banking System*. Athens: EET. (in Greek)

Karouzou, E. (2006). Institutional Framework and Agricultural Economy. In K. Kostis & S. D. Petmezas (Eds.), *The Development of the Greek Economy During the 19th Century (1830–1914)* (pp. 175–218). Athens: Alpha Historical Archive Bank. (in Greek).

Kostis, K. (1987). *Agricultural Economy and Agricultural Bank: Aspects of the Greek Economy in the Interwar Period (1919–1928)*. Athens: National Bank of Greece Cultural Foundation. (in Greek).

Kostis, K. (1997). *Collaboration and Competition: The 70 Years of the Hellenic Banks Association*. Athens: Alexandria Publications. (in Greek).

Kostis, K. (2006). Public finances. In K. Kostis & S. D. Petmezas (Eds.), *The Development of the Greek Economy During the 19th Century (1830–1914)* (pp. 293–336). Athens: Alpha Bank Historical Archive. (in Greek).

Kostis, K. (2013). *The Spoiled Children of History: The Formation of the Modern Greek State 18th–21st Century*. Athens: Polis Publications. (in Greek).

Kostis, K., & Tsokopoulos, V. (1988). *The Banks in Greece 1898–1928*. Athens: Papazisis and EET. (in Greek).

La Porta, R., Lopez-de-Silanes, F., Shleifer, A., & Vishny, R. W. (1997). Legal Determinants of External Finance. *The Journal of Finance, 52*(3), 1131–1150.

La Porta, R., Lopez-de-Silanes, F., Shleifer, A., & Vishny, R. W. (1998). Law and Finance. *Journal of Political Economy, 106*(6), 1113–1155.

Lavdas, K. A. (2006). Interest Groups in Disjoined Corporatism: Social Dialogue in Greece and European‘ Competitive Corporatism. In K. Featherstone (Ed.), *Politics and Policy in Greece*. London and New York, NY: Routledge.

McKinnon, R. I. (1973). *Money and Capital in Economic Development*. Washington, DC: Brookings Institution.

North, D. C. (1991). Institutions. *The Journal of Economic Perspectives, 5*(1), 97–112.

North, D. C. (2005). *Understanding the Process of Economic Change*. Princeton, NJ and Oxford: Princeton University Press.

Pagano, M., & Volpin, P. (2001). The Political Economy of Finance. *Oxford Review of Economic Policy, 17*(4), 502–519.

Pagoulatos, G. (2003). *Greece's New Political Economy: State, Finance and Growth from Postwar to EMU*. Houndmills: Palgrave Macmillan.

Petmezas, S. D. (2003). *The Greek Agricultural Economy during the 19th Century*. The regional dimension, Heraklion: University Publications of Crete. (in Greek).

Petmezas, S. D. (2006). Agricultural Economy. In K. Kostis & S. D. Petmezas (Eds.), *The Development of the Greek Economy during the 19th Century (1830–1914)* (pp. 103–152). Athens: Alpha Bank Historical Archive. (in Greek).

Petrakis, P. E. (1985). *The Banking Financing of the Public and Private Sector in Greece (1844–1869)*. Athens: National Bank of Greece Cultural Foundation. (in Greek).

Petrakis, P. E. (1992). *Points of Change in the Activity of the Greek Economy (1840–1913)*. Athens: National Bank of Greece Cultural Foundation. (in Greek).

Pizanias, P. (1988). *Economic History of Greek raisins 1851–1912. Production, International Market, Price Formation, Crisis*. Athens: Research and Culture Institute of the Commercial Bank of Greece. (in Greek).
Psalidopoulos, M. (2010). Economic Thought and Policies in 19th Century Greece. In M. Psalidopoulos (Ed.). *Economists and Economic Policy in Modern Greece*. Athens: Midnight editions. (in Greek).
Psilos, D. D. (1964). *Capital Market in Greece*. Center for Economic Research, Research Monograph Series, No. 9, Athens.
Rostow, W. W. (1960). *The Stages of Economic Growth: A Non Communist Manifesto*. Cambridge: Cambridge University Press.
Riginos, M. (1987). *Production Structures and Wages in Greece, 1909–1936*. Athens: Educational and Research Foundation of the Commercial Bank of Greece. (in Greek).
Sakellaropoulos, T. (2003). *Essays on Economic and Social History*. Athens: Dionikos. (in Greek).
Shaw, E. S. (1973). *Financial Deepening in Economic Development*. New York, NY: Oxford University Press.
Svoronos, N. (1985). *Overview of modern Greek history*. Athens: Themelio. (in Greek).
Tsotsoros, S. N. (1993). *The Formation of Industrial Capital in Greece (1898–1939): The Slow Industrialization* (Vol. I). Athens: National Bank of Greece Cultural Foundation.
Williamson, O. E. (1985). *The Economic Institutions of Capitalism*. New York, NY: Free Press.
Williamson, O. E. (1996). *The Mechanisms of Governance*. New York, NY: Oxford University Press.
Vergopoulos, K. (1978). *State and Economic Policy in the 19th Century*. Athens: Exantas. (in Greek).
Zolotas, X. (1964). *Monetary Balance and Economic Development: The Greek Economy over the Last Fifteen Years, Problems and Perspectives*. Athens: Bank of Greece. (in Greek).

CHAPTER 3

The Geostrategical Settings and the Systemic Risks

3.1 Introduction

The economic and social world environment is changing very rapidly. One would say that the speed of change in economic and social developments is the main feature of the twentieth and especially the beginning of the twenty-first century. Moreover, the Covid-19 crisis has been described as an accelerator (Petrakis, 2020) and an amplifier for existing developments, has brought these changes more quickly. These changes concern all participants in the world economic process. At the same time, the critical time for a society and economy almost never arises only from the peculiarities that derive from its intrinsic space. Usually, there is a conjuncture that involves the interaction of external and endogenous forces.

This chapter aims to present the Greek economy in the context of wider geostrategic developments in the wider region of Southeastern Europe. The production system, as it operates in the wider area of the Greek economy and society, like any economy and society, operates in an international environment shaped by international economic and political relations. Therefore, the study of the terms of formation of the complex concept of National Power has an important priority, because it ultimately determines the terms of the game at the global level and in the background of the picture the terms of international exchange of the products of the productive system. At the same time, it is particularly useful to detect the systemic risks that the Greek economy faces over time and

P. E. Petrakis and P. C. Kostis, *The Evolution of the Greek Economy*,
The Political Economy of Greek Growth up to 2030,
https://doi.org/10.1007/978-3-030-47210-8_3

which have determined to a significant extent the productive model of the economy and the behavior of Greek society.

The structure of this chapter is as follows: in Sect. 3.2 of the chapter, the main geostrategic developments concerning the area of Southeast Europe are presented. In Sect. 3.3, the concept and evolution of national power is presented. Finally, Sect. 3.4 presents the systemic risks facing the Greek economy over time, while describing how they affect its economic performance. Finally, data on the Covid-19 pandemic are presented in Sect. 3.5 and the global and domestic consequences are commented on.

3.2 The Geostrategical Settings

The cultural and historical history of Southeast Europe is an integral part of European culture, influenced throughout the centuries by the cultural characteristics of the various societies that constitute the region. These cultural characteristics differ significantly as the countries that constitute Southeastern Europe are influenced by social attitudes and influences coming from the Eastern Mediterranean, but also from Central, Western and Eastern Europe.

Southeastern Europe and especially the Balkans are considered an area of exceptional geopolitical and geostrategic importance as they are located at the crossroads of three continents (Africa, Asia, and Europe). The geopolitical and geostrategic importance of the region have been important elements for intercultural development and the particular characteristics of the countries in this region. During the three thousand years of their history the Balkans have been developed as the crossroads of different cultures, which led to two main results (Sotirovic, 2019): (a) the presence of a large number of national minorities in the various countries (Hungarians in Romania, Bulgarians in Turkey, Albanians in Greece, Albanians and Bulgarians in Serbia and Montenegro, Czechs in Bosnia-Herzegovina, Serbs and Hungarians in Croatia, and (b) the existence of many different religions and Churches. Over the years, the Balkans have experienced alternate imperial drives, as well as competing ideologies and contradictory social, political and economic systems. The fact that the members of these societies live in an area of high international tensions, led them to seek a way out of the constant internal and external pressures, developing nationalist perceptions. At the same time, the Southeast Europe societies accepted many imported institutions, rules and customs or habits, which in many cases were reformed in accordance with local traditions and necessities.

At the same time, Southeastern Europe has always been a geographical area where there were strong economic and cultural convergences and conflicts. In recent decades, significant national and cultural tensions remain in this area, such as: Serbia Kosovo, FYROM (today North Macedonia)—Greece, Greece—Cyprus—Turkey, Ukraine—Russia, Georgia—Russia, Turkey—Kurdish populations, Middle East—Suez. At the same time, the region is an area of economic development and diffusion of economic interests. On all sides, there are geographical and political influences and upheavals, since these tensions fluctuate broadly.

In particular, for the Greek economy, tension with Turkey puts pressure on economic activity, since it is certain to put increasing pressure on defense spending, etc. The evolution of Turkish aircraft activity in the Aegean, especially after 1974, is characteristic. Another typical example is the hypothetical existence of oil deposits in Southeast Europe, including Cyprus. Obviously, the Covid-19 crisis has re-organized the relevant priorities, with oil prices falling, etc. but general trends remain. These issues could trigger new rounds of tension. In addition, the Greek economy and society are close to parts of the world in which international influence has not taken a definite form (Eurasia) and as a result they have a status of claimed areas. If we add to this fact the revisionist attitude of Turkey toward the Treaties of Lausanne (1923) that shaped the geographical boundaries of present-day Turkey, they form a picture of an international environment with several turbulence, not found in most of the other countries of the European Union. This environment leads to disproportionately high investments in the military sector: aircraft and frigates for the Greek side (equipment expenditure as a share of defense expenditure was 12.3% in 2019), aircraft carriers and anti-aircraft systems for the Turkish side (equipment expenditure as a share of defense expenditure was 38.6% in 2019) (NATO, 2019). In fact, there are estimates that defense spending in the two countries will increase in the coming years for both Greece and Turkey. Therefore, new problems of strategic choices arise, expressed by the initiatives of the Chinese in the form of the Silk Road for the commercial connection with the Balkans and the interests of Russia (especially in Serbia) which has also developed strong relations with Turkey with a significant presence on Syria. Essentially, Greece is called upon to identify where the new or emerging international centers of influence are located and to decide how and to what extend to connect with them (e.g., Russia).

In general terms, the economic situation of a national economy is not the only condition for the development of the standard of living of citizens has an impact and is being influenced by the process of development that the economy is to follow. The reason for this is that an eventual unfortunate military conflict with a neighbor country could drive the standard of living of its citizens to collapse.

However, the picture of relations that are being developed in Southeastern Europe is, of course, not only a scene of conflict. To a higher degree, it is a field of development of economic relations.

Greece is the largest foreign investor in Albania in the last 15–20 years. Greek investments in Bulgaria total 2.28 billion euros, while Bulgaria is the fifth largest importer of Greek products and the 11th in exporting products to Greece. Northern Macedonia is Greece's third-largest trading partner, with Greek investments totaling nearly 474 million euros, while Greece is its country's third largest supplier. The stock of Greek investments in Romania amounts to 1.36 billion euros, while about 500 companies of Greek interests operate in the country. Total Greek investments in Serbia amounted to 1.5 billion euros and there are 150 active Greek businesses in the country. Greek exports to Bosnia and Herzegovina totaled 80 million euros in 2017 and included aluminum and aluminum products, building materials, fruits, vegetables, and plastics.

At the same time, the port of Piraeus is one of the deepest ports in the Mediterranean and with the shortest distance from Suez Canal where the Chinese now have a decisive presence. Also, the Port of Thessaloniki is the closest hub to the Balkans and Southeast Europe. Alexandroupolis Port connects or will connect, via rail, Bulgaria and Romania.

Thus, the area of the Balkans and S.E. Europe is also a privileged area of the development of foreign trade for the Greek economy. Table 3.1 presents the imports and exports of the Greek economy to and from the economies of Southeast Europe for 2017.

Exports of products and services to Southeast European countries accounted for 24.7% of total exports for 2017 while the corresponding figure for imports was 10.6%. As a percentage of all trade to and from countries in Europe and Central Asia, the percentage for exports is 36.7% and for imports 16.1%.

The result of the great exposure of the Greek economy in the Southeast European region was that the region was a source of economic instability

Table 3.1 Trade between the Greek economy and the countries of SE Europe (2017)

	Export (US$ thousand)	*Export Partner Share (%)*	*Import (US$ thousand)*	*Import Partner Share (%)*
Albania	521,124.57	1.62	100,818.72	0.18
Bosnia and Herzegovina	90,435.5	0.28	12,910.39	0.02
Bulgaria	1,521,239.36	4.73	1,788,817.23	3.23
Croatia	87,417.22	0.27	69,057.33	0.12
Cyprus	1,947,210.84	6.06	418,875.2	0.76
Hungary	154,295.11	0.48	474,911.83	0.86
Romania	955,423.26	2.97	978,352.07	1.77
Serbia, FR(Serbia/Montenegro)	334,967.08	1.04	191,244.88	0.35
Turkey	2,206,671.94	6.86	1,618,328.87	2.93
Ukraine	140,992.24	0.44	207,153.01	0.37
Southeast Europe	7,959,777.12	24.75	5,860,469.53	10.60
Europe and Central Asia	21,682,489.28	67.43	36,350,491.24	65.73
World	32,154,816.41	100	55,300,597.55	100

Source World Bank—World Integrated Trade Solution and authors' calculations and creation

for the economy during the 2008 crisis. As a result, exports in the region were reduced, while the stability of the Greek banking system was fluctuated since there is a significant number of Greek bank branches in the wider region. In contrast to the Covid-19 crisis, the region has shown stabilizing effects since, with the exception of Turkey, the other countries have not suffered very great damage.

In the future, significant geostrategic developments are expected in the region that may change the prevailing balances. For example, serious national issues such as the refugee and migrant crisis in the eastern Greek islands and the issue of Cyprus, as well as the exploitation of energy deposits. Also, Kosovo remains a constant source of unrest in the Balkans, although having very low risk. The most serious change noted is the one regarding Greek-Russian relations due to the Russian-Turkish approach. This issue, of course, needs much more analysis since it relates to the Greek-American, the Greek-Turkish and the Turkish-Russian relations and the views of public opinion in Greece on the Russian factor. All these developments should be taken into account although it is generally considered that the risk of creating serious transnational problems with serious economic consequences, although progressively increasing, is still low.

3.3 The National Power

National power is the comprehensive expression of all the potential that a nation possesses at a given time to promote internally and internationally the achievement of national goals, regardless of the difficulties it faces (Kelly, 1994 [1992]).

The question of national power has an international political character, and is generally involved with individual considerations, which leads to criticism of the way in which indicators of national power are constructed. The purpose of this analysis is not to contribute to the discussion of what factors should be taken into account when attempting to evaluate a similar indicator, but to obtain a picture of Greece in relation to its competitors. What is understandable, however, is that the concept of shaping the power of a state mechanism nowadays has a wide content and covers key areas of human activity. Thus, it covers wealth and standard of living, war capability, technological capability, the growth potential, and represents human capital, energy security, and the conditions of organization and operation of human society.

Bialoskorski, Kiczma, and Sulek (2019) calculate the national power of economies based on Sulek model i.e., by calculating the national power through economic, military, and geopolitical power. For the calculation of economic power, the gross domestic product of economies is used as a measure of the produced product, the population as a measure of demographic factors and the wider geographical area as a spatial factor. For the calculation of the military power, the factors used are the military spending as a percentage of GDP as a military and economic factor, the number of active soldiers as a demographic and military factor and the wider geographical area as a spatial factor. Finally, the calculation of geopolitical power uses the arithmetic mean of economic power and twofold the military power (to indicate the significance of the military factor in shaping the current distribution of power). Bialoskorski et al. (2019) calculate this indicator for 1992 and 2017 for 195 countries in the following way:

$$\text{Economic Power} = \text{GDP}^{0.652} + \text{Population}^{0.217} + \text{Geographical area}^{0.109}$$

$$\text{Military Power} = \text{Military Expense}^{0.652} + \text{Military Population}^{0.217} + \text{Geographical area}^{0.109}$$

$$\text{Geopolitical Power} = (\text{Economic Power} + (2 * \text{Military Power}))/3$$

Table 3.2 shows the scores of the index for Southeast European countries and the ranking of countries among all 195 countries.

Greece is being presented as the second largest national power in the region for 2017, following Turkey. Of course, it should be noted that Greece is one of the countries in which the level of national power deteriorated in 2017 compared to 1992. This deterioration concerns a reduction of the score by 36.93% in economic power (reduction by 26 positions in international ranking), by 7.5% in the military (maintaining the 34th position among 195 countries) and by 16.36% in the geopolitical power (reduction by 10 positions in the international ranking). The crisis of 2008 played, as expected, a role in this, which led to a significant reduction in GDP and the military spending.

It should be noted that all the economies included in the above tables have lost positions in the world rankings compared to 1992, in all the individual power indices (with the exception of Turkey, which slightly improved its ranking in the economic power index), highlighting the influences of the recent global financial crisis in the wider region. However, it is clear that the role of the Greek economy in this broader context of relations has been and remains particularly important.

3.4 The Systemic Risks

Since the birth of the Greek state, economic growth is accompanied by deep national, social, and macroeconomic crises (Petrakis, 2011). This is a process that has consequences on the conditions of accumulation of capital, labor and the rest of growth factors.

The major negative events in the Greek economy and society during long historical periods are depicted in Table 3.3. As such can be considered wars, revolts, hostilities abroad (outside the Greek territory), or internal conflicts (wars of the Greek state—Greco-Turkish wars, Balkan wars, civil wars, epidemics—Covid 19, etc.), periods of great economic crises with external or internal origin. The criterion to include these events in Table 3.3 is their impact on domestic economy. The magnitude of these negative figures is of unimaginable scale according to current events: (i.e., Greco-Turkish war of 1897, World War I and II, the German Occupation of 1941–1944, the civil war of 1946–1949, etc.). It should be noted that

Table 3.2 Ratings in the national power (1992 vs. 2017)

	1992						*2017*					
	Economic Power		*Military Power*		*Geopolitical Power*		*Economic Power*		*Military Power*		*Geopolitical Power*	
	Score	*Ranking*	*Score*	*Ranking*	*Score*	*Ranking*	*Score*	*Ranking*	*Score*	*Ranking*	*Score*	*Ranking*
Turkey	7.72	*(18)*	9.29	*(13)*	8.77	*(16)*	10.99	*(17)*	7.70	*(22)*	8.80	*(20)*
Greece	3.61	*(31)*	3.97	*(34)*	3.85	*(33)*	2.27	*(57)*	3.69	*(34)*	3.22	*(43)*
Ukraine	4.49	*(29)*	8.65	*(17)*	7.26	*(21)*	2.50	*(52)*	3.29	*(40)*	3.03	*(45)*
Romania	1.68	*(51)*	2.83	*(45)*	2.45	*(46)*	2.86	*(47)*	3.04	*(43)*	2.98	*(46)*
Hungary	1.69	*(50)*	2.41	*(50)*	2.17	*(53)*	1.69	*(63)*	1.06	*(69)*	1.27	*(68)*
Croatia	–	*(–)*	–	*(–)*	1.44	*(6)*	0.88	*(69)*	0.73	*(85)*	1.09	*(55)*
Bulgaria	0.70	*(74)*	2.81	*(46)*	2.11	*(54)*	0.90	*(82)*	0.73	*(76)*	0.79	*(78)*
Serbia	–	*(–)*	5.72	*(24)*	–	*(–)*	0.71	*(95)*	0.59	*(85)*	0.63	*(87)*
Cyprus	0.25	*(111)*	0.45	*(90)*	0.38	*(87)*	0.25	*(134)*	0.34	*(104)*	0.31	*(109)*
Bosnia Herzegovina	–	*(–)*	–	*(–)*	–	*(–)*	0.34	*(121)*	0.21	*(116)*	0.25	*(117)*
Albania	0.09	*(137)*	0.18	*(112)*	0.15	*(111)*	0.24	*(137)*	0.14	*(124)*	0.18	*(125)*
North Macedonia	0.16	*(126)*	–	*(–)*	–	*(–)*	0.21	*(141)*	0.14	*(123)*	0.17	*(126)*

Note Presentation of the countries in the table has been made based on the score in the geopolitical power in 2017
Source Bialoskorski et al. (2019) and authors' creation

Table 3.3 Negative incidents in the Greek economy and society: 1831–2020

		1831–1878	*1879–1938*	*1939–1953*	*1954–1974*	*1975–2020*
Wars	Ext. origin	5	5	6	–	–
	Int. origin	7	3	8	–	–
Severe economic crises	Ext. origin	5	5	4	2	9
	Int. origin	5	4	4	–	8
Severe political crises	Ext. origin	1	2	–	–	–
	Int. origin	4	3	–	7	–
Incidents to number of years ratio		0.57	0.37	1.57	0.45	0.38

Note All events are included in the calculation presented by units relative to the number of years of their duration. If in one year 2 events take place, they are presented in the Table with a single unit. As negative episodes we consider wars, uprisings, very serious international crises, etc. Their presentation is based on whether they have endogenous or exogenous origin, that is, whether their birth appears to be within or outside the Greek territory. The incidence of negative events in Greece is particularly high. Indeed, the cumulative appearance of endogenous and exogenous events, creates an increased density of phenomena of instability in the economic and social environment. A detailed description of the events is given in the Appendix to this chapter, in Table 3.5
Source Authors' own creation

these events took place in a weak economic structure with low levels of extroversion.

High frequency of negative events are depicted for the pre-1974 period. Since 1975, however, a period of relative stability is presented, until the debt crisis of 2010 broke out.

In addition, if one observes the number of years from 1833 to 2016 (based on the availability of data from Maddisson Database 2018) during which the Greek economy is experiencing recessionary conditions, she will notice that during 78 of these 183 years (i.e., 42.6% of this total period) the Greek economy is experiencing conditions of decline in GDP per capita (Table 3.5).

In fact, compared to other economies it appears that the Greek economy has a smaller number of recessionary years only compared to developing economies such as Venezuela, Colombia, Indonesia, Uruguay, Brazil, and South Africa, and has the highest percentage of recessionary years compared to all European and other developed economies presented in Table 3.4.

Table 3.4 Number of recessionary years during the period 1833–2016

	Number of available annual data of GDP per capita changes for the period 1833–2016 (A)	*Number of years under conditions of declining GDP per capita (B)*	*Percentage years under conditions of declining GDP per capita in comparison to total available data (B)/(A) (%)*
Venezuela	183	89	48.6
Colombia	146	70	47.9
Indonesia	175	83	47.4
Uruguay	145	67	46.2
Brazil	166	75	45.2
South Africa	152	68	44.7
Greece	183	78	42.6
Spain	166	70	42.2
Argentina	141	59	41.8
Italy	183	76	41.5
United States	183	75	41.0
Portugal	169	69	40.8
Chile	183	74	40.4
Netherlands	183	71	38.8
Japan	146	56	38.4
United Kingdom	183	69	37.7
Finland	156	58	37.2
Australia	183	68	37.2
France	183	67	36.6
Switzerland	165	60	36.4
Canada	146	52	35.6
Denmark	183	65	35.5
Norway	183	64	35.0
Belgium	170	58	34.1
Austria	146	44	30.1
Germany	166	50	30.1
Sweden	183	55	30.1
Poland	142	39	27.5

Note The above table includes only those economies for which data are available for the period from 1833 onwards (although some of the economies show some discontinuities or the data begin a little later). Countries are classified according to the result of the third column of the table
Source Maddison database (2018) and authors' own calculations and creation

Obviously this demonstrates the fact that Greek society lives constantly under the pressure of the limited ability to finance what it perceives as its needs. In fact, the reality is more negative. In the 190 years period since the formation of the Greek state, only two brief intervals would be identified as not subject to intensive inflationary pressures: The period of reconstruction after World War II and Greek civil war, which lasted until the first oil crisis (1953–1973) and the first decade of Eurozone membership 2000–2007. Just one generation, the one born and raised in the 1960s and 1970s, did not experience any serious social or economic turbulence during its upbringing (in the first 15 years of life). Typical is the response of Professor Reinhart (University of Maryland), which when in October questioned about the state of the Greek debt and the prospects opened, replied: "Greece, since its independence in 1830, is in a state of bankruptcy almost 50% of the time. Does that mean anything to you?"

Those observations would have a certain value if we assumed that the upbringing of this generation did not bear the marks of their parents' experiences, an assumption that is, of course, implausible. Consequently, risk as a component of economic reality is also a component of the personal, social and economic lives of Greeks, ever since the creation of the Greek state. Essentially, the society's survival terms have competed with its development terms.

The role of macroeconomic experiences in individual investment behavior, and by extension in the attitude of a society toward investment, was primarily investigated in response to the effects of the great depression of 1929 (Friedman & Schwartz, 1963). The starting point is the assumption that people do not have stable attitudes toward risk. Instead attitudes are formed according to personal experiences (Hertwig, Barron, Weber, & Erev, 2004). Indeed, Malmendier and Nagel (2011) demonstrated that households with experience of higher capital markets returns are less risk averse: they participate to a greater extent to capital markets and allocate a larger part of their wealth to such investments. Moreover, households with experience in periods of higher inflation tend to invest a smaller fraction of their assets in bond markets, while they tend to retain more cash and prefer investments of shorter maturities. Such human behavior can be interpreted either by the formation of endogenous development preferences, where the risk depends on the returns of hazardous past investments (Palacios-Huerta & Santos, 2004), or by learning, when the existing perceptions depend on real past experiences.

The existence of systematically high levels of risk weights on the domestic production structure (data refer to years previous those of the current crisis):

(a) The prevalence of small and medium traditional type enterprises that form a weak private sector.
(b) The absence of innovation in business.
(c) The formation of weak institutions with a precarious character and ad hoc features, which means that they are created in order to deal with specific situations and not to help the economic system operate.
(d) The prevalence, from time to time, of conditions of "banking liquidity panic" (1931, 1991, 2010–2011).

The existence of systematically high levels of risk influences other sectors, such as foreign policy and foreign economic relations (Fey & Ramsay, 2010), creating a constantly volatile international relations environment with domestic consequences, i.e., Communist North threat (until 1990), eastern threat (Turkey), the Cyprus problem, etc. Systemic risks should include those of the Covid-19 that increase risk and uncertainty on a global basis (see next section).

3.5 The Global and Domestic Consequences of Covid-19: The Systemic Risks

The outburst of Covid-19 was geographically located in Wuhan, China in December 2019 and in less than three months, it was recognized as a pandemic on March 11, 2020 by the World Health Organization (2020) and grew into a global threat to citizens' health, putting the healthcare systems and economies of the countries to a strong test. The effects of the pandemic concern all human activities and it is difficult to control them and assess the risk of their expansion. This makes it particularly difficult to predict the next day of the healthcare crisis, as the properties of the virus are not fully understood—isolation of people is the only weapon against the virus—and they can change; political responses will be uneven, often delayed and possibly incorrect, and the reactions of businesses and households are uncertain (Carlsson-Szlezak, Reeves, & Swartz, 2020).

The extent of the social and economic dislocation of States around the world as a result of the pandemic creates conditions for the most severe post-war global crisis, affecting employment and production, consumer and investment confidence, demand and supply, and its chains, particularly, in critical sectors such as transport, trade, and tourism. At the same time, people are dominated by fear and uncertainty and States are closing their borders. This is undoubtedly a turning point in the modern history of mankind. The economic crisis that will follow will not even be close to the 2008 crisis, as it affects the whole world in a systemic way. People do not work, shops are closed and every day it's like Sunday (Bremmer, 2020).

The economic effects of the pandemic are expected to spread over the medium to long term, reducing the growth rates of countries globally and shaping a new economic environment on the next day of the crisis. In particular, the perceived vulnerability of global supply chains, coupled with the reduced manufacturing activity of recent decades in developed Western countries, will increase self-sufficiency and protectionism policies (Shilling, 2020). However, the hope that this promotes domestic jobs and incomes will be shattered, as national and empirical obstacles have historically proved to restrict economic growth. At the same time, fiscal policy is expected to become active as monetary policy is proven to be weak. Thus, in addition to measures to boost employment and incomes affected by the recession and the redistribution of wealth through increased taxation, there are likely to be significant infrastructure costs, notably in economies such as Greece and Italy, resulting in a further surge in the countries' public debt.

Global supply will continue to exceed international demand, reducing prices and interest rates. Low inflation rates, possibly even deflation, will reduce the trend to consumption and investment, further limiting economic recovery (Shilling, 2020). This negative development will be accompanied by the inability to repay private debt and the impending bankruptcy of many companies, which will result in stricter borrowing criteria and a shift of investment funds to secure, even of very low yield, assets (government bonds).

The epidemiological crisis also advocates different incentives and behaviors that may become permanent. Individuals—especially older people, even after relaxing restrictive measures—are expected to minimize leisure trips and mass gatherings, placing the tourism, food, and leisure industries under strain. Distance work and education, with a wide application during the quarantine period, may increase over time compared to pre-pandemic levels (Shilling, 2020). This will lead to structural reclassifications in the economies of the countries to the benefit of certain sectors (such as information technology) and to the detriment of others (such as tourism and transport). At the same time, consumer uncertainty and subsequent cost postponement can be consolidated, with long-term effects on economic activity.

In the political field, amid the pandemic, unfavorable conditions increase the acceptance rates of state leaders (Bremmer, 2020), as the world joins government policies and the need for a strong leader to manage this crisis arises. It is true, however, that a prolonged freeze of economies—which is damaging to the supply side, with immediate strong effects on the real economy—is a new ground for policy-makers, unlike their experience on financial crisis management (Carlsson-Szlezak et al., 2020). The poor handling of the epidemiological crisis and the development of a serious health issue in a new economic crisis, with long-term consequences for citizens, will result in political responsibilities and political costs.

Although decisive measures are now taking place within States after the initial delayed response, the world lacks an effective leadership that will lead the global agenda. That is why, in the first global crisis facing this world, the international community's response is inadequate and far from coordinated. On the contrary, it is deeply politicized (Bremmer, 2020). The epidemiological problem can be exacerbated by international economic and commercial competition between States and the possible, financially tempting, hasty lifting of the restrictions against the spread of the virus.

The unprecedented global pandemic has created a double global crisis: health care and the ensuing economic crisis. A double crisis that creates simultaneous failures that reinforce each other. Covid-19 may mark a radical transformation, seen only once in a century, shattering past assumptions (Mishra, 2020). This was the case at the beginning of the last century, when optimism that the progress of humanity was irreversible and that the free world market for goods, capital, and labor is the best insurance against war. Both were denied by the Great War and the subsequent Great Recession, leading to a new stand in arts, science and philosophy, but also in economics. At that time it was difficult to understand the main causes, as they were set in motion decades ago and had been neglected. This is also the case at the present time, where all the components of the disaster at the beginning of the twentieth century are present on a larger scale (Mishra, 2020). Covid-19, as a follow-up to the 2008 economic crisis, which caused deeper and greater damage than the Great Recession, can only be the first of many shocks ahead (Mishra, 2020).

Appendix: Negative Episodes in Greece

Table 3.5 gives a brief chronology of the crises of exogenous (A) and endogenous (B) origin for the Greek economy from the foundation of the Greek state to the present day (1831–2018). Brief comments and bibliographical references are given, which were kindly prepared for the needs of this work by Riginios (Prof. of NKUA) and Progoulakis (Scientific Associate of the Department of Economics, NKUA).

Crises of Exogenous Origin

A1 Anglo-American stock market crisis (1836–1837) due to the instability of the banking system (Sobel, 1999, p. 32).

A2 Agricultural crisis and railway bubble: The crisis of 1847–1848 in Europe combines elements of the crisis of old and new type. Old type: decline in agricultural production, rising prices of food, declining demand for industrial products, expansion of the recession throughout the economy. New type: over-investment in railways and then stock price collapse.

For the agricultural crisis see E. Labrousse (1992, p. 185).

A3 Revolutions in France, Germany and Austria. See Hobsbawm (1962, p. 150).

A4 Crimean War (see also B3).

A5 Financial crisis in England, Italy and Germany. The crisis is mainly American and is related to the fall of the "barons" of the railways (Geisst, 2004, p. 74).

A6 Russian-Turkish War—Bankruptcy of Egypt: The Russo-Turkish War ended in 1979 with the Congress of Berlin. The main result for Greece was that, after continuous consultations, it annexed Thessaly and part of Epirus, in 1881 (Kofos, 1977, p. 353). It was not a negative event.

Table 3.5 Negative episodes in Greece based on their exogenous or endogenous origin

Year	*Exogenous origin (A)*	*Endogenous origin (B)*
1831		Assassination of Kapodistrias, governor of Greece (B1)
1836 1837	Anglo-American stock market crisis (A1)	
1847	Agricultural crisis and railway bubble (A2)	
1848	Revolutions in France, Germany and Austria (A3)	First forced circulation of the drachma (B2)
1854 1855 1856 1857	Crimean Wae (A4)	Occupation of Piraeus by the Anglo-French (B3)
1862		Dethronement of Otto (B4)
1866 1867		Cretan Revolution (1866–1868)—Holocaust of Arkadi, 1866 (B5)
1868		Second forced circulation of drachma (B6)
1870		Massacre in Dilesi and international defamation of the country (B7)
1873	Financial crisis in England, Italy and Germany (A5)	Lavrion Issue (B8)
1876 1877 1878	Russian-Turkish War—Bankruptcy of Egypt: 1878 (A6)	1877: Third forced circulation—Recession to the country's centers of trade, especially in Ermoupolis: (B9)
1884		An economic crisis that combines aspects of old-style crises (poor harvesting) and elements of capitalist-type crises (stock market and credit crises). The first crisis of a new type in Greece (B10)
1890	Bankruptcy of Argentina—Baring crisis (A7)	
1893		Bankruptcy—Crisis of raisin exports—devaluation of the drachma (B11)
1897		Defeat in the war against the Ottoman Empire (B12)

(continued)

Table 3.5 (continued)

Year	*Exogenous origin (A)*	*Endogenous origin (B)*
1898		Obligation to pay compensation—International Financial Control (B13)
1907	Stock Exchange and Credit Crisis in New York (A8)	
1912		Balkan wars (B14)
1913		
1914	World War I (A9)	
1915		
1916		The culmination of the National Schism: Greece is divided in two, with the royal government in Athens and the Venizelos government in Thessaloniki (B15)
1917		
1918		
1920	Collapse of New York and London stock markets (A10)	Great Powers impose an economic blockade on Greece—Devaluation of drachma (B16)
1922		Asia Minor disaster and 1st forced loan (B17)
1923	Hyperinflation (A11)	
1929	Collapse of the New York Stock Exchange (A12)	
1931	Britain abandons the "Gold Standard"—bank bankruptcies in Austria and Germany (A13)	
1932		Abandonment of the "Gold Standard"—bankruptcy—restriction of imports and attempt to stabilize the currency (B18)
1933	USA abandons the Gold Standard (A14)	
1936		Dictatorship of Metaxas by order of King George II (B19)
1939	World War II (A15)	
1940		War of 1940—Occupation (B20)
1941		
1942		

(continued)

Table 3.5 (continued)

Year	*Exogenous origin (A)*	*Endogenous origin (B)*
1943		
1944		
1945		
1947		Continuous depreciation of the drachma—The gold pound plays the role of national currency, while the drachma is limited to small transactions (B21)—1946–1949: Civil war (B22)
1948		
1949		
1950		
1951		
1952		
1953		
1967		Dictatorship (B23)
1968		
1969		
1970		
1971	Dollar depreciation—End of Bretton-Woods era (A16)	
1972		
1973	First oil crisis (A17)	
1974		
1979	Second oil crisis (A18)	
2008	Financial crisis (A19)	Financial crisis
2009		
2010		
2011		
2012		
2013		
2014		
2015		
2020		Covid-19 pandemic

Source Authors' own creation

A7 Bankruptcy of Argentina—Baring crisis. The crisis erupted when Baring Bank, an Argentine bondholder, failed to place them in international markets, was about to bankrupt, and been saved thanks to the intervention of the British government. It was the first time that the British government had intervened to save a bank from the risk of bankruptcy: (Finch, 2001, p. 346; Kindleberger, 1993, p. 163).

A8 Stock Exchange and Credit Crisis in New York. Stock manipulation by J. P. Morgan and subsequent bankruptcies. This crisis led the government to the creation of the Federal Reserve System (Sobel, 1999, p. 297).

A9 World War I: During the war, European funds fled to the United States, which lend their European allies (Finch, 2001, p. 347).

A10 Collapse of New York and London stock markets. Reported by Kindleberger (1993, p. 16).

A11 Hyperinflation in Germany: Under the pressure of the needs to pay for war reparations, and the political chaos in which the country finds itself, the German government prints large sums of money resulting in hyperinflation. In November 4 trillion marks was exchanged for $1 (Kindleberger, 1993, 301).

A12 Collapse of the New York Stock Exchange (28/10/1929). A brief bibliography on the Great Recession in P. Temin (2003).

A13—A14: Britain (1931) and the United States (1933) abandon the "Gold Standard": B. Eichengreen (1995) refers to the "gold standard" and the problems it created to get out of the 1929 crisis.

A15 World War II: During the war, and in order to avoid the credit crunch that followed World War I, European allies borrowed weapons and other goods from the United States under the law of borrowing, assuming that after the victory they will be able to return the items provided to them. The value of the amounts borrowed ($50 billion) was greater than the total government spending from 1933 to 1939.

A16 Dollar depreciation—End of Bretton-Woods era: In August 1971, the US government abolishes the convertibility of the dollar into gold (1 ounce = $35), and two years later the Bretton-Woods treaty, which provided for a fixed exchange rate between currencies, is abolished. Welcome to the world of floating exchange rates (Eichengreen, 2007, p. 242).

A17 First Petroleum Crisis: Rising oil prices from manufacturing countries caused a 2% drop in GDP in OECD countries and a global redistribution of wealth (Aldcroft, 1993, p. 326). According to Kostis (1997, p. 134), the second "gave the deathblow to the Greek economy".

A18 Covid-19 crisis started from China at the end of 2019—beginning of 2020, affecting its production structure after it appeared in Hubei province, which is characterized by a complete industrial infrastructure and has a population of around 59 million inhabitants. When Covid-19 extended to the West, it raised supply and demand issues and increased uncertainty. In Greece the first case was registered on 26 February 2020. The total number of cases confirmed in the country by 6 May is

2663 and 147 deaths. The epidemiological crisis has brought the global economy a rapid 'sudden stop' for the main economies, comparable to the 2008 recession. By 6/5/2020, 3,679,544 cases are recorded, and deaths worldwide are 257,793.

Crises of Endogenous Origin

B1 The assassination of Kapodistrias by the Mavromichali family of Mani is due to the rupture of the governor with the armed local authorities who had become powerful during the Independence Struggle. The attempt of the state to take control on the autonomous suzerainty of Mani led to the rupture and his murder (Loukos, 1984).

B2 First forced circulation of the drachma: 1848 was the first year of trial for the National Bank of Greece. The tumultuous turn of events and the revolutionary storm that caused the peoples of Europe to be upset this year and to undermine the foundations of any regime, the next step being to provoke an economic crisis and to shake public faith. Therefore, the once-reborn trade of Greece was suddenly embarrassed, and suddenly the source of the external credits depleted (Valaoritis, 1988, p. 9).

The Bank had been able (...) to repeat the redemption of its bank securities from 16 December 1849 (Sakellaropoulos, 1994, vol. II, p. 13; Valaoritis, 1988, p. 23).

B3 Occupation of Piraeus by the Anglo-French: In the context of the Crimean War (Ottoman Empire, France and England on the one hand, Russia on the other) the Greek government provoked a series of uprisings in the southern Ottoman territories. The allies, in an attempt to blackmail the country's neutrality, proceeded with its naval blockade and occupation of Piraeus, which ended three years later (Papadopoulos, 1977, p. 165).

B4 Conflict of Otto with the country's politicians, but also with public opinion ("Skiadika"). Despite the repression of the riots, Otto left Greece and was replaced by George I (Dimitrakopoulos, 1977, p. 187).

B5 The Great Cretan Revolution was suppressed by the Ottoman army, despite the acts of self-sacrifice of its fighters (blowing up the Monastery of Arkadi, 1866) after two years in 1868. The events of Crete are related to the next one (Diamantourou, 1977, 253).

B6 Second forced circulation: The second forced circulation (1868–1870) was imposed due to the fiscal needs of the state, which came in part from the Cretan revolution, and imposed its lending by the National Bank of Greece (Valaoritis, 1988, pp. 45 and 55).

B7 Massacre in Dilesi and international defamation of the country: Throughout nineteenth century robbery was an endemic phenomenon in the countryside. In 1870, three English travelers were kidnapped by thieves in Dilesi and then slaughtered when the required ransom had not been paid. The event resulted in the country's international defamation.

B8 The Lavrion Issue was a dispute between the Greek state and the Italian-French company Ilarion Rou & Co., which took on international proportions due to the interference of foreign governments. The issue arose when the Greek government challenged the company's rights over the "estuaries," i.e., the minerals who were on the surface of the area given to it for exploitation, arguing that the contract only gave the company the right to exploit the subsoil. The estuaries were supposed to contain significant amounts of gold, and "Greeks swam in an imaginary ocean of millions" (Platanopoulos, 1976, p. 15). Finally, the company was acquired in 1873 by Syggros, establishing the Lavrio Metallurgical Company (Platanopoulos, 1976, p. 19). The game with "Lavria" is the first bubble of the Greek stock market, before it was even founded.

B9 Third forced circulation—Recession to the country's centers of trade (especially in Ermoupolis): The third forced circulation is due to the need to finance war preparations, in view of a possible new Greek-Turkish war (Valaoritis, 1988, p. 70).

B10 The first crisis of new type in Greece: Valaoritis speaks of the "commercial and industrial crisis that erupted from Monday, 1883," which made impossible to lift the forced circulation (Valaoritis, 1988, p. 92).

B11 Bankruptcy—Crisis of raisin exports—depreciation of the drachma: Valaoritis mentions bankruptcy (1988, p. 131). For the crisis of raisins, the only essentially exportable product of the Greek state, Pizanis (1988, p. 108).

B12 Defeat in the war against the Ottoman Empire. For the "unfortunate" war, which illustrated all the disorganization of the army (Pikros, 1977, p. 127).

B13 Obligation to pay compensation—International Financial Control. For the terms of the agreement, see Valaoritis (1988, p. 172).

B14 The First and Second Balkan Wars resulted in a doubling of the Greek state, both in area and population. For economic and political side effects see Economou (1977, p. 289) and Svolopoulos (1977, p. 335).

B15 National Schism. See Leontaritis (1978, p. 18).

B16 The Great Powers impose an economic blockade on Greece. Depreciation of the drachma: On the occasion of the referendum that approved the return of the pro-German King Constantine, the Great Powers exclude Greece from international credits. On the incapacity of external borrowing during the critical period 1920–1922: (Alogoskoufis and Lazaretou, 2002, p. 133).

With the forced loan, the banknotes were cut in half. The old owner was getting a new half value, and government bonds which with the inflation that followed the disaster lost all value: (Bank of Greece, 1978, 33)

B17 Asia Minor Disaster. See Llellyn-Smith (2002).

B18 Abandonment of the gold standard, bankruptcy, restriction of imports, and attempt to stabilize the currency: See Alogoskoufis and Lazaretou (2002, p. 144).

B19 Dictatorship of Metaxas by order of King George II. See Petraki (2006).

B20 The War of 1940—Occupation: There is no exact estimate of the catastrophes of war and occupation, and perhaps the numbers mentioned are exaggerated. Let's stick to an indicator: according to official sources, the losses in construction amount to 406 thousand, almost the ¼ of pre-war building wealth (Magriotis, 1949, p. 130).

B21 Between 1944 and 1953 there were four depreciation of the drachma (Bank of Greece, 1978, p. 237 et seq.).

B22 Civil War: If the Asia Minor military campaign cost 37 thousand dead and the war of the '40s 15 thousand, the dead of the civil war, only in its last phase, reached 40 thousand (Margaritis, 2000, p. 50). In 1948, there were more than 800,000 "civil-war" refugees (Laiou, 1992).

References

Aldcroft, D. H. (1993). *The European Economy, 1914–1990*. London: Routledge.

Alogoskoufis, G., & Lazaretou, S. (2002). *The Drachma: From Finikas to the Euro*. Athens (in Greek).

Bank of Greece. (1978). *The First Fifty Years of the Bank of Greece*. Athens (in Greek).

Bialoskorski, R., Kiczma, L., & Sulek, M. (2019). *National Power Rankings of Countries 2019*. Warsaw: Oficyna Wydawnicza, ASPRA-JR.

Bolt, J., Inklaar, R., de Jong, H., & van Zanden, J. L. (2018). *Rebasing 'Maddison': New Income Comparisons and the Shape of Long-Run Economic Development* (Maddison Project Working paper 10).

Bremmer, I. (2020). *The Most Serious Crisis Since World War II*. Retrieved from www.kathimerini.gr/1071262/gallery/proswpa/synentey3eis/ian-mpremer-sthn-k-h-pio-sovarh-krish-meta-ton-deytero-pagkosmio.

Carlsson-Szlezak, P., Reeves, M., & Swartz, P. (2020). Understanding the Economic Shock of Coronavirus. *Harvard Business Review*. Retrieved from https://hbr.org/2020/03/understanding-the-economic-shock-of-coronavirus.

Diamantourou, I. (1977). *"The Cretan Revolution", History of the Greek Nation, Vol. III*. Athens (in Greek).

Dimitrakopoulos, Od. (1977). *The Anti-Dynastic Struggle and the Expulsion of Otto, History of the Greek Nation, Vol. III*. Athens (in Greek).

Dritsa, M. (1990). *Viomichania kai Trapezes stin Ellada tou Mesopolemou* [Industry and Banks in Inter-War Greece]. Athens: Cultural Foundation of the National Bank of Greece.

Economou, N. (1977). *"The First Balkan War", History of the Greek Nation, Vol. II*. Athens (in Greek).

Eichengreen, B. (1995). *Golden Fetters*. Oxford: Oxford University Press.

Eichengreen, B. (2007). *The European Economy Since 1945*. Princeton: Prınceton University Press.

Fey, M., & Ramsay, W. K. (2010). Uncertainty and Incentives in Crisis Bargaining: Game-Free Analysis of International Conflict. *American Journal of Political Science*. Retrieved from https://doi.org/10.1111/j.1540-5907.2010.00486.x.

Finch, Ch. (2001). *In the Market*. New York: Anneville Press.

Friedman, M., & Schwartz, A. J. (1963). *A Monetary History of the United States, 1857–1960*. Princeton, NJ: Princeton University Press.

Geisst, Ch. (2004). *Wall Street*. Oxford: Oxford University Press.

Hertwig, R., Barron, G., Weber, E. U., & Erev, I. (2004). Decisions from Experience and the Effect of Rare Events in Risky Choice. *Psychological Science, 15*, 534–539.

Hobsbawm, E. J. (1962). *The Age of Revolution, 1789–1848*. Cleveland: World Pub. Co.

Kelly, P. (1994 [1992]). *The End of Certainty: Power, Politics and Business in Australia*. St Leonards, NSW: Allen & Unwin. ISBN 1-86373-757-X.

Kindleberger, Ch. (1993). *A Financial History of Western Europe*. Oxford: Oxford University Press.

Kofos, E. (1977). *"The Eastern Crisis, 1875–1878", History of the Greek Nation, Vol. III*. Athens (in Greek).

Kostis, K. (1997). *Collaboration and Competition: The 70 Years of the Hellenic Banks Association*. Athens (in Greek).

Labrousse, E. (1992). 1848–1830–1789. Comment naissent les revolutions. In M. Magrairaz (Ed.), *Hostoire Economique*. Paris: XVIIIe-XXe siècle.

Laiou, A. (1992). Population Movements in the Greek Countryside During the Civil War. In L. Baerentzen, G. Iatrides, & O. L. Smith (Eds.), *Studies on the Civil War, 1945–1949* (pp. 67–114). Athens: Olkos (in Greek).

Leontaritis, G. (1978). *"Since 1923 of the Asia Minor Disaster", History of the Greek Nation, Vol. IED*. Athens (in Greek).

Llellyn-Smith, M. (2002). *The Vision of Ionia*. Athens (in Greek).

Loukos, Chr. (1984). *"Incorporations: The Case of the Mavromichalia", The Historical, Vol. 2*. Athens (in Greek).

Magriotis, D. (1949). *Sacrifices of Greece and Crimes of Occupation*. Athens: Odyssey (in Greek).

Malmendier, U., & Nagel, S. (2011). Depression Babies: Do Macroeconomic Experiences Affect Risk-Taking? *Quarterly Journal of Economics, 126*, 373–416.

Margaritis, G. (2000). *History of the Greek Civil War*. Athens (in Greek).

Mishra, P. (2020). Get Ready, a Bigger Disruption Is Coming: The Covid-19 Pandemic Reflects a Systemic Crisis Akin to the Seminal Crashes of the 20th Century. *Bloomberg*. https://www.bloomberg.com/opinion/articles/2020-03-16/coronavirus-foreshadow-s-bigger-disruptions-in-future.

NATO. (2019). Defence Expenditure of NATO Countries (2013–2019). *COMMUNIQUE PR/CP(2019)123*.

Palacios-Huerta, I., & Santos, T. (2004). A Theory of Markets, Institutions, and Endogenous Preferences. *Journal of Public Economics, 88*(3), 601–627.

Papadopoulos, St. (1977). *"The Crimean War and Hellenism", History of the Greek Nation, Vol. III*. Athens (in Greek).

Petraki, M. (2006). *The Myth of Metaxas*. Athens: Oceanida (in Greek).

Petrakis, P. E. (2011). *The Greek Economy and the Crisis: Challenges and Responses*. New York and Heidelberg: Springer.

Petrakis, P. (2020). *Theoretical Approaches to Economic Growth and Development. An Interdisciplinary Perspective*. Palgrave Macmillan. ISBN 978-3-030-50067-2.

Pikros, I. (1977). *The Greco-Turkish War of 1897* [History of the Greek Nation, Volume XIV: Modern Hellenism from 1881 to 1913] (pp. 125–160). Ekdotiki Athinon (in Greek).

Pizanis, P. (1988). *Economic History of Greek Raisins: 1851–1912*. Athens (in Greek).

Platanopoulos, M. (1976). *History of the Athens Stock Exchange: 1876–1976*. Athens (in Greek).

Sakellaropoulos, Th. (1994). *The Crises in Greece 1830–1857*. Athens: Kritiki (in Greek).

Shilling, G. S. (2020). A Look at Economies and Markets After Covid-19: Once the Coronavirus Is Defeated, the New Normal Will Be Marked by Much Slower Growth, the Risk of Deflation and a Distrust of Equities. *Bloomberg*. Retrieved from https://www.bloomberg.com/opinion/articles/2020-03-20/coronavirus-a-long-term-look-at-economies-and-markets.

Sobel, R. (1999). *Panic on Wall Street*. Washington, DC, USA: Beard Books.

Sotirovic, V. D. (2019). *The Geopolitics of South-East Europe and the Importance of the Regional Geostrategic Position Preface*. Mimeo.

Svolopoulos, K. (1977). *"The Second Balkan War", History of the Greek Nation, Vol. II*. Athens (in Greek).

Temin, P. (2003). *The Great Depression*. Oxford: The Oxford Encyclopedia of Economic History.

Valaoritis, I. (1988). *History of the National Bank of Greece (1842–1902)*. Athens (in Greek).

WHO. (2020). *Director-General's Opening Remarks at the Media Briefing on COVID-19—11 March 2020*. Retrieved from https://www.who.int/dg/speeches/detail/who-director-general-s-opening-remarks-at-the-media-briefing-on-covid-19—11-march-2020.

CHAPTER 4

The Formation of Idiosyncratic Structure of Institutions and Culture

4.1 Introduction

In the first and second chapter, it was found that the presence of institutions function in a retentive manner on economic growth (extractive institutions, rent seeking activities), the prevalence of hierarchical structures in the Greek economy (non-market allocation of resources) and the non-diversification of investment and production, from the establishment of the new Greek state onward.

Also, in the third chapter it was found that from the beginning of the twentieth century to the present day (110 years), only the periods of 1953–1970 and 2000–2007 could be characterized as periods that were not under the influence of strong inflationary pressures or periods of high risk. Therefore, risk and uncertainty are components of the personal, social, and economic life of the Greeks, from the birth of the Greek state to the present day.

Due to the existence of high levels of risk, economic actors avoid committing to investments that require significant amounts of money. This resulted in the prevalence of the small and medium-sized enterprises model, having as consequences: (a) the absence of innovative business activities, (b) business activity of small scale, and (c) the prevalence of "banking liquidity panic" from time to time (years 1931, 1991, 2009–2010).

P. E. Petrakis and P. C. Kostis, *The Evolution of the Greek Economy*,
The Political Economy of Greek Growth up to 2030,
https://doi.org/10.1007/978-3-030-47210-8_4

The willingness to take risk also depends on personal experiences of microeconomic history (Petrakis & Konstantakopoulou, 2015). This human behavior can be interpreted by the formation of endogenous growth preferences, where risk depends on the returns of risky investments of the past (Palacios-Huerta & Santos, 2004). The effect of risk on human behaviors is diffused through social learning, so present perceptions depend on actual experiences of the past. Thus, the Greek economy from its birth until recently faced a development characterized by events that magnified mainly its systemic risk.

These conditions have influenced and determined the way society and the economy function and behave.

The structure of the chapter is as follows: Initially, Sect. (4.2) presents the concept of the institutions and culture's optimum pattern, while the next Sect. (4.3) presents the deviations observed from this optimum pattern. In the fourth (4.4) and fifth (4.5) part, idiosyncratic institutions and idiosyncratic culture traits in the Greek economy are presented, respectively, while the sixth Sect. (4.6) presents the formation of the stagnated growth prototype in the Greek economy.

4.2 The Optimum Structure of Institutions and Culture with First and Second-Best Theory Conditions

The existence of an optimal structure of institutions which is linked to an optimal nexus of cultural values can essentially exist on a theoretical level for the sake of simplification of reality (Kafka, Kostis, Petrakis, 2020).

According to Petrakis, Valsamis, Kafka, (2016), Walras (1874) developed a general equilibrium model concerning the microfoundations of price formation. The basic assumptions underlying Walrasian Paradigm are: (a) the existence of perfect competition, (b) that the allocation of resources is Pareto optimal, (c) that there exist institutions that foster economic growth, (d) that there does not exist systemic risk, and (e) that the growth preferences of individuals and companies (or in other words growth oriented cultural background dimensions) are non-idiosyncratic. The basic assumption of perfect competition in combination with the Pareto Optimal allocation of resources in the Walrasian Paradigm and the neoclassical model in general ensures a specific framework of behavior and preferences shaping the way economic institutions operate. At the same time, under perfect information, markets are cleared and no transaction costs are incurred due to the complete contractual assumption.

However, Walrasian Paradigm rejects the interaction relationships between agents. The price mechanism is unable to incorporate the available information since some aspects of the transactions are not expressed in enforceable contracts (Bowles & Gintis, 2000). Furthermore, the role of entrepreneurship and innovation in the Walrasian Paradigm is very weak. Thus, a Schumpeterian framework is needed on the purpose to locate the emergence of innovation and entrepreneurship.

Schumpeter (1921, 1939) based his analysis on the existence of a perfectly competitive economy which is a stationary equilibrium and therefore a perfect competitive equilibrium, without making profits and without interest rates, savings, investments, and involuntary unemployment. But a capitalist economy never stagnates. Innovation is the element that causes imbalance and that, at the same time, makes it evolve. For Schumpeter (1939) equilibrium is a concept introduced in order to explain the imbalance caused by innovation. Thus, the transition to dynamic economic growth, which is disconnected from the growth of production factors, is explained.

According to Schumpeter, the role of the institutions is important, which he sees as responsible for the emergence of certain behaviors, so that they can partly be seen as the crystallization of individuals' behaviors (Festre & Garrouste, 2008, p. 379). Schumpeter (1934, pp. 60–61) also stated that "economic sociology deals with institutions," which is contrasted to economic theory dealing with purely economic phenomena and mechanisms. In the Schumpeterian competition scheme innovation plays a key role in economic change through the increase in the efficiency of the economic and institutional structure (Ülgen, 2014). Furthemore, Swedberg (2002, p. 250) argued that for Schumpeter, institutions are a necessary condition for a vigorous capitalism.

In addition, Schumpeter assumed that the preferences of the societies are generally incomplete, as well as that learning, experience, innovation, and our social environment mold the desires of the society. Schumpeter deal with the issue of how preferences are determined and concludes that in the face of ignorance concerning how much we will enjoy specific outcomes, we will not just rely on our own past experiences, but also seek guidance from the revealed preferences of other similar but more experienced consumers (Johnson, 1954). In the field of consumers' behaviors and preferences, Schumpeter adopts a very categorical attitude, according to which the producers' behaviors and activities are important because they have the strength to influence and change consumers' preferences (Croitoru, 2012).

The first basic theorem of welfare economics suggests that the market will move toward a forced equilibrium when the economy has two key features which make up a weak Pareto optimum:

(a) there are complete markets without transaction costs and perfect information.
(b) price-taking behavior prevails. In other words, there are no monopolies, and to enter and exit the market is free and easy.

When a third characteristic (the local non-compliance of preferences) is added to the two above, in which for each portfolio of complaints or services there is always another that is very close to the first but is preferable to that, then an equilibrium point can be reached that is weakly Pareto optimal.

The second basic theorem states that among all possible Pareto optimal equilibrium points we can choose and implement the achievement of some of them by realizing a lump—sun wealth redistribution and subsequently allow the economy to function without other interventions.

Thus the general theories of equilibrium, such as those of Walras (1874) and Arrow—Debreu—McKenzie (1954; 1959), in the presence of the first and second fundamental theories of welfare economics suggest a general and abstract conception of the functioning of economies.

This is a general framework, having as its main feature the dominance of the markets which is characterized by the first-best conditions. Subsequently, economic policy proposals are exported. The first-best conditions for an optimum allocation of resources are based on some stringent conditions (Lipsey, Naugle, Nowak, & Lukacs, 2017), such as that the firms are "price takers," and that there do not exist externalities and unexploited ranges of increasing returns.

The best-known deviation from this general framework of analysis includes the analysis of externalities in economies with imperfect markets and imperfect information (Greenwald & Stiglitz, 1986). But this is only (however prevalent and general) a reason for moving away from theories of general equilibrium. There are other causes which are related either to specialized aspects of the institutional background or to the cultural background or finally to the dependence of the economy on the past (path dependence) (Hoeffler Ariely & West, 2006).

Thus, second (or higher order)-best conditions are formed which shape much more than a different set of economic conditions. As Lipsey and Lncaster (1956) point out, the second-best theory demonstrated that the necessary conditions for maximizing any function do not provide guides for increasing the value of that function when all the necessary conditions cannot be satisfied. Under these conditions, the *"one-size-fits-all"* policies (Stiglitz, 2002) become extremely controversial. This creates the conditions for context specificity (Lipsey et al., 2017) which can create policies that can be implemented in the real world. The usual situation in the world is to be objective with situations where individual policies are applied and not in a general ideal situation.

In order a body of economic policy to be formed that is being applied under second-(or higher order) best policies, it is necessary to conquer the current state of the market under consideration and the firm-best conditions for real market. Then those policies that are capable of eliminating these disorders emerge.

"The General Second Best Theories (Lipsey & Lncaster, 1956) states that the 'piecemeal satisfaction' of any one first-best optimality condition is not sufficient to increase community welfare in a world in which first - best conditions are not achieved globally." This proposition may be general in nature, arguing that individual conditions that meet only certain first-best conditions do not result to an increase in the value of a (any) utility function.

Essentially the second-best theory leads to the conclusion that there are few states with general economic policy rules that are always applied. Instead, it requires special knowledge of individual markets and their relationships.

Hence, the second-best theory supports the need for individual policies that are context specific.

What caused the "*departure*" of the economic prototype from the first order to the second order conditions, i.e., what are the conditions that block the efficient allocation of resources? We are talking about the conditions that could follow "*constraints*" or "*distortions.*" It is about anything that could prevent the achievement of a perfectly competitive, price-taking equilibrium which would be characterized as Pareto efficient.

4.3 The Deviations from the Optimum Pattern on Institutions and Culture: Third-Best Theory Conditions

An "idiosyncratic growth prototype" emerges when institutions and cultures opposing to the growth process prevail, and we could characterize them as idiosyncratic. In addition, the coevolution of culture and institutions, in the case that cultural background is described as idiosyncratic, results to the formulation of idiosyncratic institutions. The implications of the prevalence of an idiosyncratic growth prototype, which deviates from the optimal pattern, have perspicuous effects on the way economies operate, with the most important, probably, being the coexistence with increased levels of uncertainty and inefficient allocation of resources.

Thus, an optimal growth pattern cannot often be met, since the existence of idiosyncratic institutions is one of the most significant reasons for the deviation from the optimal pattern (Petrakis et al., 2016). The Idiosyncratic Growth Prototype described here is a general definition of a deviation from the optimal pattern, in which idiosyncratic institutions and culture are generated. However, there is not only one possible form of deviation from optimality. Moreover, we present this idiosyncratic prototype (it will be described thoroughly below) as one that could describe better an emerging economy that faces a long period of stagnation.

On the one hand, institutional deviations from the optimal pattern is when exist extractive institutions (Acemoglu & Robinson, 2012). Economies dominated by extractive institutions are characterized by a lack of established relationships between the participants of the economic system. As a results, conditions which favor the expansion of uncertainty appear, that could be described as idiosyncratic. Factors that enhance the existence of idiosyncratic institutions are (Petrakis et al., 2016):

(a) Coordination failures, which are responsible for the appearance of externalities resulting in some costs in economic terms and the economy to deviate from the optimal equilibrium point.
(b) Information asymmetry, like coordination failures, create economic costs as their elimination requires the contracting between the principal and the agent, and as a result it is difficult to achieve market efficiency.

(c) Path dependency (history legacy), in the sense that *"history matters"* in everyday human aspect such as preferences, decisions and attitudes. To the extent that preferences are shaped by initial experiences, later preferences are path dependent (Hoeffler et al., 2006). Both the institutions and the way the economy operates are the result of a path-dependent procedure with elements of historical legacy. Based on this view, the existence of high levels of systemic risk favors societies that retain historical aspects that distort the proper functioning of the economy and create disincentives to take business action and to market efficiency in general.

On the other hand, the factors that create divergences of culture from the optimal pattern vary and might derive from both the external environment and human behavior. Petrakis et al. (2016) focus on a variety of factors that may lead to deviations of culture from the optimal pattern:

(a) Idiosyncratic cultural background: An idiosyncratic cultural background could be characterized by the existence of some specific forces that act in a peculiar manner shaping human behavior and preferences. This kind of cultural background may be represented through the analysis of several cultural dimensions which deviate significantly from the optimal pattern when persistent high systematic risk exists: (i) the prevalence of high risks in the economy creates the need for individuals to protect themselves against risk by displaying behaviors of uncertainty avoidance, (ii), the inclusion of individuals in groups in order to feel more secure, to protect themselves from uncertain situations, to secure material resources and social support (Triandis, Bontempo, Villareal, Asai,& Lucca, 1988), (iii) high time discount preferences (in uncertain environments members of society tend to be cautious about their future decisions, avoiding to withhold resources and effort over a long period of time), (iv) trust (under conditions of high systematic risk individuals lose confidence in the institutions that surround them while the level of interpersonal trust decreases, at least toward people outside the potential groups to which a person belongs), (v) power distance (under conditions of high uncertainty, inequalities in society usually increase as authority has greater power in order to overcome the problematic situation), (vi) human orientation (concepts such as justice, truthfulness, friendliness, generosity, care and kindness lose their momentum under conditions of high systematic risk).

(b) Non diversification of investment: Economies whose production and investment are one-way defined, i.e., there is a high concentration of the production process in a few sectors, fail to eliminate systematic risk and lead to an optimal growth pattern. Kuznets (1971) suggests that a country's economic growth may be defined as a long-term rise in capacity to supply increasingly diverse economic goods to its population. This argument is further empowered with the view of Grossman and Helpman (1992) who claim that for an economy to grow it has to produce an ever-increasing quantity, quality and variety of goods and services.

(c) Loss aversion behavior: The loss aversion assertion (Kahneman & Tversky, 1979) is one of the elements of the prospect theory (Kahneman & Tversky, 2000) which implies that people are twice as sensitive to risks as to gains. That is, the absolute subjective value of a specific loss is larger than the absolute subjective value of an equivalent gain (Ert & Erev, 2010). Loss aversion behavior is guided by the existence of high systematic risk levels and idiosyncratic/stagnated cultural background.

Those deviations of the institutional and cultural framework may lead to a new state of equilibrium which does not represent the optimal structure of institutions and culture. It is more a strategic equilibrium having the characteristics of Nash Equilibrium (Nash, 1950, 1951)[1] which emerges as the optimal outcome of a game between two sides. Overall, an individual can receive no incremental benefit from changing actions, assuming other players remain constant in their strategies.

The analysis of the idiosyncratic cultural and institutions framework is of great importance when it comes to determine on the economic policy to be decided, since it is obvious that when an economic policy is developed and implemented, the actual background to which it refers is crucial.

It is a fact that moving away from first order conditions leads to various economic prototypes with varying degrees of distortions. Ng (1977) focuses his attention when information costs are not negligible. This is a condition that can be described as a third-best condition.

Ng (1977) considered that the problem posed by the risk of "generality in shaping general policy rules" and arising from the second-best theories is likely to conclude that for every economy with special geographic and time-specific characteristics, a special policy of economic development is needed. Hence, he articulated what he called the third-best theory.

By the third-best theory he argued that when neither the third best nor the best second theory can be achieved and there are "informational poverty conditions" then the fulfillment of the first-best conditions is the best policy available. So we should depart from the first-best conditions only when there are strong reasons for this.

The theoretical conflict between Lipsey and Lancaster and Ng continues today with unabated intensity (Lipsey et al., 2017; Lipsey & Ng, 2017). The final conclusion drawn from the analysis of Lipsey and Lancaster is that the current status quo must be maintained (whatever it may be), in specific contexts. Finally, the conclusion drawn from Ng's analysis is that if the first and second-best conditions have been disturbed and conditions of informational weakness prevail, that is, third-best conditions, as many of the first-best policy conditions as possible should be fulfilled.

In conclusion, an idiosyncratic production prototype is characterized by strategically Nash equilibria with second and third order policy conditions.

4.4 Idiosyncratic Institutions in the Greek Economy

Whereupon, four issues that describe idiosyncratic institutions in the Greek economy in a fairly satisfactory way are being presented. It is about the relationship between capital and labor shares, the appropriation rules and the role of elites, the high transaction costs and oligopolies in the Greek economy.

4.4.1 The Distortion of the Relative Price of Capital/Labor Ratio

The distribution of factor shares was an issue that started to absorb the attention of economists since its beginnings in the 1920s, but all attempts had to overcome issues of measurement and comparability. Some years later there were some studies, such as those of Phelps-Brown and Weber (1953) or Johnson (1954) who concluded that the wage shares are constant, a fact that was highly accepted during that period. Later, academic interest in Bowley's law begin to resurface (Gollin, 2002, 2008) doubting the constancy of wage shares. Recent empirical evidence shows that the wage share has substantially and significantly declined since the 1980s. Similar is the situation for Greek economy (Fig. 4.1).

From the mid-1960s to the early 1990s, the relative size of the gross operating surplus was constantly increasing, indicating (a) the transformation of Greek productive activity from labor-intensive to capital-intensive and (b) the change in the social balance of powers at the expense of the labor factor which has been observed mainly since 1989. It should be noted that the conclusion on the validity of this last ratio is drawn from the fact that the intensity of the change (abrupt change) is not reasonable to believe that it is due to a rapid change in the productive structure of the economy in the period 1987–1993. Apparently, therefore, it is due

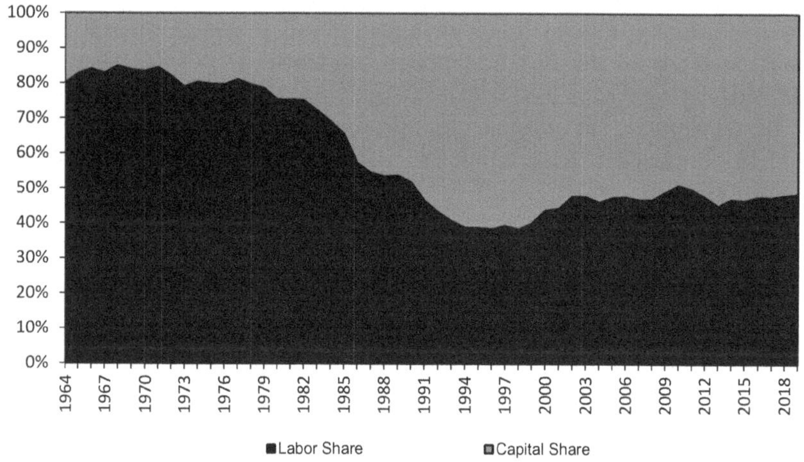

Fig. 4.1 Estimates of the share of gross operating surplus (capital share) and compensation of employees (labor share) in the Greek economy (1960–2019) (*Note* Labor share results from the division of compensation of employees divided by the sum of compensation of employees plus gross operating surplus of enterprises and households. Capital share results from the division of gross operating surplus of enterprises and households divided by the sum of compensation of employees plus gross operating surplus of enterprises and households. *Source* AMECO Database and authors' calculations)

to the rapid formation of new conditions of distribution of the produced wealth in terms of social balance of power. In addition, there has been a stabilization in the relationship between them over the last twenty years.

4.4.2 *The Appropriation Rules and the Role of Elites*

The term elite means the maintenance of a large part of power by a small part of society, a power which is independent of the democratic electoral process of a state. Usually it is about members of the society who are directly related to economic policy-making and have a significant influence on government policy decisions, as they usually hold strong positions in businesses and organizations and are directly related to decision and policy centers (think tanks or policy discussion groups). Elites include some large industrial and financial complexes.

Elites exert pressure on state power with the aim of achieving their own goals. Members who make up a group of elites are usually close to the rulers and this is also one of the reasons why their interests are easily achievable. Also, elites usually consist of a small number of members (Petrakis, 2020).

In the case of Greek society, as in many societies, it is understood that a large number of interest groups it is active at all levels (professional, economic, political, ideological, etc.). This fact, combined with the relatively small size of the country, but also due to the fact that many of the interests promoted are conflicting, constitute obstacles to the equal distribution of income. Specific pressure groups, usually those that already have authority and the ability to push power, manage to extract benefits unlike other groups in which the lack of pressure capabilities does not help them to derive beneficial results from their mobilizations.

Organized interest groups can often harm the economy through defending specific interests that are at odds with the "common good." Specific changes that become not only necessary but also beneficial, such as the adoption of new technology in the production of a product, which will reduce the need for human resources, may not be promoted due to interests of guilds. This does not promote change and improvement of processes for the benefit of companies but also for the benefit of society. This avoidance of adaptation to new conditions, hinders evolution, does not make obvious the need for change, adjustment of needs and processes, thus slowing the evolution and further adaptability of the country to new conditions.

DiCaprio (2012) brings together the influence of elites on the economic development of the societies to which they belong, in the following: (a) their ability to control and trade the desired resources, especially those of high monetary value, (b) the way in which they influence the distribution of resources, which is also the most direct way through which they influence the process of development and growth, (c) the political influence they exercise, although they may not hold positions of power, (d) the fact that institutions designed by the elites themselves usually promote the participation and flow of information and strengthen the position of a particular group within the governmental structure, (e) their ability to frame the way in which issues are perceived, and (f) their ability to influence public opinion by diffusing or holding information.

From the above, it is reasonable to assume that such actions (avoiding adaptation to changes) create a negative dynamic in society and the economy. When rapidly developing countries follow developments and adapt directly to them, then they create the conditions for development and progress, for the discovery of new technologies, products, etc. Societies that are not able to follow will have less room to adapt and deal with external upheavals that will arise as they lag behind in readiness, speed of evolution and adaptation and contact with new conditions.

If each group is individually active in order to defend specific interests, this can not only work negatively for the efficient functioning of the economy but also for the equal distribution of income (Olson, 1982). More specifically, if members of each group use whatever means available to achieve their objectives, this implies political choices which, although economically ineffective for society as a whole, will give an advantage to organized groups, since the costs of policies fall in a way that is not proportionate to individuals who are not members of the group. In addition, there is a possibility that the cost of negotiation and slow decision-making will make society unprofitable.

4.4.3 High Transaction Costs

One of the main sources of institution weakness, as it is represented in the property rights obscurity, derives from the Greek state success consequence from the Ottoman regime and it is referred to the inland state. This land, which was the most productive, accounted for the 85.16% of the total geographical area of the newborn Greek state. The land by definition belonged to the state and was used as collateral to external financing. At the same time, the land was used for agricultural production and—later on—inherited by the farmers' children; as a result a complex system of property rights was developed. In turn, this required lawyers and civil engineers resolving the serious property rights problems.

These conditions are still very present in the Greek state. It is worth noticing that (a) one of the current main obstacles of the Troika proposals in utilizing the state-owned property is the absence of clear property rights on land, and (b) the main existing obstacles for future development of the tourism sector is the absence of land registry, clearly defining publicly owned land and cultivated land (i.e., the territories that can be exploited for mining, quarrying, housing, or any other entrepreneurial use, including tourism infrastructure development).

The numerous modern expressions of this phenomenon range from construction in areas outside urban planning zones, to intellectual property piracy, to an ever-changing tax system and the re-selling of public transport registration licenses.

However, the causes of this obscurity regarding property rights should not be sought exclusively in economic facts, but also (a) in basic cultural characteristics, (b) in the characteristics of the transactions and, (c) in the basic wealth-producing resources.

In addition, market operation information efficiency is low (and, hence, extends the obscurity in property rights) or encounters structures designed to create obscurity. Therefore, asymmetrical information is both a product and a result of this obscurity. A financial system based on lending-borrowing relationships is favored, while arm's length financial transactions (i.e., systems based on the fact that both parties in the deal are acting in their own self-interest and are not subject to any pressure or duress from the other party) are avoided.

Prevailing extracting institutions create symptoms which can be easily recognized in today's Greek economic life. There are three major areas to focus upon: (a) the transaction costs in the economy, (b) the property rights obscurity, and (c) the poor contracting procedures. Transaction costs can be revealed or not. Revealed transaction costs include permission costs, additional taxes on specific transactions such as transfer of property ownership, etc. Corruption costs are an additional "revealed" transaction cost. Unrevealed transaction costs origin from bureaucratic procedures, required days for getting entrepreneurial licenses, etc.

4.4.4 Oligopolies

The Greek economy is also characterized by the emergence of oligopolistic sectors. This is a serious question of the structure of the economic system related to the organization of economic institutions, the way the economy is organized and, ultimately, directly concerns the distribution of income and wealth in the country.

The Greek market has an oligopolistic structure in many areas. A typical example of the oligopolistic sector in Greece is the retail food market, where 10 department store chains control over 85% of the market. (Melas, 2009). Typical examples are telecommunications, industry, procurement, financial services and basic necessities (Table 4.1).

The table shows that 33 sectors of the Greek economy have a narrow oligopolistic structure. It is noteworthy that sectors such as manufacture and more specifically tobacco products, tobacco and LPG bottling, air transport, and the leather and fur trade have an oligopoly concentration of more than 98%, which is evidence of an extremely narrow oligopoly.

4.5 Idiosyncratic Cultural Traits in the Greek Economy

The cultural dimensions and social psychological stereotypes prevailing in Greek society have a very long life span that goes beyond the establishment of the modern Greek state (Petrakis, 2011). This does not mean that they are immobilized and consolidated through time, although their systematic presence is being generally observed, not only in the Greek economy but in all societies of the world, not as defined just by national borders. In general, they are the cognitive constructions that connect the past with the present and define the future.

The cultural characteristics of societies reflect psychological and social stereotypes, which have been created in the long past and are the factors shaping institutions and transactions in the present (Petrakis 2011). Cultural values show a stability over time. The different social and political processes that form the cultural background of each society, respectively, direct the character of those involved. In general, cultural stereotypes are very resistant to change and redefinition (Johnston, 1996).

Eight basic social psychological stereotypes prevail in Greek society. We consider that these stereotypes have remarkable social and economic

Table 4.1 Highly concentrated sectors in the Greek economy (2016)

	CR4
Manufacture (Tobacco Products)	100
Manufacture (Tobacco)	99.98
Manufacture (LPG Bottling)	99.87
Air Transport	99.61
Trade (Leather—Fur)	98.06
Manufacture (Metallurgical Products)	89.14
Telecommunications	85.08
Trade (Furniture—Lighting)	82.62
Manufacture (Fabric Items)	81.73
Trade (Minerals-Mines)	81.69
Tourism (Business Yachting—Cruising)	80.83
Shipping	79.75
Trade (Dealerships—Imports—Exports)	77.82
Investment Services Companies	74.93
Trade (Yarn—Fabrics)	71.68
Manufacture (Petroleum & Coal Products)	69.82
Manufacture (Leather—Fur)	67.16
Manufacture (Newspaper—Magazine Publications)	65.5
Manufacture (Transportation—Shipyards)	62.57
Financial services	61.85
Manufacture (Drinks)	61.75
Trade (Supermarkets—Stores)	60.99
Trade (Professional Equipment)	60.86
Manufacture (Machinery)	58.75
Manufacture (Wood—Cork & Products)	58.32
Manufacture (Furniture)	57.96
Trade (Home—Professional Devices)	56.76
Trade (Fuel—Lubricants—Liquids)	55.83
Manufacture (Electrical Appliances—Lighting)	55.31
Manufacture (Electrical—Electronic Material)	54.31
Manufacture (Various Products)	53.07
Technical-Building	52.69
Manufacture (Non-Mineral Products)	51.01

Notes The table shows that 33 sectors of the Greek economy have a narrow oligopolistic structure. It is noteworthy that sectors such as manufacture and more specifically tobacco products, tobacco and LPG bottling, air transport, and the leather and fur trade have an oligopoly concentration of more than 98%, which is evidence of an extremely narrow oligopoly

Source Data from ICAP for the needs of this study and authors' calculations and creation

Table 4.2 Hierarchy of prevailing social psychological stereotypes in Greek society

	Prevailing stereotypes	*Non-prevailing stereotypes*
1	Collectivism	Individualism
2	Orientation to the present	Future orientation
3	Dominance of uncertainty	Risk taking and active management of uncertainty
4	Non-orientation to performance	Performance orientation
5	Accepting inequalities	Seeking equality
6	Lack of trust	Trust
7	Masculinity	Femininity
8	Religious influence neutral to negative	Religious promotional factors

Source Petrakis (2011)

reflections on the productive and social environment of the Greek economy and are directly related to its peculiarities (Table 4.2).

An important question raised by the Covid-19 pandemic is whether it is possible to influence attitudes that make up social stereotypes. Obviously, we know that social stereotypes show relatively little mobility of change. On the other hand, however, and because the shock is exogenous and massive with systematic characteristics and serious health effects, it is highly likely that it has an impact on human behavior. However, these impacts are difficult to be seen, and at least for the time being, there is a mixed effect.

In particular, the success of managing the epidemiological crisis has strengthened the credibility of collegiality and trust in institutions (Dianeosis, 2020) but has also enhanced privacy through the isolation provided for by the social responsibility policies and the distance learning and working methods.

Furthermore, it is clear that Covid-19 has significantly increased uncertainty and reduced the visibility of the future, so it can clearly work in the direction of strengthening present preferences while increasing uncertainty.

At the same time, a crisis of this kind creates high efficiency demands from the institutional and operational framework of the economy and thus strengthens efficiency demands.

The question is whether it increases or reduces confidence in people and their transactions. It is obvious that it operates by destroying structure, but if the social experiment of dealing with the crisis is proved successful, then the degree of confidence will increase. Religious sentiment is under considerable pressure, especially because in Greek society there was a conflict between the rational scientific community and the religious institutional framework.

It should be noted that a significant impact of the prevailing social pattern is to reduce the rate of population growth. It is obvious that the growth rate of the population is also due to economic—real reasons. Characteristically, the level of economic development and the effects on the general environment formed by its development (maternity protection, economic prospects, etc.) are mentioned and constitute a more general attitude that prevails in developed countries. However, these purely real economic reasons have also been incorporated as elements of the Greek cultural background and influence the decision of fertility which is a personal decision. Thus, the prevailing social stereotypes and especially the orientation to the present, the dominance of uncertainty and distrust (low social capital) contribute to reduced fertility.

The impact of this cultural background extends to a number of economic aspects that generally operate with an anti-development character. The main direction of this is the fixation on what is familiar, the lack of competition and control, the prevalence of inertia from uncertainty and therefore anxiety to undertake risky ventures (entrepreneurship) and finally, the lack of trust and generally low levels of social capital.

Does the cultural background have a long-term anti-cyclical developmental effect or a cyclical anti-developmental effect? During the prosperity phase of the economy certain "anti-developmental" aspects of social values prevail. Thus, strong family cohesion (a) reduces the spatial mobility that the child will move around and (b) affects the longitudinal mobility of vocational guidance. For example, parents who are doctors and lawyers, despite the saturation of their specialties, influence their reproduction, not allowing the "signals" of oversaturation (unemployment, wage reduction) to influence the choices of younger generations. The lack of performance orientation also contributes to the creation of social organizations that involve excessive expenditure of resources without evaluation. The dominance of uncertainty leads to the shortening of investment horizons and consequently to the denial of innovation. In the recession phase, this social model itself "generates" lines of defense against its change. Thus during the Great Recession of 2008 it is obvious that collectivism and in particular in-group collectivism (family) contribute to the reduction of the negative effects of the crisis, as in the case of unemployment or wage reduction. The fact that in the very difficult phase of the recession the cultural background operates "rescue," gives it the ability to survive, possibly even stronger.

From the context of cultural dimensions particular emphasis is placed on the lack of orientation toward the future, in the sense that the also important dimensions of (a) protection of collectivism, (b) uncertainty avoidance, (c) lack of performance orientation, and (d) lack of trust, are easily understood.

Particular emphasis should be placed on the impact that the specific cultural model that prevails in Greek society has on the prevailing motivation framework. When a society is not characterized as future-oriented (as is the Greek society) there is no organization of "goals and objectives" and therefore there is no activation of incentives. Thus, the only factor in the formation of motivation remains the basic framework of human needs, which corresponds to earlier levels of development, so that incentives with a developmental nature cannot be activated.

4.6 The Idiosyncratic Growth Prototype of the Greek Economy

The nexus of idiosyncratic institutions and preferences in a society is what motivates or prevents its members from taking innovative initiatives. The differences between countries in terms of levels of technological development and the investment capacity stem largely from the unequal existence of idiosyncratic institutions and the idiosyncratic preferences that prevail.

The coevolution of preferences and institutions, in the case where the former is designated as idiosyncratic preferences, leads to idiosyncratic institutions forming an Idiosyncratic Growth Prototype (Petrakis et al., 2016, Kafka et al., 2020). The emergence of new institutions is associated with cultural innovation (Bowles, 2009). However, such a development is usually the result of complex and numerous processes that do not take place together, but are differentiated in terms of time and space. The adaptation of new preferences is a process that reflects the changes in human behavior following influences that the individual has accepted (Bowles, 1998). Culture and institutions being complements is essential for the survival of the latter in a long-term pattern. Otherwise, where coevolution is interrupted by rapid change of institutions then the efficiency of the economic system is conditional.

The evolution of social structure is of particular importance, which leads the small "initial" differences to prevail and be perpetuated over time (Petrakis et al., 2016). Thus, the population is constantly in a situation where influences from the past affect the preferences of individuals and the development of institutions in general. However, the coevolution of preferences and institutions in most cases is not synchronized. Incompatibility can take the form either of time progression (institutions reach an equilibrium that is compatible with equilibrium preferences at a point in time where preferences have already changed). Incompatibility, however, can be the result of incomplete transformation of preferences into institutions which can be due to many reasons (ineffective political process, hidden preferences, etc.).

Thus, understand the Greek growth process by employing a path dependence evolutionary model with two distinct characteristics: extractive institutions and non-market mechanisms of allocation of resources (Petrakis et al., 2016). It has been showed that according to institutions and preferences coevolution interactions there will be second round effects on institutions (generation of systematic risk) and preferences: (non-diversification of investment behavior and idiosyncratic cultural background consistent by: uncertainty avoidance, in-group collectivism, high discount preferences, and loss aversion). The formation of the second round idiosyncratic institutions and preferences perpetuates the existence of extractive institutions and non-market mechanisms of allocation of resources. Thus, an idiosyncratic growth prototype is generated and is prevailing with low performance on entrepreneurship and innovation (Fig. 4.2).

This stagnated growth prototype has no endogenous energy to break the barriers to growth (Kafka et al., 2020). Institutions always affect preferences and vice versa, through the coevolution pattern that they follow and has a long-lasting ability to survive (Fig. 4.2). When idiosyncratic institutions and preferences prevail in an economy, there are barriers produced that hinder innovation outcomes. The growth policy concerns should be devoted to whether we can approach a growth performance pattern with endogenous ability to sources of growth (Petrakis et al., 2016). Consequently, attention should be paid to the design and implementation of pro-growth structural changes with reference to institutions and preferences which would take into account their coevolution process.

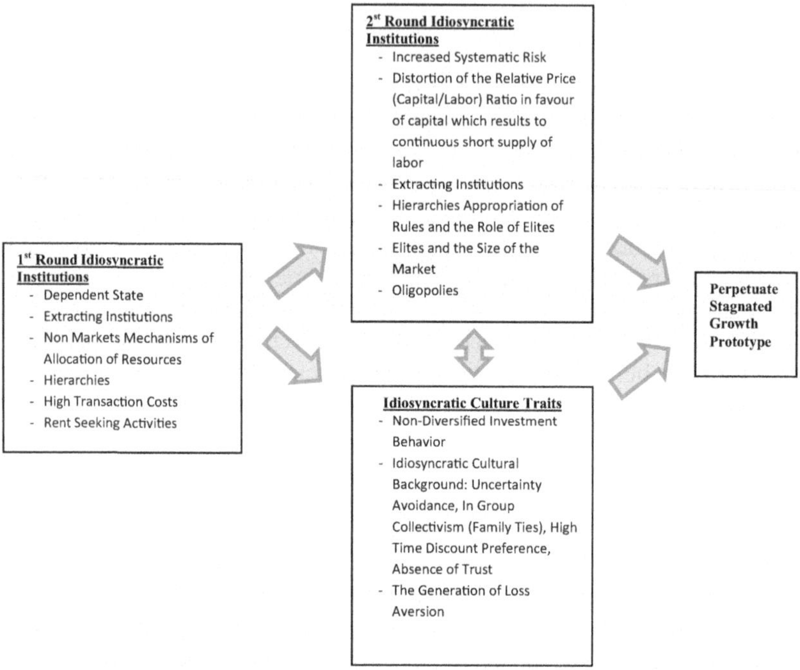

Fig. 4.2 The Idiosyncratic Growth Prototype (*Source* Authors' creation)

Otherwise, we have to rely on the importation of growth (e.g., inward flows of capital, incoming innovation) creating a pro-growth prototype that will promote growth.

Notes

1. Nash Equilibrium is the solution to a game in which two or more players have a strategy, and with each participant considering the opponent's choice, he has no incentive, nothing to gain, by switching his strategy. In the Nash Equilibrium, each player's strategy is optimal when considering the decisions of other players. Every player wins because everyone gets the outcome he/she desires. To quickly test if Nash equilibrium exists, reveal each player's strategy to the other players. If no one changes his/her strategy, then Nash Equilibrium is proven.

References

Acemoglu, D., & Robinson, J. A. (2012). *Why Nations Fail: The Origins of Power, Prosperity, and Poverty*. New York, NY: Crown.

Arrow, K. J., & Debreu, G. (1954). Existence of an Equilibrium for a Competitive Economy. *Econometrica, 22*(3), 265–290.

Bowles, S. (1998). Endogenous Preferences: The Cultural Consequences of Markets and Other Economic Institutions. *Journal of Economic Literature, 36*(1), 75–111.

Bowles, S., & Gintis, H. (2000). Walrasian Economics in Retrospect. *Quarterly Journal of Economics, 115*(4), 1411–1439.

Bowles, S. (2009). Did Warfare Among Ancestral Hunter-Gatherers Affect the Evolution of Human Social Behaviors? *Science, 324*(5932), 1293–1298.

Croitoru, A. (2012). *Schumpeter, J. A., 1934 (2008), The Theory of Economic Development: An Inquiry into Profits, Capital, Credit, Interest and the Business Cycle*. New Brunswick, NJ and London: Transaction Publishers.

Dianeosis. (2020). *How Greeks Live In Pandemia? Dianeosis*. (in Greek).

DiCaprio, A. (2012). Introduction: The Role of Elites in Economic Development. In A. H. Amsden, A. DiCaprio, & J. A. Robinson (Eds.), *The Role of Elites in Economic Development* (pp. 1–18). Oxford, UK: Oxford University Press.

Ert & Erev. (2010). On the Descriptive Value of Loss Aversion in Decisions Under Risk. *Judgment and Decision Making, 8*(3), 214–235.

Festre, A., & Garrouste, P. (2008). Rationality, Behavior, Institutional and Economic Change in Schumpeter. *Journal of Economic Methodology, 15*(4), 365–390.

Gollin, D. (2002). Getting Income Shares Right. *Journal of Political Economy, 110*(2), 458–474. https://doi.org/10.1086/338747.

Gollin, D. (2008). Labour's Share of Income. In S. B. Durlauf, L. E. Blume (Eds.), *The New Palgrave Dictionary of Economics*. London: Palgrave Macmillan.

Greenwald, B., & Stiglitz, J. E. (1986). Externalities in Markets with Imperfect Information and Incomplete Markets. *Quarterly Journal of Economics, 101*, 229–264.

Grossman, G. M., & Helpman, E. (1992). *Protection of Scale* (NBER Working Paper No. 4149). Cambridge, MA: National Bureau of Economic Research.

Hoeffler, S., Ariely, D., & West, P. (2006). Path Dependent Preferences: The Role of Early Experience and Biased Search in Preference Development. *Organizational Behavior and Human Decision Processes, 101*(2), 215–229.

Johnson, S. M. (1954). Optimal Two-and Three-Stage Production Schedules with Setup Times Included. *Naval Research Logistics Quarterly, 1*, 61–68.

Johnston, L. (1996). Resisting Change: Information-Seeking and Stereotype Change. *European Journal of Social Psychology, 26*, 799–825.

Kafka, K. I., Kostis, P. C., & Petrakis, P. E. (2020). Why Coevolution of Culture and Institutions Matters for Economic Development and Growth? In R. MYonk(Ed.), *Economic-Financial Development and Cultural Transformation*. London: IntechOpen. ISBN 978-1-78985-938-6.
Kahneman, D., & Tversky, A. (1979). Prospect Theory: An Analysis of Decision under Risk. *Econometrica, 47*(2), 263–291.
Kahneman, D., & Tversky, A. (2000). *Choices, Values and Frames*. New York, NY: Russell Sage Foundation and Cambridge University Press.
Kuznets, S. (1971). *Economic Growth of Nations: Total Output and Production Structure*. Cambridge, MA: Harvard University Press.
Lipsey, M. K., Naugle, D. E., Nowak, J., & Lukacs, P. M. (2017). Extending Utility of Hierarchical Models to Multi-Scale Habitat Selection. *Diversity and Distributions, 23*(7), 783–793.
Lipsey, R. G., & Lncaster, K. (1956). The General Theory of Second Best. *Review of Economic Studies, 24*(1), 11–32.
Lipsey, R. G., Ng, Y.-K. (2017, May). Concluding Comments to the Debate. *Pacific Economic Review, 22*(2), 213–228. Wiley Blackwell.
McKenzie, L. W. (1954). On Equilibrium in Graham's Model of World Trade and Other Competitive Systems. *Econometrica, 22*(2), 147–161.
Melas, K. (2009). *Stunned Europe*. Athens: Exantas. (in Greek).
Nash, J. F. (1950). The Bargaining Problem. *Econometrica, 18*, 155–162.
Nash, J. F. (1951). Non-Cooperative Games. *The Annals of Mathematics, Second Series, 54*(2), 286–295.
Ng, Y. K. (1977). Towards a Theory of the Third Best. *Public Finance / Finance Publique, 32*,1–15.
Olson, M. (1982). *The Rise and Decline of Nations*. New Haven, CT: Yale University Press.
Palacios-Huerta, I., & Santos, T. (2004). A Theory of Markets, Institutions, and Endogenous Preferences. *Journal of Public Economics, 88*(3), 601–627.
Petrakis, P. (2011). *The Greek Economy and the Crisis*. Springer Verlang.
Petrakis, P. E., & Konstantakopoulou, D. (2015). *Uncertainty in the Entrepreneurial Decision Making: The Competitive Advantage of Strategic Creativity*. New York, NY: Palgrave Macmillan.
Petrakis, P. (2020). *Theoretical Approaches to Economic Growth and Development. An Interdisciplinary Perspective*. Palgrave Macmillan. ISBN 978-3-030-50067-2.
Petrakis, P. E., Valsamis, D. G., & Kafka, K. I. (2016). From an Optimal to a Stagnated Growth Prototype: The Role of Institutions and Culture. *Journal of Innovation & Knowledge, 2*(3).
Phelps-Brown, P., & Weber, B. (1953). Accumulation, Productivity and Distribution in the British Economy, 1870–1938. *Economic Journal, 63*, 263–288.

Schumpeter, J. A. (1921). *The Theory of Economic Development*. Cambridge: Harvard University Press.

Schumpeter, J. A. (1939). *Business Cycles, A Theoretical, Historical and Statistical Analysis of Capitalist Process*. New York, NY: McGraw-Hill.

Stiglitz, J. E. (2002). *Globalization and its Discontents*. London: Penguin Books.

Swedberg, Richard. (2002). The Economic Sociology of Capitalism: Weber and Schumpeter. *Journal of Classical Sociology, 2*(3), 227–255.

Triandis, H. C., Bontempo, R., Villareal, M. J., Asai, M., & Lucca, N. (1988). Individualism and Collectivism: Cross-Cultural Perspectives on Self-Ingroup Relationship. *Journal of Personality and Social Psychology, 54*, 323–338.

Ülgen, F. (2014). Schumpeterian Economic Development and Financial Innovations: A Conflicting Evolution. *Journal of Institutional Economics, 10*(2), 257–277. https://doi.org/10.1017/S1744137414000022.

Walras, L. (1874). Principe d'Une Théorie Mathématique de L' Échange. *Journal Des Économistes, 34*, 5–22.

PART II

The Evolution of Sustainability, Governance, Inclusivity, Culture and Economic Growth in the Greek Economy

CHAPTER 5

Sustainable Development

5.1 Introduction

The United Nations Agenda 2030 on Sustainable Development (Transforming our World: The 2030 Agenda for Sustainable Development) was signed at the 70th session of the General Assembly in September 2015. It is the successor to the Millennium Development Goals (MDGs) which had been in place between 2000 and 2015. The new agenda aims to build on the work of its predecessor, while building on the lessons and experience of recent years in implementing policies and measuring results. The two programs differ widely in the scope of the objectives and the approach adopted to their implementation. In particular, the Millennium Goals put at the center issues such as tackling poverty, combating AIDS, and reducing child mortality worldwide, in absolute terms. On the other hand, the agenda for Sustainable Development is much more ambitious. It is not only aimed at solving pre-existing problems but also at reshaping the economic and social system in a way that prevents problems and ensures the preservation of the natural environment and resources so that future generations are not deprived of opportunities and means of economic development and quality living. In other words, Sustainable Development seeks to meet the needs of modern (and future) generations without jeopardizing the ability of future generations to meet their own needs.

P. E. Petrakis and P. C. Kostis, *The Evolution of the Greek Economy*, The Political Economy of Greek Growth up to 2030,
https://doi.org/10.1007/978-3-030-47210-8_5

Obviously, the Covid-19 crisis has come to change the priorities of human society by putting health issues first. In a way, the current issues raised by Covid-19 for societies do not differ significantly from environmental issues. The similarity lies in the fact that both issues have an external origin in terms of the economic system and concern supply conditions in the economic system and above all the supply conditions of the labor factor since they first affect productivity and then the availability of the workforce.

However, the objectives of Sustainable Development as set out in Agenda 2030 are very broad and we do not intend here to address this in particular, even though we recognize the value of the framework it sets. In this book, we have chosen to pay attention to some of those who we consider to be particularly important for the Greek economy.

In this chapter we are therefore paying attention to matters concerning the environment, renewable energy sources, natural resources and formerly on population evolution, recognizing the role of epidemics/pandemics as black swans in the operation of the economic system. In this section, we are thus giving importance to environmental issues, renewable energy sources, natural resources and formerly on the population evolution.

In addition, some of the objectives also related to additional factors also found in the 2030 Agenda are developed in the following chapters, such as those relating to sustainable governance, inclusive growth, social enterprises, and dynamic growth.

Sustainable Development requires environmental sustainability. Promoting the use of renewable energy sources that can provide an opportunity to boost the economy significantly (notably by reducing the cost of producing or importing energy from other economies), the existence and rational use of natural resources—as national resources can give a competitive advantage—and sufficient population evolution.

This chapter presents the above factors for Greece, thereby highlighting opportunities and threats. Greece has made significant efforts to improve the state of the environment in recent decades and is increasingly using renewable energy sources.

Section 5.2 shows the extent to which the Greek economy has achieved the Sustainable Development Goals set by the United Nations. Section 5.3 presents the state of the environment for Greece, while the next section (Sect. 5.4) shows the use of renewable energy sources. Section 5.5 analyses the natural resources available in Greece, which either already provide or are expected to provide significant comparative advantages in the future. Finally, Sect. 5.6 presents demographic developments in Greece, and more specifically the way in which the natural and migration balance has evolved over recent decades, since these are a critical area from which destabilizing pressures can emerge on the possibilities of preserving the development perspective in the Greek economy. Finally, Sect. 5.7 presents the global epidemics—of the twentieth and twenty-first century—as black swans in terms of their impact on the functioning of the economic system.

5.2 The Attainment of Sustainable Development Goals

The United Nations (UN) has set 17 action targets to achieve sustainable development globally by 2030. The action areas cover 5 major sections on human needs (poverty, hunger, health, education, gender equality), planet earth (water, sustainability, climate, seas, biodiversity), prosperity (energy, economy, infrastructure, inequality, cities), peace (security), and cooperation (means of implementing sustainable development policies). Specific quantified targets and indexes have been set to achieve these objectives.

The Organization for Economic Cooperation and Development (OECD) has calculated the distance between each country and achieving these objectives by 2030. On the basis of these figures, Greece has, over time and not only since 2015 when the 17 UN targets were set, covered 49% (compared to 58% for the OECD) of the distance from a minimum position covered by all OECD countries to the desired end-point of full achievement of the OECD objectives (common to all countries) by 2030. It should be noted that Greece, together with Mexico, Chile and Turkey, have the lowest rates of coverage of the sustainable development objectives.

On the basis of the analytical data, which also reflect the progress of Greece to date in sustainable development, it appears, for example, that the relative poverty rate (population with an income below 50% of median income) coincides with the OECD average, at the same time as Greece has low per capita income, low productivity and faces high unemployment. Greece does not have problems with hunger, obesity, or good health, but there are significant high smoking rates and not satisfactory levels of gender equality. There are also low levels of lifelong education and training, there is high proportion of young people who do not work, study or train, and at the same time R&D expenditure is low. In addition, there are problems related to sewage, rubbish, recycling, and high carbon dioxide emissions, although a high level of biodiversity protection applies. In addition, Greek cities are characterized as densely populated but also by high levels of air pollution. Finally, the rates of criminality in the country are low, while there is no great trust in institutions.

Obviously, it should be noted that economic development cannot be sustainable unless it is balanced and accompanied by progress, for all citizens, in all areas that define humanity in its entirety, including caring for the planet we live in. It is difficult for a country to perform well in sustainable development if it does not perform well in the economy. It is thus also difficult to achieve the sustainable development goals by 2030, as the strong economic foundations are lacking. Surely, the economic situation is expected to improve in the coming years (see Chapter 12), thus correcting the distortions that exist between the sustainability and development objectives.

5.3 The Environment

The environmental situation of Greece varies according to the sector under consideration and its monitoring is a necessary step toward continuous improvement. Many indexes show an improvement in time, but not in all. This improvement is partly due to the inherent characteristics of the country (morphology, density and population distribution) but also to the policy measures implemented, many of which are EU policies.

The Environmental Performance Index (EPI) provided by the Yale University, the Columbia University and the World Economic Forum (Wendling et al., 2018) ranks 180 countries on 24 performance indexes across ten issue categories covering environmental health and ecosystem vitality. These metrics provide a gage at a national scale of how close countries are to establish environmental policy goals. The EPI offers a scorecard that highlights leaders and laggards in environmental performance, gives insight on best practices, and provides guidance for countries that aspire to be leaders in sustainability. The EPI index tracks two fundamental dimensions of sustainable development: (1) environmental health, which accounts for 40% of the total score of the EPI, which rises with economic growth and prosperity, and which concerns factors such as air quality, water sampling, and the heavy metals, and (2) ecosystem vitality, which accounts for 60% of the total score of the EPI, which comes under strain from industrialization and restructuring as it consists of sub-indicators related to biodiversity and habitat, the forests, the fisheries, the climate and energy, the air distribution, the water resources, and the agriculture.

Figures 5.1, 5.2, and 5.3 show the relative image of the environmental performance of Greece compared to the other OECD economies for 2018, concerning the overall EPI index (Fig. 5.1), but also the environmental health (Fig. 5.2) and the ecosystem sustainability (Fig. 5.3).

Greece ranks 22nd among 180 countries in the 2018 Environmental Performance Index. For the two main sub-indexes, Greece ranks 21st in

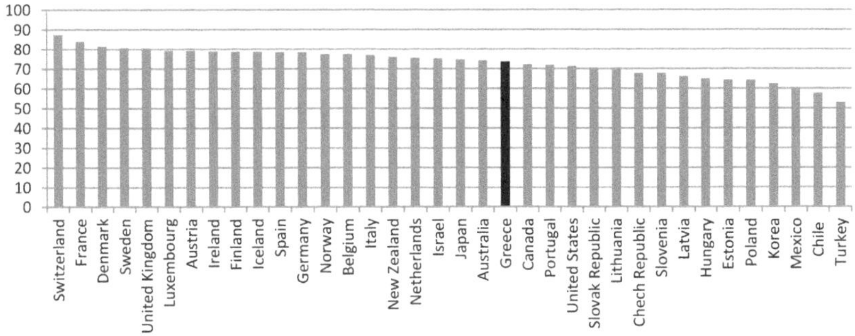

Fig. 5.1 Environmental Performance Index (2018) (*Source* Wendling et al. [2018] and authors' creation)

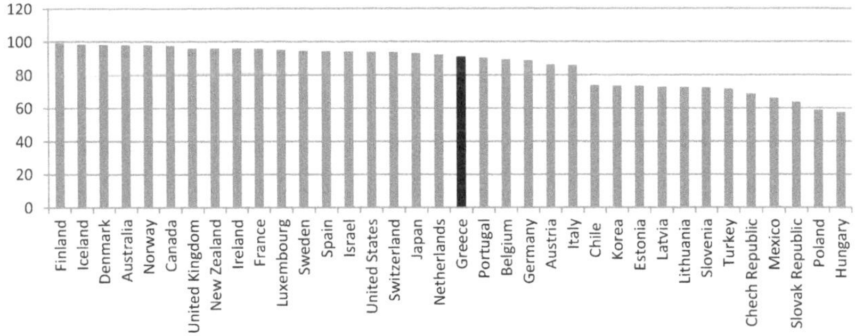

Fig. 5.2 Environmental health (2018) (*Source* Wendling et al. [2018] and authors' creation)

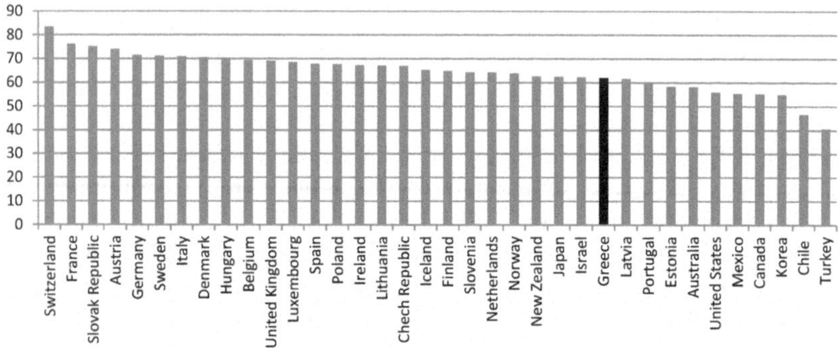

Fig. 5.3 Ecosystem vitality (2018) (*Source* Wendling et al. [2018] and authors' creation)

the environmental health sub-index, and 47th in the ecosystem sustainability position. The biggest distinction is that it is ranked first in the global water and pollution sub-index, while the worst performance is achieved in the climate and energy sub-index (where it takes 133rd place) and in the air pollution sub-index (where the 105th position is taken).

In particular, the situation of the nature and biodiversity of Greece is quite satisfactory compared to the rest of Europe, with the country making significant progress in recent years. In recent years there has been a large reduction (35%) in Greece's ecological footprint[1] (with Greece occupying one of the last places in Europe) and a corresponding downward trend in the carbon footprint of agriculture, livestock, forestry, and fisheries. By comparison, terrestrial ecosystems seem to be in a better situation than marine ecosystems, which are under pressure mainly due to overfishing and illegal fishing practices. A positive development is the recent increase in marine protected areas that have been included in the NATURA 2000 network. The progress made in the development of forest maps is particularly positive, which will have made a decisive contribution toward monitoring and protecting Greek forests.

Air quality in Greece has generally improved in recent decades. The reduction in total national emissions of the main pollutants is significant mainly due to cleaner electricity generation (reduction of lignite plants in the overall energy mix, reduction of air emissions by secondary measures, energy savings, RES), and the use of vehicles with newer cleaner engines, etc.

In terms of water management, water quality in Greece is generally considered to be particularly good. In terms of ecological status, coastal water bodies are predominantly in very good to good condition, rivers in good to moderate condition, while lakes and transitional water bodies are predominantly in moderate and/or unknown state due to insufficient data and lack of an observation station. Finally, the vast majority of groundwater bodies are in good condition both in terms of quality (85%) and quantity (80%). In addition, swimming water quality was and remains excellent.

With regard to the climate change mitigation action in Greece, in 2016 being the year for which the latest data are available, the overall greenhouse gas emission reductions have continued both due to the gradual transition of the energy system to a low-emission system; and because of the reduced activity due to the economic crisis. In particular, emissions decreased in 2016 by 3.703 kt CO2 compared to 2015 (4th largest decrease in the EU after the UK, Spain, and Italy according to EEA data). This is the direction of the national energy and climate planning for 2030 and more broadly toward 2050. The 2030 greenhouse gas emission reduction target is expected to be combined with targets for energy savings and the development of renewable energy sources, within the framework of the European institutional framework.

Finally, the waste management sector remains the most problematic. Greece, due to the chronic problem of illegal landfills and the lack of adequate infrastructure for managing hazardous industrial waste, has been convicted with substantial fines. There are also a number of legal landfills, which operate with significant problems or do not even work due to local reactions. At the same time, municipal waste recycling rates remain stable at around 14%, one of the lowest rates in the EU, with many problems in the functioning of recycling structures.

5.4 The Renewable Energy Sources

The energy potential of the Greek economy is low, due to the fact that it is characterized as an energy importer, but it acts as a transit point for energy traffic, particularly from the Caspian to Europe, mainly through the following projects: (a) the Burgas–Alexandroupolis natural gas pipeline; (b) the Trans Adriatic Pipeline (TAP) which transports natural gas from the Caspian region to Europe and passes through Northern Greece, Albania, and the Adriatic Sea before ending on the coast of southern Italy;

(c) the South Stream for the transportation of Russian natural gas through the Black Sea to Bulgaria, Serbia, Hungary, Italy, and Austria; (d) the Interconnector Turkey–Greece–Italy (ITGI) interconnecting Turkey with Italy; and (e) the Eastern Mediterranean (EastMed) pipeline, which aims to transport natural gas directly from the Eastern Mediterranean deposits to the European gas system through Greece.

However, Greece is characterized by a significant potential to use renewable energy sources. The sun, the air, and the mountains of water within and surrounding the country are suitable for the use and production of hydroelectric, wind and solar energy (Fig. 5.4).

As a result of this turn to renewable energy sources, Greece is one of the nine countries in the world producing more than 20% of their electricity from solar and wind energy for 2018,[2] according to the report on the Global Situation in the renewable sources sector of the REN21 network (GSR).[3] On the basis of this report, solar energy has a critical role in Greece (8.2% of electricity generation), while Greece is classified among the best five solar thermal markets for the year 2018 and achieves steady growth every year, reaching an all-time high record in export volumes from the solar thermal industry.

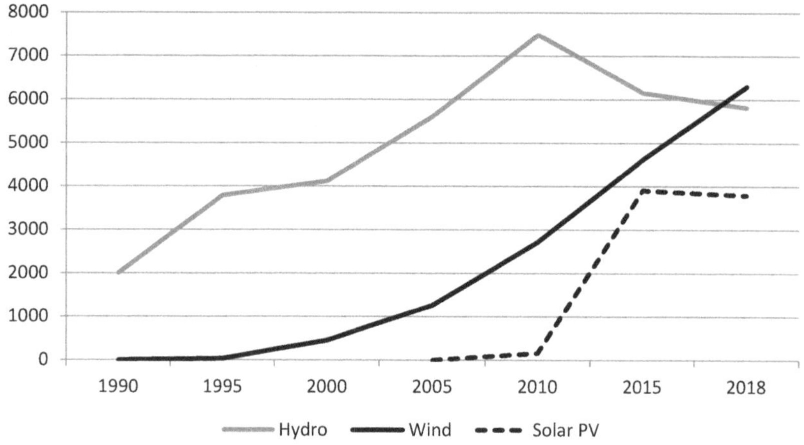

Fig. 5.4 Renewable electricity generation by source (non-combustible), Greece 1990–2018 (in Gigawatt hours—GWh) (*Source* IEA [2019] and authors' creation)

In fact, renewable energy sources are an appropriate area for attracting investment. Greece has a strong interest in investing in renewable energy both from Greek companies and from large foreign energy groups. This trend comes as a result of recent successful tenders by the Energy Regulatory Authority for the assignment of installed renewable energy capacity, based on competitive selling prices, and also due to new European targets for greater penetration of renewable energy sources. According to the 2019 Annual Report on the Greek Energy sector by the Institute of Energy for SE Europe (IENE, 2019), the total investment potential for wind farms by 2027 is €8.2 billion; for solar farms is €5.5 billion and for all other forms of renewable energy—including small hydroelectric, solar thermal, biomass and geothermal—is €1.4 billion. In other words, investments totaling more than €15 billion over the next 10 years or €1.5 billion a year.

5.5 The Natural Resources

Greece has always been a place rich in natural resources. In ancient Greece, the island of Sifnos and the mountains of Thrace were areas of significant silver and gold mining, while silver existed in Lavrio, Attica. These materials were used to create coins and jewelry, while their limited quantity in other countries has since made Greece an important trading partner for many other countries.

Today, Greece still has a wealth of natural resources that characterize it, making it one of the richest places in the wider region of Southeast Europe. Tsirambides and Filippidis (2012) in their assessment estimate the total value of the reserves of energy mineral resources of Greece at about €1.5 trillion; the total value of the indicated reserves of the industrial minerals and rocks is €60 billion, the total value of the indicated reserves of the metallic minerals is €72 billion, the total value of the indicated reserves of the energy mineral raw materials is €1362 billion (of which €268 billion belong to lignite which is exploited for decades to produce only electricity), the indicated oil reserves are 10 billion barrels with current value of €685 billion and the corresponding natural gas is 3.5 trillion m3 with a current value of €409 billion.

In more detail, the Greek economy relies heavily on the production of petroleum products,[4] although the raw material is in its largest proportion an imported product. These products are the first ranked export product of the Greek economy, accounting for around 32% of total exports in

2018. Greece has a stock of about 10 million barrels of oil. There are also estimates by the US geological Society that there are still around 22 billion barrels of oil in the Ionian Sea, off western Greece, and another 4 billion barrels in the northern Aegean Sea.

There are also estimates that the largest gas reserves in Europe (Bruneton, Konophagos, & Foscolos, 2011) are located in Greece. Considering that Greece is currently importing gas from Russia (6000 km away), finding a deposit would be particularly crucial for the future of the Greek economy.

Also, although Greece does not have a large production of mineral metals, it is one of the world's leading producers in the production of nickel and bauxite. Indeed, in these minerals Greece is the leading producer country at a European Union level. Moreover, almost all of the country's biggest companies are major players in its mining industry. In addition, there is production in the Greek land of lignite, iron ore, lead, zinc, magnesite, marble and salt, and there are gold mines.

Furthermore, the geographical location and climate of Greece are favorable factors for the development of agriculture, in particular products such as grapes, olives,[5] tobacco, and various types of cereals, such as maize, wheat and barley and products such as feta cheese,[6] barley, sugar beets, tomatoes, wine, tobacco, potatoes, beef, and dairy products. Another important agricultural product coming from Greece is cotton, with Greece being the only country that produces it in the European Union. Obviously, the Greek economy's agricultural production is not as effective as it could be because only one third of the country is suitable for cultivation (the other two-thirds consist of forests and scrubs where education is less sustainable). At the same time, the level of rainfall observed is not considered to be particularly high and there are artificial hindrances such as unsustainable farming methods. It should be noted that the entry of the Greek economy into the Eurozone has gained a great deal of benefit to the country's agricultural industry, as it opened up the profitable European market for Greek agricultural products, while at the same time EU subsidies have helped in particular the development of the country's agricultural sector. Forest land accounts for about one-fifth of Greek land, but forest products are not particularly important for the Greek economy.

At the same time, the abundance of tourist attractions in Greece combined with the prevailing climate make the country particularly dependent on its tourism industry. The islands are a main morphological characteristic of the Greek region and a constituent part of the country's culture and tradition. The Greek territory comprises 6000 islands and islands scattered in the Aegean and Ionian Seas, of which only 227 are inhabited. This is a unique phenomenon on the continent of Europe. The Greek archipelago has 7500 km of coastline—over the entire 16,000 km of the country—which is very diverse and is suitable not only for swimming, but also for diving, exploring, water skiing, sailing and windsurfing. Some of the oldest European civilizations (Cycladic, Minoan, etc.) have developed in the Greek islands, so they have unique archaeological sites, unique architectural heritage and charming local traditions of a long-time and multi-faced culture. Together with the excellent climate, the safety of the Greek seas and the short distances between ports and coasts, these elements have made the Greek islands famous and extremely popular to Greek and foreign visitors. At the same time, the continental backbone of the country is covered by a rare natural beauty, offering plenty of winter tourism options. Virgin forests, national parks, imposing mountains, impressive caves, deep-shaded gorges and lakes hosting rare habitats, and unique ecosystems are the gift of the Greek land.

5.6 The Population

The population of a society is growing with the birth and inflow of immigrants and is decreasing with the deaths and outflows of migrants. The difference between births and deaths is the natural balance and the difference between immigration flows and inflows is the migration balance. The sum of the two balances reflects the change in a population.

The Greek population increased significantly in the post-war period, a trend observed in all developed countries in the world. More specifically, from 8.3 million people in 1960 it reached around 10.7 million people in 2018, and it had reached 11.2 million people in 2011 (Eurostat, 2020a). The general characteristics which have led to the current size of the Greek population, and which are expected to determine significantly and its future size, can be summarized as follows: (a) characteristics relating to the fertility of women, relating to the number of births, (b) the average age and life expectancy associated with the number of deaths, and (c) the migration balance.

In Greece, fertility has been particularly restricted in recent decades and the overall birth population has also been reduced. This is mainly due to an improvement in the role of women in Greek society, with women's participation in education and in the labor market as a main expression, which appears to be linked negatively to fertility. Women born after the end of the nineteenth century have less and less children and do not ensure their reproduction, that is to say, each mother is not replaced, taking into account the current mortality conditions, by a daughter. The average age in acquiring the first child was in 2017 (generation of 1985) at 31 years and the corresponding average age for 1992 (generation of 1965) was 25.8 years (Eurostat, 2020b). At the same time, any postponement of births for later because of unfavorable socioeconomic conditions by generations who were at the age of 25–35 in the years of crisis (i.e., women born in the mid-1980s onward) will probably lead to an acceleration of the trend toward a reduction in the number of children, due to a reduction in both of available reproductive time and of the biological ability to procreate. These conditions are expected to result in an even smaller number of children expected to be brought to the world by women born after 1985. In particular, while in 1960 each mother gave birth to an average of 2.23 children, the figure for 2017 was 1.38 children (World Bank, 2020a). At the same time, the trend of increasing the proportion of women who never make children continues for generations born after 1965, as is the continuing decline in families of multiple children, as the births of the fourth and more children, who accounted for 13.4% of all births in 1960, and in 2017 reached only 3.6% (Eurostat, 2020b) is expected to stabilize at 2% in the mid-next decade.

Another characteristic of the Greek population is that it is aging progressively, as the average age of the population was 31.2 years in 1960 and reached 44.6 years in 2018 (Eurostat, 2020c). In addition, life expectancy at birth has increased significantly, from 69 years in 1960 to 78.8 years for men in 2017 and from 73 years to 83.9 years for women (Eurostat, 2020d). As a result of the aging population, the number of deaths in Greek society has increased significantly, since in 1960 annual deaths were less than 60,563 persons, in 2017 the respective figure was 124.501 (Eurostat, 2020e). Indeed, estimates of the rate of people over 65 years of age in the total population indicate that this percentage, from 21.8 in 2018 to reach 33.8% in 2050 (Eurostat, 2020f), a condition which is expected to place a heavy burden on the Greek insurance system.

As a result of these developments, the natural balance (births–deaths) has fallen significantly in Greek society since 1960 onward. Indeed, the natural balance has been negative since 2011 and has contributed to the decline in Greece's total population. Figure 5.5 shows the natural balance and the individual development of births and deaths in the Greek society.

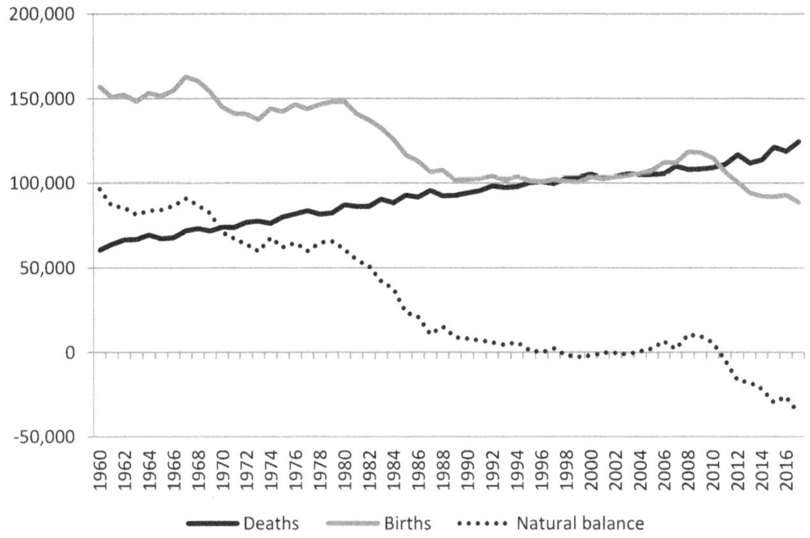

Fig. 5.5 The natural balance in Greek society (1960–2017) (individuals) (*Source* Eurostat data [2020b, 2020e] and authors' calculations and creation)

After the Second World War, the Greek population was characterized as homogeneous, as in 1960 the non-holders of Greek nationality were 52,495 people; in 2015 the figure was 1,242,514 people (World Bank, 2020b). In fact, the majority of these foreigners comes from the former socialist countries and the less developed regions of the world. It is also estimated that a significant proportion of foreigners have entered Greece illegally and do not hold a residence permit. More specifically, in the first 30 years or so after the end of the Second World War, there was a large wave of Greek migration to the outside world to find job opportunities. From the late 70s to the late 80s, this trend was reversed, due to the return of a significant proportion of migrants from previous decades, making the migration balance positive during this period. Greece turned into a country of influx of migrants mainly during the period from the early 90s till the end of 2000s, when the number of migrants almost quadrupled from 1989 to 2010. Over the last decade, which concerns the years of the major crisis in the Greek economy, positive migration balances have been reversed as part of the foreign and economic migrants established in the past decades have returned to their country, while migrants from less developed regions have continued to flow. At the same time, during this period, there is a large "brain drain," with graduates mainly of tertiary education left to seek work and opportunities which were limited in Greece during the crisis.

Figure 5.6 shows the migration balance for the Greek economy combined with the course of the number of inflows and outflows of migrants to the Greek economy.

Result of the above developments: (a) aging of the population, (b) low fertility, (c) an increase in the number of migrants, and (d) the total population of Greece is declining over time. Indeed, the estimates for the future show a trend that is expected to continue in the coming years.

Figure 5.7 shows the evolution of the natural and migration balance in relation to the evolution of the total population of Greek society, from 1960 to 2017, while at the same time presenting estimates on the evolution of the population until 2050.

The large reduction in the natural balance has contributed significantly to the decline in the population since 2011, a trend which is expected to continue for all years up to and including 2050, giving rise to important

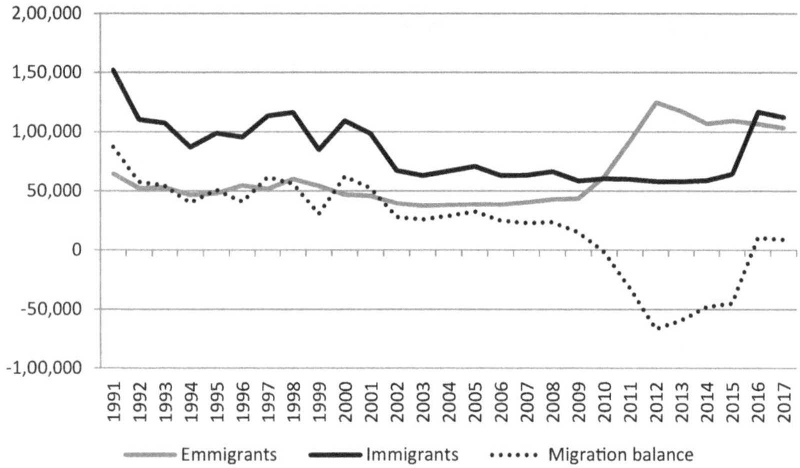

Fig. 5.6 Migration balance in Greek society (1991–2017) (individuals) (*Source* Eurostat [2020g] and authors' calculations and creation)

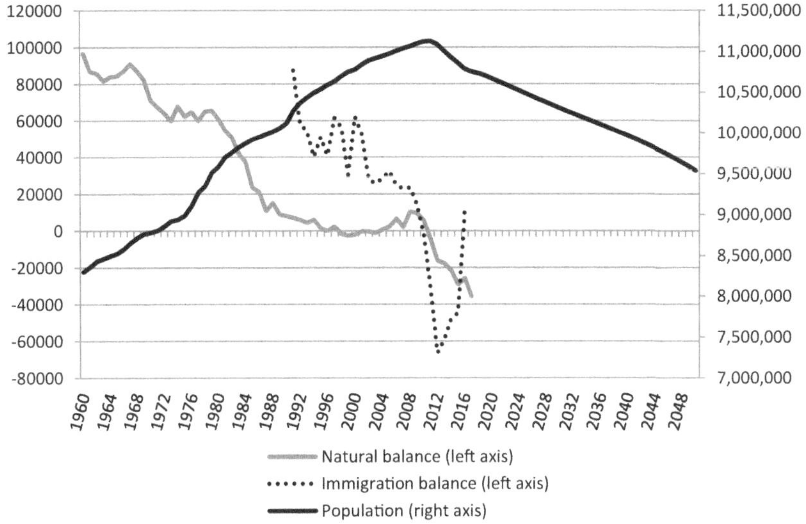

Fig. 5.7 Natural and migration balance and population evolution (*Source* Eurostat data [2020b, 2020e, 2020g], Oxford Economics [2020] and authors' calculations and creation)

issues that must be resolved. The population of Greek society is declining considerably, while at the same time aging significantly, leading to a situation which is expected to result in major problems in the productive structure of the economy, as not only will there be insufficient numbers of active people to work, but at the same time the product produced will probably not be sufficient to meet the requirements of the aging population who will not be able to work.

5.7 Pandemics and Epidemics as Black Swans

Just as people have spread across the globe, the same has happened with infections. Pandemics (global epidemics) are mostly disease outbreaks through the transmission and spread of human infection. Historically, many major epidemic and pandemic outbreaks of diseases have been recorded since ancient times, causing crises linked to huge negative impacts on health, the economy, society and the safety of national and global communities. They also caused considerable political and social upheaval (Qiu, Rutherford, Mao, & Chu, 2017).

Some of the key features of a pandemic are broad geographical expansion, transport, innovation, and severity of the disease, high rates of attack and surge, minimal public immunity, infectivity and transmissibility, which help us to better understand the concept, after looking at the similarities and differences of each case (Qiu et al., 2017). Its classic definition is defined as "an epidemic occurring worldwide, or in a very large area, crossing international boundaries and usually affecting a large number of people" (Last, 2001).

In recent history, in the twentieth century, three influenza pandemics emerged over several decades, the most serious of which was the so-called "Spanish flu" (caused by the A(H1N1) virus), which is estimated to have caused 20–50 million deaths in 1918–1919. Milder pandemics were subsequently emerging between 1957 and 1958 (the Asian flu caused by the A(H2N2) virus) and in 1968 (the "Hong Kong flu" caused by the A(H3N2) virus), which are estimated to have caused 1–4 million deaths each (WHO, 2020). The first twenty-first century influenza pandemic emerged in 2009 and was caused by the influenza A(H1N1) virus. It was the first pandemic for which many States had developed comprehensive public health action plans to reduce disease and deaths (WHO, 2020). The second is the ongoing pandemic (Covid-19), whose consequences are still to be assessed.

Covid-19, like previous pandemic events, are events that are outside the scope of normal expectations and are therefore exceedingly difficult to predict. Despite the warnings about humanity's lack of preparedness to manage the outbreak of a new pandemic (Dhillon, Srikrishna, & Beier, 2017; GPMB, 2019; Walsh, 2017) and the fact that past disasters serve as a guide to what the future holds us, when it will occur, what extent it will have and how dangerous it can be to human health, it is impossible to assess. As the world entered the 2020s, the event that no one expected was the outbreak of a deadly pandemic (Nathan, 2020). It is characteristic that in the World Economic Forum's latest report on the greatest risks facing the planet, in terms of the likelihood and magnitude of their effect, the threat of a disease is not perceived as high in either category (WEF, 2020). Indeed, in recent years there has been a reduction in resources earmarked for the prevention and response of epidemic and pandemic crises (Walsh, 2017).

Pandemics, apart from rare and unpredictable events, can have a huge impact on people's health and the economy, but also on the functioning of societies, the time horizon of which cannot be known in advance, as it is determined by the specific properties of the virus (Bloom, 2020). In addition, comparing new pandemics with older forms, often does not equip us with the necessary knowledge to manage the new crisis, due to the different "behavior" of different viruses (Osterholm, 2020). Above all, a rapidly moving, extremely deadly pandemic can cost—even in modern times—the lives of tens of millions of people (Global Preparedness Monitoring Board, 2019). Secondly, according to estimation by the World Bank, the annual global cost of a medium-to-serious critical pandemic is estimated at around USD 570 billion, or 0.7% of the global GDP. A profoundly serious pandemic, such as the Spanish flu in 1918, could cost up to 5% of the global GDP or around $4 trillion (World Bank, 2016). A crisis on this scale creates widespread destruction, instability, and insecurity.

If we add to the above findings the people's ex-post effort to rationalize the occurrence (e.g., underdeveloped health conditions) and the impact of pandemics (e.g., globalization), but also the belief that these could have been foreseen (e.g., scenario analysis), then the pandemics are "Black Swan" phenomena (Taleb, 2007). According to Taleb (2007), Black Swan events can be positive or negative and fulfill three characteristics: (1) They are out of range of normal expectations, (2) they have a huge impact, and (3) they lead to us creating explanations to show that the event was predictable.

Pandemics appear as inevitable obstacles to social welfare and economic progress. Three elements that have always strengthened the spread of lethal diseases, from the days of the plague to the present, have been scientific-medical ignorance, interconnected commercial networks and population concentration. Developed tourism has also been added to this in the modern world. The effects of Covid-19 will be very different from those of pathogens in the past, which have affected much poorer populations than today's people and with less knowledge of things like viruses and bacteria. Today's societies are cognitively improved, but their development and dependence on the globalized market and urbanization make them both richer and more vulnerable. The economies most likely to be affected by pandemic events are those with a higher degree of integration with the world market (Verikios, Sullivan, Stojanovski, Giesecke, & Woo, 2011). And as global economic integration continues, along with the integration of developing and underdeveloped regions, the cost of the outbreak of pandemics will increase. It is characteristic that Chinese imports and the money spent by Chinese tourists (in terms of global GDP), in relation to the SARS epidemic period (2003), are, respectively, three and eight times more today (Tilton, 2020).

The emergence of health crises in the form of Black Swan pandemics in today's hyperconnected world is more likely and more acute than ever (Taleb, 2007), as it is sufficient that only a few people, being a carrier, travel from one place to another. Covid-19, which in a short time has evolved from endemic to epidemic and then to pandemic, is and is being perceived as a Black Swan event (Halliburton, 2020; Nathan, 2020). It is even stronger than the Great Recession of 2008 (Lonski, 2020). This new pandemic is one of the biggest crises of confidence in the modern world, causing markets to be disturbed more rapidly than by other historical events, such as the Great Recession of 1929 or the crisis of 2008 (Wells, 2020).

Notes

1. Ecological footprint is a way to measure the effects of human activities on earth. It is the demand and consumption measure that measures meeting the needs of a society, as well as the waste and greenhouse gases that it produces daily on productive marine and land areas. It also assesses all the natural resources needed to support the physical needs of a population or individual through the technology, lifestyle and habits of each country.
2. These nine countries are Denmark, Uruguay, Ireland, Germany, Portugal, Spain, Greece, United Kingdom, and Honduras.
3. Since 2005 and every year, the Renewable Energy Policy Network has published the renewable Global Status Report. This is a collection of figures that measure the performance of many states over a large number of renewable energy technologies ranging from photovoltaic to geothermal energy and wave generators.
4. Petroleum oils derived from bituminous minerals (excluding crude oils) containing 70% or more of the oil.
5. The best variety of olives is cultivated in Greece for olive oil production. However, Greece accounts for only 4% of the global olive oil industry. Similarly, in Italy and Spain, small olive oil producers merged into global competitive clusters and replaced their machines with more efficient new technologies. As a result, these two countries now cover almost all the world's olive oil supply, unlike Greek production, which, despite its many advantages, maintains the least profitable part of the supply chain.

6. Feta cheese is becoming increasingly popular throughout the world, while it is mandated by an E.U. ruling to come from Greece. However, Greece holds only 28% of the world market for feta cheese. Over the past decade, companies from the USA, France, Denmark, and other countries invested in their own food research and production equipment and managed through feta cheese variations to gain the largest market share.

References

Bloom, B. (2020). Interview with Dr. Barry Bloom. *Goldman Sachs Top of Mind, 86*, 4–6. Retrieved from https://www.goldmansachs.com/insights/pages/coronavirus.html.

Bruneton, A., Konophagos, E., & Foscolos, A. (2011). Economic and Geopolitical Importance of Eastern Mediterranean Gas Fields for Greece and the E.U. Emphasis on the Probable Natural Gas Deposits Occurring in the Libyan Sea Within the Exclusive Economic Zone of Greece. *Mineral Wealth, 160*, 7–22.

Dhillon, R. S., Srikrishna, D., & Beier, D. (2017). The World Is Completely Unprepared for a Global Pandemic. *Harvard Business Review*. Retrieved from https://hbr.org/2017/03/the-world-is-completely-unprepared-for-a-global-pandemic.

Eurostat. (2020a). *Database*. Retrieved from http://appsso.eurostat.ec.europa.eu/nui/show.do?dataset=demo_pjanind.

Eurostat. (2020b). *Database—Live Births by Mother's Year of Birth (Age Reached) and Birth Order*. Retrieved from https://db.nomics.world/Eurostat/demo_fordager.

Eurostat. (2020c). *Database—Population: Structure Indicators*. Retrieved from http://appsso.eurostat.ec.europa.eu/nui/show.do?dataset=demo_pjanind.

Eurostat. (2020d). *Database—Life Expectancy at Birth by Sex (sdg_03_10)*. Retrieved from https://ec.europa.eu/eurostat/cache/metadata/en/sdg_03_10_csmsip2.htm.

Eurostat. (2020e). *Database—Deaths by Age and Sex (demo_magec)*. Retrieved from https://appsso.eurostat.ec.europa.eu/nui/show.do?dataset=demo_magec&lang=en.

Eurostat. (2020f). *Database*. Retrieved from http://appsso.eurostat.ec.europa.eu/nui/show.do?dataset=proj_18np&lang=en.

Eurostat. (2020g). *Database—Migration and Migrant Population Statistics (migr_imm8, migr_emi2)*. Retrieved from https://ec.europa.eu/eurostat/statistics-explained/index.php/Migration_and_migrant_population_statistics.

Global Preparedness Monitoring Board. (2019). *A World at Risk: Annual Report on Global Preparedness for Health Emergencies*. Geneva: World Health Organization.

Halliburton, B. C. (2020). COVID-19 Is a Black Swan. *Forbes*. Retrieved from https://www.forbes.com/sites/forbesbooksauthors/2020/03/19/covid-19-is-a-black-swan/#1541df1d7b4b.

IEA. (2019). *Renewables Information 2019*. Paris: IEA. Retrieved from https://www.iea.org/reports/renewables-information-2019.

IENE. (2019). *The Greek Energy Sector, Annual Report 2019*. Retrieved from https://www.iene.gr/articlefiles/file/meletes/iene-meleti-2019.pdf.

Last, J. M. (2001). *A Dictionary of Epidemiology* (4th ed.). New York: Oxford University Press.

Lonski, J. (2020). *Coronavirus May Be a Black Swan Like No Other*. Moody's. Retrieved from https://www.moodysanalytics.com/-/media/article/2020/weekly-market-outlook-coronavirus-may-be-black-swan-like-no-other.pdf.

Nathan, A. (2020). 2020's Black Swan: Coronavirus. *Goldman Sachs Top of Mind, 86,* 4–6. Retrieved from https://www.goldmansachs.com/insights/pages/coronavirus.html.

Osterholm, M. (2020). Interview with Dr. Michael Osterholm. *Goldman Sachs Top of Mind, 86,* 8–9. https://www.goldmansachs.com/insights/pages/coronavirus.html.

Oxford Economics. (2020). *Global Economic Model*.

Qiu, W., Rutherford, S., Mao, A., & Chu, C. (2017). The Pandemic and Its Impacts. *Health, Culture and Society, 9,* 1–11.

Taleb, N. N. (2007). *The Black Swan: The Impact of the Highly Improbable*. New York: Random House.

Tilton, A. (2020). Interview with Dr. Andrew Tilton. *Goldman Sachs Top of Mind, 86,* 10–11. https://www.goldmansachs.com/insights/pages/coronavirus.html.

Tsirambides, A., & Filippidis, A. (2012). Energy Mineral Resources of Greece. *Journal of Environmental Science and Engineering B, 1,* 709–719.

Verikios, G., Sullivan, M., Stojanovski, P., Giesecke, J., & Woo, G. (2011). *The Global Economic Effects of Pandemic Influenza: Centre of Policy Studies/IMPACT* (Centre Working Papers g-224).

Walsh, B. (2017). The World Is Not Ready for the Next Pandemic. *TIME*. Retrieved from https://time.com/magazine/us/4766607/may-15th-2017-vol-189-no-18-u-s/.

WEF. (2020). *The Global Risks Report 2020*. Insight Report 15th Edition.

Wells, P. (2020). S&P 500 Suffers Its Quickest Fall into Bear Market on Record. *Financial Times*. Retrieved from https://www.ft.com/content/d895a54c-64a4-11ea-a6cd-df28cc3c6a68.

Wendling, Z. A., Emerson, J. W., Esty, D. C., Levy, M. A., de Sherbinin, A., et al. (2018). *2018 Environmental Performance Index*. New Haven, CT: Yale Center for Environmental Law & Policy. Retrieved from https://epi.yale.edu/.

WHO. (2020). *Past Pandemics*. http://www.euro.who.int/en/health-topics/communicable-diseases/influenza/pandemic-influenza/past-pandemics.
World Bank. (2016). *World Bank Group Launches Groundbreaking Financing Facility to Protect Poorest Countries Against Pandemics* (Press Release).
World Bank. (2020a). *Database, Fertility Rate, Total (Births Per Woman)*. Retrieved from https://data.worldbank.org/indicator/SP.DYN.TFRT.IN.
World Bank. (2020b). *Database, International Migrant Stock, Total*. Retrieved from https://data.worldbank.org/indicator/SM.POP.TOTL.

CHAPTER 6

Sustainable Governance

6.1 Introduction

The changes in the international economic system and in geopolitical power relations over the last decades have had a decisive impact on the ways in which states are now involved in shaping the economy. The globalization of markets, special competitions, the Covid-19 pandemic, new environmental and regional challenges, as well as the divisions emerging at socioeconomic and cultural level, redefine the role of the state. The current global economic crisis is also contributing to the adjustment of the state function in relation to the economy. Popular approaches to date, which have given priority to market mechanisms and their ability to self-regulate, are beginning to lose momentum. The conditions for a general consensus are gradually emerging on the new forms of regulation and action which the states are now called upon to take while simultaneously there are fears that overstaffing their role could threaten the privacy of citizens.

The importance and, ultimately, the meaning of seeking more effective and democratic methods of governance (political and economic) lies in the fact that governance can not only influence the performance and form of the economic system at present, but it essentially shapes incentives and institutions for the future distribution of resources and incomes within society. Let us not forget that institutions, as entities, in their capacity to evolve and enjoy broad acceptance and influence, by their very nature are

P. E. Petrakis and P. C. Kostis, *The Evolution of the Greek Economy*,
The Political Economy of Greek Growth up to 2030,
https://doi.org/10.1007/978-3-030-47210-8_6

the most effective tools to address the biggest systemic problems, such as economic inequality, discrimination, and a reduced sense of justice within societies, the gradual elimination of natural resources, etc. If we are to be able to exploit these institutions' potential as a society, then we must recognize the importance of good and sustainable governance and make them a political priority for the coming years.

The concept of sustainable governance promotes a long-term view of public policy in such a way as to take into account the interests of future generations. Some approaches, mechanisms, and frameworks make it easier than others to design and implement long-term policies with positive results in the future. For example, increased confidence in the political system and institutions and the conditions for political stability are more favorable to this. The focus on the longevity of policies and the consideration of the interests of the next generations stems from the international community's assumption that current economic development in the current period should not hinder future development, nor should it pass on debts and problems to the coming societies.

This chapter aims to present the quality and sustainability of governance in Greece, highlighting many of the weaknesses that characterize it. A good effort to measure the quality of governance is the World Governance Indicators formulated by the World Bank from 1996 to today (Kaufman, Kraay, & Mastruzzi, 2009). The quality of institutions is measured using indicators such as voice accountability, political stability, government efficiency, regulatory quality, rule of law, and control of corruption. These indicators can reflect the performance of the Greek economy in a historical and comparative perspective and thus obtain useful conclusions on the quality of political institutions related to the sustainability of governance.

The quality of political institutions has a significant impact on economic growth. Policies that channel the social product to groups with a disproportionate political influence over others are contributing to the discrediting of the political system (Petrakis, 2011). In this way, any reform effort toward adapting an economy to the requirements of international competition is invalidated, while in the long term the potential for economic growth is restricted. The vicious circle is complemented by incentives for counter-productive and non-institutional economic action, as positive expectations are missing. The extent of tax evasion in Greece is a sign of the vicious circle. The crucial point, however, of the negative impact of political institutions on economic growth is the redistribution of the social product.

The structure of the chapter is the following: Sect. 6.2 shows the evolution over time of the voice accountability indicator for the Greek economy compared to the OECD average, followed by the corresponding developments in the political stability (Sect. 6.3), government efficiency (Sect. 6.4), regulatory quality (Sect. 6.5), rule of law (Sect. 6.6) and control of corruption (Sect. 6.7) indicators.

6.2 Voice and Accountability

The voice and accountability indicator measures the extent to which citizens of a country are involved in the government's selection process, as well as the degree of freedom of expression of associations and the Press. It reflects the perception of the extent to which citizens of a country can participate in the selection of their government, as well as freedom of expression, freedom of association, and free media.

This is essentially an aspect that expresses the existence of the problem of "representation" which has a significant impact on modern complex societies. This issue refers to whether those who represent the citizens in parliament adequately represent and effectively promote the collective interests of those who voted for them. The issue of representation is linked to the existence of a democratic system and its interconnection with the economic system and economic development, the role of elites and pressure groups, the cultural background of policy-makers and the role of the media.

With regard to the media, apart from the significant benefit of providing general information and entertainment, they inform society of (a) all the political events that are happening (policies being implemented, inform on laws in force or changing) either locally or globally, and (b) the profiles of the government members and their actions, to allow them to decide whether to re-vote or replace them. Also, the media have succeeded in educating the illiterate masses of the countryside and eliminate the distances that separate the place of residence of a member of a society from the centers of policy. For these reasons, media freedom is a reflection of the success of governance and the success of the democratic regime, making the system more accountable so that it can respond better and be citizen-friendly (Fig. 6.1).

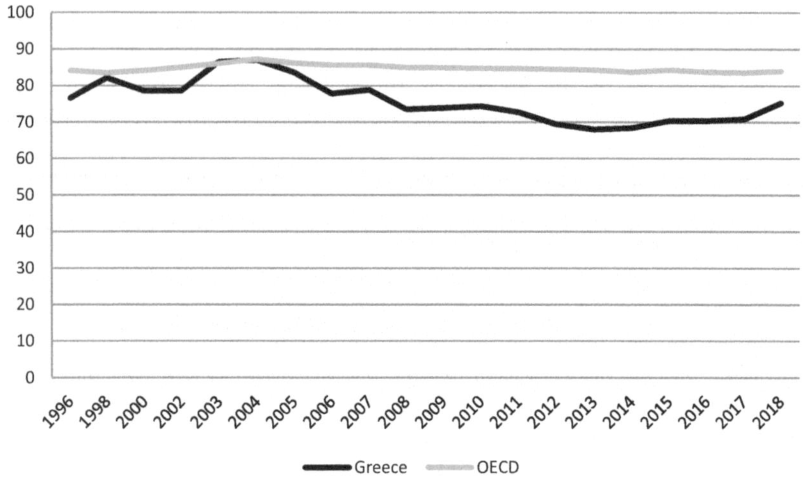

Fig. 6.1 Voice and accountability—Greece vs OECD (1996–2018) (*Source* World Bank [2019] and authors' calculations and creation)

While in this indicator Greece ranks the same as the OECD average up to and including 2004, it has since and until 2014 diverged significantly, while in 2015 and 2018 there is a significant recovery effort. For 2018, Greece with a score of 75.37, it ranks 29 among the 36 OECD countries (the OECD average score is 83.98), with only Latvia, Korea, Poland, Israel, Hungary, Mexico and Turkey getting a lower score. The highest values in this indicator are achieved by Norway, New Zealand, Switzerland, Finland, Denmark and Sweden.

6.3 Political Stability and Absence of Violence/Terrorism

The indicator of "political stability" measures the likelihood that the government will be destabilized by constitutional or violent means, including terrorism.

Especially in the case of Greece, political risk varies over time to a high level. Most research on the greatest risks to the Greek economy concludes that political instability and political risk are one of the greatest threats.

More specifically, according to a survey carried out by ALCO research company in 2016, in collaboration with consultants Fidel & Fortis Management Consultants, the five most important risks of the senior Greek companies are: (a) political instability (81%), (b) security-related threats (62%), (c) natural disasters (56%), (d) financing difficulties (55%), and (e) continuous changes in the institutional framework (48%). Also, according to Allianz Global Risk Barometer for 2019 (Allianz, 2020), the political risk is one of the 10 biggest risks to the Greek economy, and in particular to Greek companies. In addition, according to the Economist, political instability in Greece combined with rising unemployment and social tension was during the crisis the important factors that contributed to the increased risk of Greece leaving the Eurozone.

Figure 6.2 shows the evolution of the Political Stability and Absence of Violence/Terrorism indicator for Greece compared to the OECD average from 1996 to 2018.

While in this indicator Greece is ranked the same as the OECD average up to and including 2002, since then, at a peak in the year 2009, it has significantly deviated, while since then it has been relatively stable. Obviously, the overall performance of around 40 units throughout the

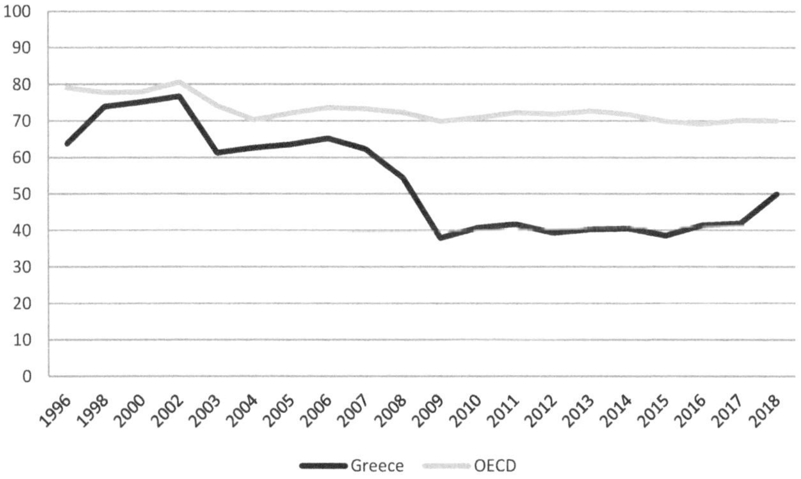

Fig. 6.2 Political stability and absence of violence/terrorism—Greece vs OECD (1996–2018) (*Source* World Bank [2019] and authors' calculations and creation)

period of severe recession is very low, when the OECD average is around 70 units. For 2018, Greece with a score of 50 ranks 32 as among the 36 OECD countries (the OECD average score is 70), with a score higher than the UK, Mexico, Israel, and Turkey alone. The highest values in this indicator are achieved by New Zealand, Iceland, Luxembourg, Switzerland and Norway.

6.4 Government Effectiveness

The indicator of "efficiency of the state" measures the quality of public services, the ability of politicians to provide services, and independence from political pressures. It records perceptions of the quality of public services, the quality of public administration and the quality of its political formulation and implementation, as well as the credibility of the government's commitment to announced policies.

Figure 6.3 shows the evolution of the Government Effectiveness indicator for Greece compared to the OECD average from 1996 to 2018.

In this indicator, Greece has fallen significantly below the OECD average in all years, and since 2004 the diverging trend has been growing

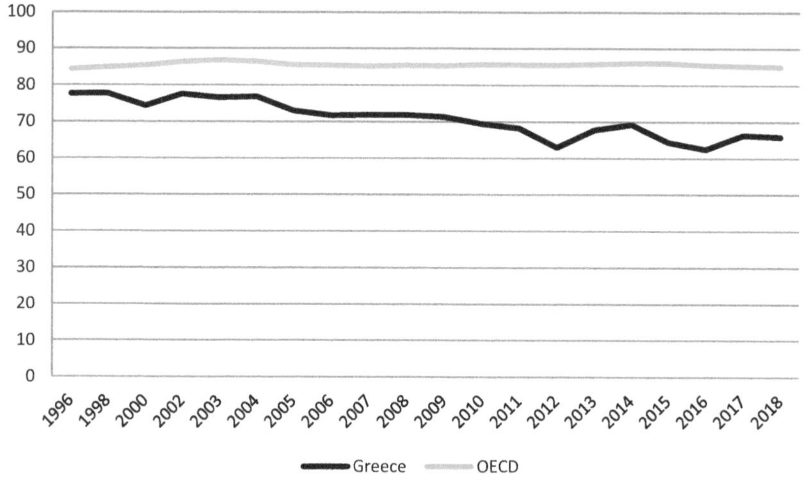

Fig. 6.3 Government effectiveness—Greece vs OECD (1996–2018) (*Source* World Bank [2019] and authors' calculations and creation)

reaching a peak in 2012 and 2016. For 2018, Greece with a score of 65.87 ranks 34 as among the 36 OECD countries (the OECD average score is 84.98), with a higher score than Turkey and Mexico alone. The highest values in this indicator are achieved by Switzerland, Finland, Norway, Denmark, and the Netherlands.

Possibly, the data from this indicator may have improved since the Covid-19 crisis, which as it is generally accepted, its treatment served as a very good international good practice.

6.5 Regulatory Quality

The indicator of "regulatory interventions" measures the government's ability to design and implement reforms and policies that strengthen and promote private sector development.

Figure 6.4 shows the evolution of the Regulatory Quality indicator for Greece compared to the OECD average from 1996 to 2018.

As in the indicator of governance efficiency, Greece has fallen significantly below the OECD average in all years, and since 2004 the diverging path is growing peaking in 2016. For 2018, Greece with a score of 64.42

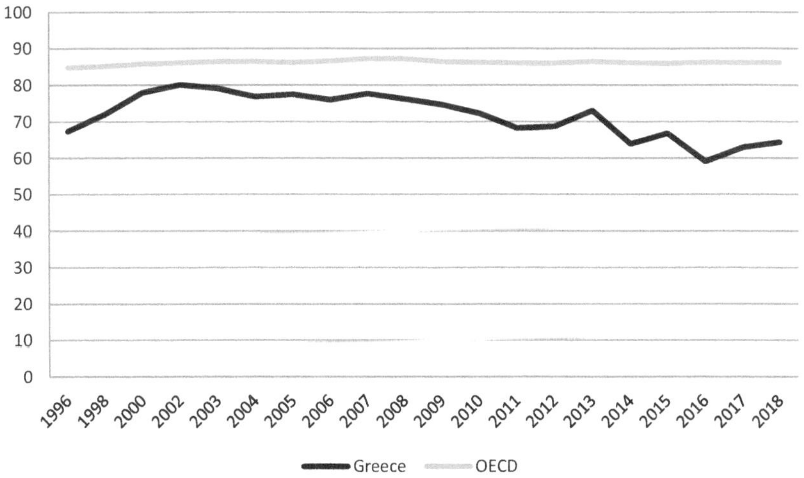

Fig. 6.4 Regulatory quality—Greece vs OECD (1996–2018) (*Source* World Bank [2019] and authors' calculations and creation)

ranks 34 as among the 36 OECD countries (the OECD average score is 86.07), with a higher score than Turkey and Mexico alone. The highest values in this indicator are achieved by the Netherlands, New Zealand, Australia, Sweden, Finland, and Switzerland.

6.6 Rule of Law

The rule of law indicator measures the extent to which citizens trust the laws of society, including the quality of property rights, police and justice. At the same time, it records perceptions of the extent to which the actors of the administration trust and comply with the rules of society, and respect the conventions (written and unwritten), on citizens' rights in property, policing, justice, and the prevention of crime.

Figure 6.5 shows the evolution of the Rule of Law indicator for Greece compared to the OECD average from 1996 to 2018.

In this indicator too, the performance of Greece has been rather poor over time and even appears to deviate significantly from the OECD average over the period considered. While in 1996 the score was exactly at the level of the OECD average (close to 84 points) since then there

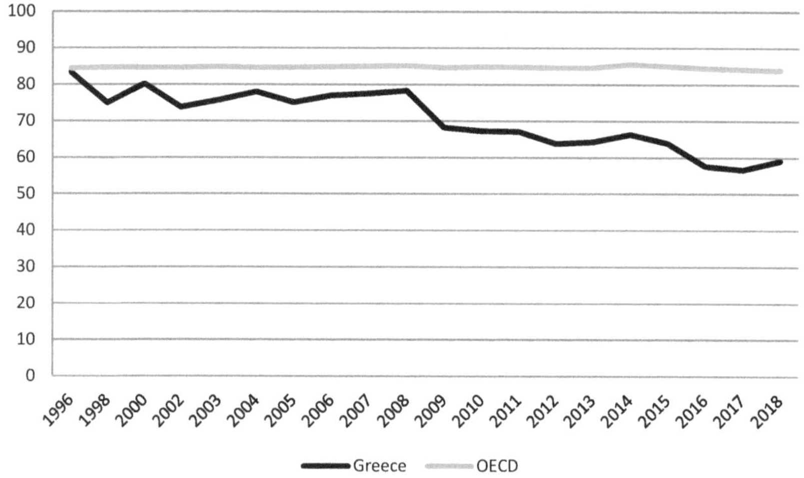

Fig. 6.5 Rule of law—Greece vs OECD (1996–2018) (*Source* World Bank [2019] and authors' calculations and creation)

has been a steady deterioration, with the result that in 2017, Greece has obtained the lowest value over time (score 56.73). For 2018, Greece with a score of 59.13 ranks 34 among the 36 OECD countries (the OECD average score is 83.83), with a score higher than Turkey and Mexico alone. The highest values in this indicator are achieved by Finland, Norway, Switzerland, Sweden, and New Zealand.

6.7 Control of Corruption

Corruption is a transaction cost in the economic system (which is unrecorded). In international literature there are a number of studies analyzing the phenomenon of corruption, the diversification of which makes it difficult to choose a definition that fully reflects the concept. Corruption is generally defined as the abuse of public authority for private benefit. It is used by journalists and politicians as a general concept including all forms of abuse of power, whether in the public or private sector. It also includes nepotism or selfless policies that allow companies, politicians, civil servants, or business executives to evade accountability (Petrakis, 2011).

In recent decades, significant efforts have been made at global level to reduce and combat corruption by national governments and international organizations. The establishment of a specialized anti-corruption center (Anti-Corruption Knowledge Centre), the creation of transparency committees in all countries at a rapid pace, pan-national investigations and the establishment of a special international anti-corruption committee are key instruments in the global strategy for highlighting and combating this phenomenon. However, achieving this objective requires it to be measured to diagnose problems and assess the results.

Corruption is mainly measured by research using questionnaires. It is easy to see that any attempt to measure corruption cannot be accurate and successful. However, as a result of anonymous questionnaire completion, it can provide an approximate picture of the phenomenon in each country.

The existence of corruption requires the presence of specific conditions. For the existence of corruption, there is a need for a society to take such action and for the conditions to either encourage or simply allow such events. For example, when bureaucracy creates delays and heavy costs for citizens, while the institutional framework for control and penalties is not strict and effective, citizens are easily motivated to find non-institutional methods for settling their obligations/operations.

The absence of effective sanctions in the event of infringements and widespread lawlessness in the functioning of the State are detrimental both to the rights of the citizen and to public interest.

The World Bank's corruption indicator measures the extent to which public power is exercised to obtain the same benefit, including both small and large forms of corruption. This is a measure of the perception of the country's ability to control all kinds of corruption, and the extent to which the public sector is controlled by private interests, making the exercise of power ineffective and inefficient.

Figure 6.6 shows the evolution of the Control of Corruption indicator for Greece compared to the OECD average from 1996 to 2018.

In this indicator, Greece's performance is fairly problematic over time and even appears to deviate significantly from the OECD average over the period considered from 1998 onward. Since 2012, there has been some stability, while in 2018 there has been little improvement. For 2018, Greece with a score of 55.77 ranks 34 among the 36 OECD countries (the OECD average score is 81.44), with a score higher than Turkey and Mexico alone. The highest values in this indicator are given by Finland, New Zealand, Denmark, Sweden, and Norway.

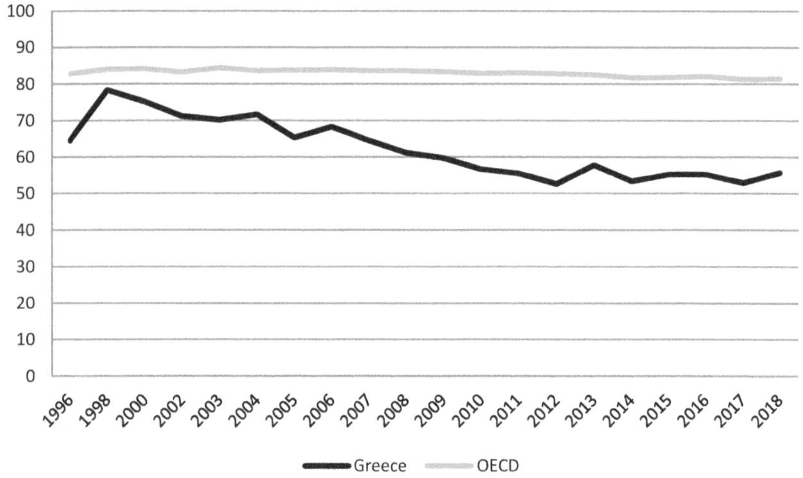

Fig. 6.6 Control of corruption—Greece vs OECD (1996–2018) (*Source* World Bank [2019] and authors' calculations and creation)

References

Allianz. (2020). *Allianz Risk Barometer 2020 (Appendix for 34 Countries)*. Munich: Allianz Global Corporate & Specialty SE. Retrieved from https://www.agcs.allianz.com/news-and-insights/reports/allianz-risk-barometer.html.

Kaufmann, D., Kraay, A., & Mastruzzi, M. (2009). *Governance Matters VIII: Aggregate and Individual Governance Indicators 1996–2008*. Washington, DC, USA: World Bank Working Paper.

Petrakis, P. E. (2011). *The Greek Economy and the Crisis: Challenges and Responses*. New York and Heidelberg: Springer.

World Bank. (2019). *The Worldwide Governance Indicators*. Retrieved from https://info.worldbank.org/governance/wgi/.

CHAPTER 7

Inclusivity

7.1 Introduction

The well-being of citizens that feeds economic development is largely shaped by indirect non-income factors which are, however, essential for the exploitation and creation of economic opportunities. Key examples are education, health, infrastructure, social engagement, social cohesion, impartial justice, etc. Everyone must have the same opportunities and be able to exploit them.

However, despite the increase in prosperity and wealth for most societies and economies in the world, there have been a number of problems that prevent inclusivity in terms of exploiting opportunities by all. For example, in most developed economies there are issues related to high-income disparities, to the reduction of the size of the middle class, to non-equal opportunities between men and women, to access education, etc. The Covid-19 crisis has intensified several of these trends.

This chapter presents issues related to the issue of inclusivity in Greek society, in particular compared to the EU-28 average, which relate to labor market conditions, issues related to income distribution and observed inequalities, the level of poverty, and the quality of education.

The structure of the chapter is the following: Sect. 7.2 presents the concept of inclusive growth and Sect. 7.3 presents issues related to the labor market, in particular wages, employment, the level of unemployment and long-term unemployment, and gender pay gaps. Next

P. E. Petrakis and P. C. Kostis, *The Evolution of the Greek Economy*,
The Political Economy of Greek Growth up to 2030,
https://doi.org/10.1007/978-3-030-47210-8_7

(Sect. 7.4) there are issues related to income distribution and observed income inequalities in society, while in the next Sect. 7.5 issues are presented related to the level of poverty and the proportion of the population at risk of poverty or social exclusion. Finally, Sect. 7.6 presents issues related to the level and quality of education while in Sect. 7.7 some aspects of inclusivity are analyzed which were affected by the Covid-19 crisis.

7.2 The Concept of Inclusive Growth

Not all growth models produce positive results for the society; just as they do not all ensure environmental sustainability. It is noted that in countries in the developed world, despite high productivity and economic-development rates, social polarization, and unrest is growing together with economic inequality and mistrust toward political systems.

Moreover, increased income inequality is associated with reduced inter-generational and social mobility. Children of poor families tend to remain poor, while children of rich families tend to be the opposite. The social problem that arises is not only moral but also has an economic-development aspect. Do people with high intellectual capabilities not require the ability to show them? But society is therefore poorer than the specific protagonists of economic development. Countries such as Finland and Denmark have low levels of income inequality and high social mobility. At the same time, countries of southern Europe such as Italy and others such as the United Kingdom are experiencing high levels of income inequality and, respectively, low social mobility.

The literature relating to the effects of income inequality is expanding, with the main body of research showing that inequality was and is a serious factor in creating unsustainable growth.

This creates the need to develop the concept of Inclusive Growth. So far, it seems that the richest share of the population in the world has benefited greatly from globalization and increased productivity. At the same time, however, the middle and lower classes of developed countries have been severely affected. International competition has led to a reduction in wages and jobs for unskilled workers who have been affected also by the economic crisis in recent years. At the same time, there has been a decline in the share of national income from work in many countries in the developed world over recent decades, which shows that labor productivity is growing faster than it is rewarded, as well as that the share of national income going to capital rather than to work is increasing.

This increase in economic inequalities within countries, in addition to the possible direct negative effects on growth from an economic point of view, gives rise to a high level of concern and a sense of injustice for citizens who feel neglected, sidelined and not involved in the benefits of economic development in their countries. At the same time, the prospect of a better future for their children is now questioned by many parents in the developed world, experiencing the effects of technological change and automation on labor markets, along with the increase of precarious, flexible, and low-quality jobs. The public's dissatisfaction with all these issues is expressed in the political arena, with the radicalisation of the population, political polarization, and social division even in the most developed countries. Increasing support for protectionist and nationalist policies, anti-systemic political candidates and marginal ideologies reveal insecurity and a decline in the confidence of societies in their political systems. Stagnation or even worsening living conditions for large sections of the population has created the feeling that political elites are not sufficient to provide effective solutions.

One of the greatest challenges for the international community in the upcoming years is therefore to adapt the institutional, systemic, and economic organization of societies in a way that ensures inclusive economic growth, by allowing increasingly large parts of society to participate in the process and the benefits of this growth, thus ensuring security and stability. It has now been understood and recognized by the major international cooperation organizations, but also by many governments, that economic growth as simply recorded by GDP growth does not necessarily translate into sustainable improvements in the quality of life of citizens. While the growth of the national economic "pie" is absolutely essential, it does not guarantee the possibility of improving the living conditions of the entire society. On the contrary, what is important for spreading the benefits of development into a society is ultimately the effectiveness of the mechanisms and channels for the distribution and redistribution of the income and opportunities that have been put in place.

Income distribution rules, the availability of economic opportunities, economic security, and quality of life are the key criteria against which a society will judge the effectiveness of the economic policy of the political leadership concerned. This exchange between the economy and society produces political, economic and social results, positive or negative in line with the balance established between the two. On the one hand, growth of economic prosperity on a broad social basis stimulates growth, increasing domestic consumption and demand, investment confidence, entrepreneurship and jobs. On the other hand, the deterioration of the quality of life of citizens can bring about a significant reduction in consumer demand, in savings and investments, wage stagnation, and high unemployment, thereby also reducing the rate of economic growth. The issue of inclusive growth therefore essentially relates to maintaining the foundations of economic growth itself.

7.3 Human Capital and Labor Market

This section includes three issues related to human capital and the labor market. These are the human resources income, employability and unemployment issues and gender gaps.

7.3.1 Income

Figure 7.1 shows the evolution of the monthly minimum wage for Greece compared to the EU-28 average for the period from 1999 to 2019.

Since 1999, the minimum wage in Greece has been increasing steadily, with the last increase being on July 1, 2011, where it reached €876.62 for 12 payments per year (and €751.39 for 14 payments per year). This minimum wage was valid until February 29, 2012. On March 1, 2012, the minimum wage was reduced by 22% for workers over 25 years of age and by 32% for workers between 18 and 25 years of age (creation of a sub-minimum wage). On February 1, 2019, for the first time since July 2011, the minimum wage was increased by 10.91% for workers over 25 years of age and by 27.22% for workers between 18 and 25 years of age (abolition of the sub-minimum wage). It was established, regardless of age, at €758.33 for 12 payments per year (and €650 for 14 payments per year).

7.3.2 Employment and Unemployment

Unemployment in Greek society has three main sources: (1) it is of structural nature due to changes in the international division of projects, (2) due to the decline in levels of economic activity (demand) due to

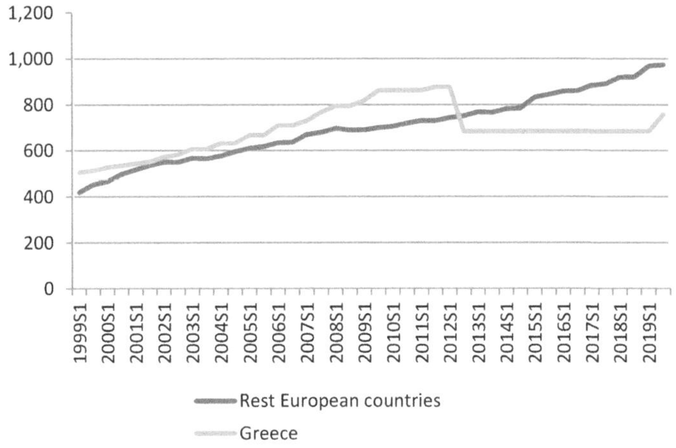

Fig. 7.1 Monthly minimum wages (1999–2019, semester data) (*Note* This is an average of the following countries: Belgium, Czech Republic, Germany [until 1990 former territory of the FRG], Estonia, Ireland, Spain, France, Croatia, Latvia, Lithuania, Luxembourg, Hungary, Malta, Netherlands, Poland, Portugal, Romania, Slovenia, Slovakia, United Kingdom. *Source* Eurostat [2020a] and authors' calculations and creation)

the economic downturn resulting from the fiscal adjustment programs, and (3) due to structural interventions of the fiscal and competitive consolidation program; reducing the role of the public sector in the economy.

Figure 7.2 shows the proportion of the population working in relation to the total working population for Greece and the EU-28 average for the period from 2000 to 2018.

It is evident that over time the percentage of the working population in Greece is below the corresponding size of the EU-28. However, this relationship has deteriorated significantly since the crisis in the Greek economy.

The trend in the unemployment rate in Greece and, in particular, in the youth unemployment rate is similar. Figure 7.3 shows the evolution of the overall unemployment rate and the youth unemployment rate in the ages from 20 to 29 for Greece and the EU-28, from 2000 to 2018.

It is obvious that the outbreak of the crisis had devastating effects on the course of the unemployment rate in Greece, which has been rising

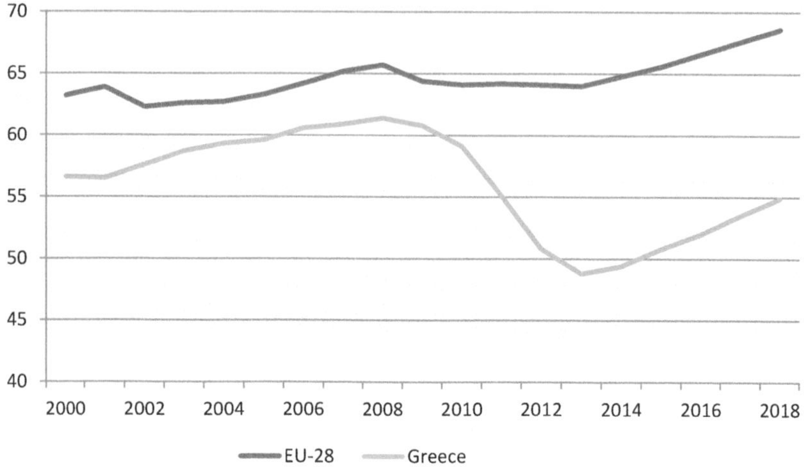

Fig. 7.2 Employment rate in Greece and EU-28 (2000–2018) (%) (*Source* Eurostat [2020b] and authors' creation)

sharply since 2009, a trend which has not been followed to the same extent for the EU-28. The problem was even more acute for young people aged 20–29, for whom the unemployment rate was reached 47.4% in 2013, when the EU-28 rate was 27.5%. However, since 2014, there has been a considerable effort to reduce the unemployment rate.

Long-term unemployment mainly affects people who have been unemployed for 12 months or more. Long-term unemployment rates are generally lower in countries which have achieved high GDP growth rates in recent years, while they can also be low at the beginning of an economic downturn due to the entry of young unemployed at the beginning of a crisis—who are not yet considered to be long-term unemployed. Thus, long-term unemployment is beginning to emerge in cases of protracted economic crises, as is the case in the current economic crisis in several countries (OECD, 2013).

Figure 7.4 describes the duration of unemployment in the Greek economy.

The structure of the rise in unemployment is clearly mainly due to the increase in the long-term unemployed, revealing the serious structural problem of the economy. The highest increases between 2008 and 2012 are in the number of people unemployed between 12 and

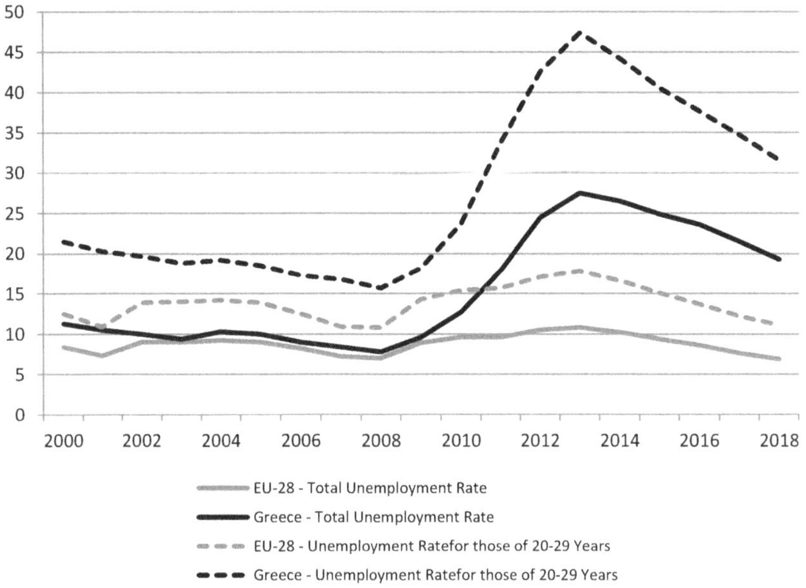

Fig. 7.3 Total unemployment rate and youth unemployment rate in Greece and EU-28 (2000–2018) (%) (*Source* Eurostat [2020c] and authors' creation)

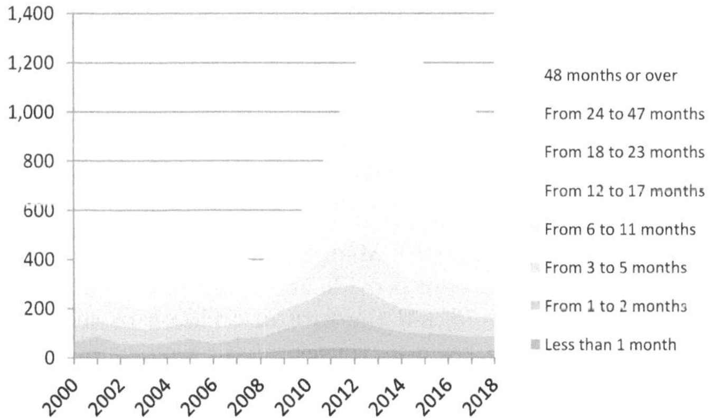

Fig. 7.4 Unemployment duration in Greece (thousands of people) (2000–2018) (*Source* Eurostat [2020d] and authors' creation)

17 months (318%), between 18 and 23 months (396%), and between 24 and 47 months (370%). Indeed, although the number of unemployed in the Greek economy has been decreasing since 2013, it appears that the number of long-term unemployed remains significantly high.

7.3.3 Gender Equality

Women are charged with multiple roles, such as wifes, mothers, and carers of the elderly, while at the same time working, so that they are unable to spend the time needed for their social engagement. The exceptions, and not the rule, are cases of redistribution of family responsibilities between partners and redistribution of family time to women.

The gender pay gap is the difference between the average annual earnings between women and men, and minly concentrated on three types of disadvantages faced by women: lower hourly earnings, fewer hours of work in salaried jobs, and lower employment rates (for example, career breaks for childcare or family care). In Greece, the gender pay gap (European Commission, 2018) is 41.4% for 2014 (latest available data), while the European average is 39.6%. This is due to the combination of lower wages (27 to 37% in the EU), with the least hours of paid work (9 to 28% in the EU) and the lowest employment rate.

At the same time, the average hourly pay of women in Europe is 16.2% lower than that of men (European Commission, 2018), which means that, annually, women work without pay 59 days more than men, while the figure for Greece is 12.5%.

The significant pay gap between men and women is due mainly to five reasons (European Commission, 2018): Firstly, the fact that the best-paid management posts are mainly occupied by men, who are promoted more often than women. This trend is rising in high positions, where women account for less than 6% of Managing Directors. Secondly, women overtake more tasks that do not provide an income on a larger scale than men, such as the household and the care of children or relatives, with reflection in the labor market. On a weekly basis women spend 22 h in such actions, while men only 9 h. Thirdly, women tend to spend more frequent periods away from the labor market and interrupt their careers to take care of children or relatives. These interruptions affect not only hourly earnings, but also have an impact on future earnings and pensions. Fourthly, women tend to be over-represented in areas such as teaching or sales offering lower hourly rates. Fifthly, wage discrimination, which, although illegal, continues to reinforce the gender pay gap.

7.4 Distribution of Income and Wealth

A meaningful understanding of the relationship between politics and the economy is a key point in shaping an integrated approach to the political economy, development, and growth. The initial allocation of resources that shapes the de facto political power, and thus political institutions, ultimately results in a new allocation of resources and a specific economic performance of the system through the formation of economic institutions (Petrakis, 2011).

The issues of the distribution of income and resources are directly linked to the system of political institutions operating in the economy, the main product of which is the observed allocation of resources.

Income inequality in a geographical area is valued by various methods (Atkinson, 1970; Cowell, 1977; Sen, 1973). More acceptable and frequently used indicators are: The S80/S20 index, the Gini coefficient,[1] the Hoover index, the Theil index and the Atkinson index.

The S80/S20 income quintiles measures the relative inequality in income distribution, compares the equivalent disposable income held by 20% of the richest people to that held by 20% of the poorest and is affected by the extreme prices of income distribution. For a better capture of the economic inequality, the income distribution gap indicator (Gini coefficient) is used as a complement, which, unlike the income distribution index (S80/S20) in income quintiles, is not affected by the extremes of income distribution. The income distribution inequality index (Gini coefficient)[2] is defined as the ratio of the cumulative population shares, broken down by income level, to the aggregate share of total income of the whole population.

The course of the two indexes for the Greek economy compared to the EU-28 average is presented in Fig. 7.5 for the period 2005–2018.

Both indicators are presented over time in relation to the average of the countries of the European Union of 28, showing that income inequalities in Greece are quite high. Indeed, the recent economic crisis has significantly worsened the two indicators for the Greek economy, which is particularly evident in the period 2010–2016. This trend is not followed by the average of the EU-28 countries where only a slight deterioration occurs in the year 2014. However, it should be noted that since

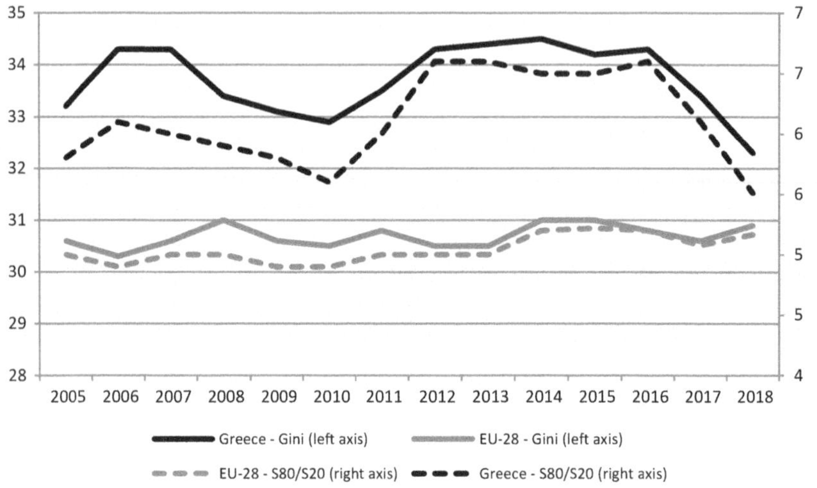

Fig. 7.5 The income distribution index (S80/S20) in income quintiles and the Gini coefficient of equivalised disposable income (*Source* Eurostat [2020e, 2020f] and authors' creation)

2018, there has been a significant degree of convergence with the EU-28 average.

More specifically, for the S80/S20 index, while in 2010 it had a value of 5.6 for 2010, in 2012 to 2016 it was 6.6 (while for the EU-28 average the value was close to 5) falling back in 2018 to 5.5 (while the EU-28 average is 5.17). This means that for 2018, the share of the income of the richest 20% of the population is 5.5 times higher than the share of the income of the poorest 20% of the population.

Respectively, there is a change in the Gini coefficient, both in relation to Greece and in relation to the EU-28 average. For Greece, the Gini coefficient was estimated in 2018 at 32.3% (while the corresponding value for EU-28 was 30.9).[3]

One way of reducing income inequalities is through income redistribution. Income redistribution takes place through different mechanisms which focus mainly on fiscal policy responsibilities. In particular, income redistribution mechanisms are divided into:

1. Transfer payments: such unemployment benefits, disability benefits, social security programs, pensions.
2. Progressive (or non-progressive) taxation through which higher incomes face higher levels of taxation.
3. Public provision of social services: Education and health are the main examples of social services in Greece.

Although taxes and social transfers have a direct effect on income distribution, public provision of social services is an indirect way of redistribution and has a more long-term character.

Figure 7.6 shows the relationship between social benefits to households and the Gini coefficient for the period 2000–2018 for OECD countries (342 overall remarks).

The relation between social transfers and inequality is negative. This means that countries with more resources in transfer payments have lower levels of income inequality. Obviously, in the case of the Greek economy, this relationship has not been valid in recent years, mainly because of the effects of the recent economic crisis and the subsequent fiscal contraction. More specifically, as shown in Fig. 7.7, while during the recent crisis

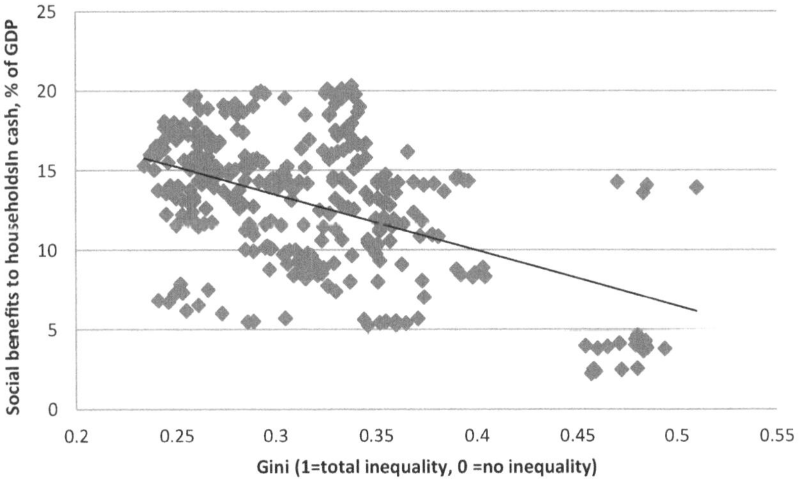

Fig. 7.6 Social benefits to households and the Gini coefficient in OECD countries (2000–2018) (*Source* OECD [2020a, 2020b] and authors' calculations)

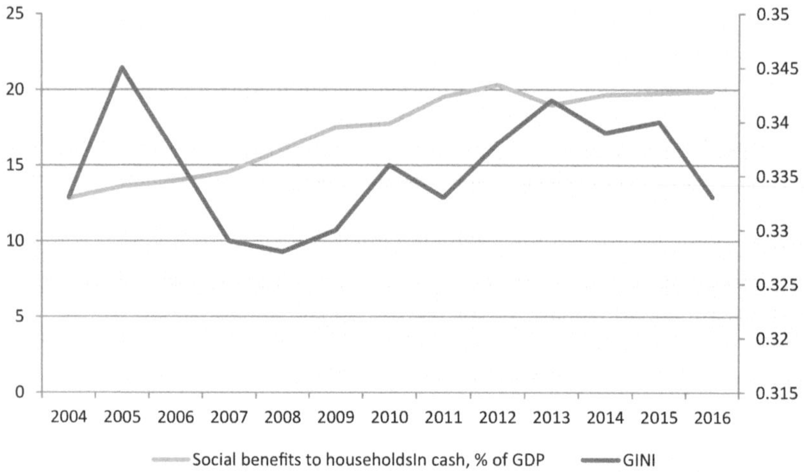

Fig. 7.7 Social benefits to households (left axis) and the Gini coefficient (right axis) in Greece (2004–2016) (*Source* OECD [2020a, 2020b] and authors' creation)

transfers to households as a percentage of GDP are increasing over time, at the same time the income inequality as expressed by the Gini coefficient increases.

7.5 Poverty

The effects of the recent economic crisis, which led to the high rise in unemployment combined with the gaps in the social protection system, have led to a marked increase in poverty in Greece in the years of the major crisis, although since 2013 there has been a significant improvement.

Of course, this is a problem that pre-existed in the Greek society, since, although until the end of the last decade social expenditure in Greece has been converging to the EU's average levels, high spending has been in line with the persistence of major gaps in protection, leading to the performance of the social protection system (and in particular of non-pension benefits) in the field of poverty reduction being very low (Dianeosis, 2016).

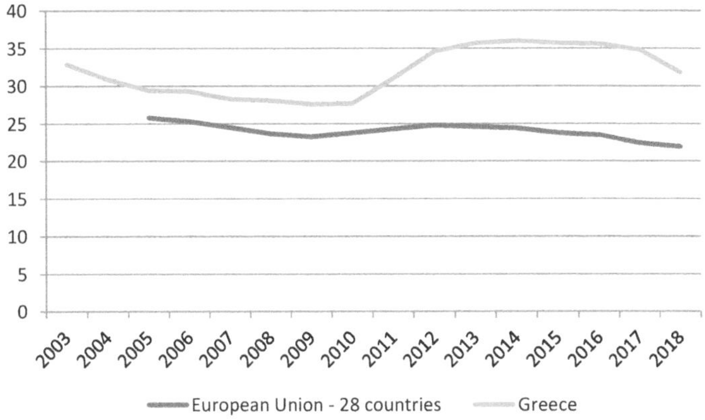

Fig. 7.8 People at risk of poverty or social exclusion (% of total population) (*Source* Eurostat [2020g] and authors' creation)

Figure 7.8 shows the percentage of population at risk of poverty or social exclusion in Greece and the averages for EU-28 countries from 2003 to 2018.

There is also only a slight decrease (after 2013) in the number of people who are at risk of being impoverished. This decline seems to be due to public-sector subsidized action, but above all to the gradual increase in employment which has occurred with the public sector as the main producer. On the basis of the Hellenic Statistical Authority data (2019) following their Survey on Income and Conditions of Living in Households, in 2018, the population at risk of poverty or social exclusion reached 31.8% in Greece in 2018 (3,348,500 people of the country's population), while the figure for the EU-28 was 21.9% in 2018.

In fact (Hellenic Statistical Authority, 2019), it appears that the risk of poverty or social exclusion is higher in the case of ages 18–64 (35.0%), while from the ages 18–64 at risk of poverty or social exclusion it is estimated that 33.0% are Greeks and 56.5% are foreigners living in Greece. Also, the rate of the population at risk of poverty living in households without material deprivation and without low-intensity work is 8.5%. At the same time, the percentage of the population who, while not at risk of poverty, live in households with material deprivation but with no low-intensity work is 8.3%.

In addition, Fig. 7.9 presents the share of persons with an equivalised disposable income, before social transfers, below the at risk of

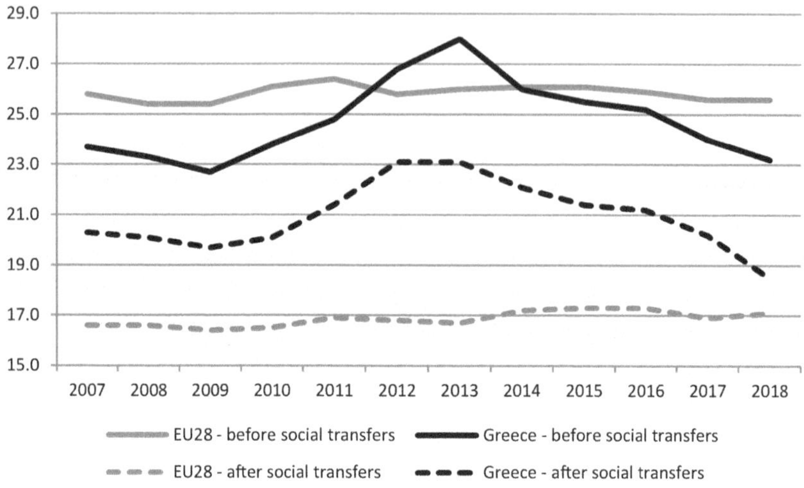

Fig. 7.9 People at risk of poverty rate before and after social transfers (% of total population) (*Source* Eurostat [2020h, 2020i] and authors' creation)

poverty threshold. Retirement and survivor's pensions are counted as income before transfers and not as social transfers. At the same time, the share of persons with an equivalised disposable income below the risk-of-poverty threshold, which is set at 60% of the national median equivalised disposable income (after social transfers), is presented.

For the population at risk of poverty in Greece, it can be seen that it is above the EU-28 average in 2012 and 2013 alone. Compared to Fig. 7.5, this suggests that in Greece—compared to the EU-28—a large part of the population is in a situation of social exclusion.

In 2018, 18.5% of Greece's total population was at risk of poverty, while the figure in the EU-28 was 17.1%. This index, which in 2005 (with a reference period of income in 2004) reached 19.6%, showed an upward trend until 2012 where it was estimated at 23.1% and started to fall from 2014.

Figure 7.9 also shows the satisfactory effectiveness of social transfers (including pensions) in the Greek economy compared to the EU-28. After social transfers, the population-at risk of poverty rates for the EU-28 are considerably lower than those for Greece. By way of illustration, for the year 2018 the percentage of the population removed from the risk of poverty is 4.7% for Greece, while for the EU-28 it is 8.5%, despite the fact that social transfers in Greece increased during the crisis (see Fig. 7.6).

7.6 Education

The education system in Greece has some major problems due to repeated and stereotyped inward behavior (Petrakis, Kostis, & Valsamis, 2013). Its main problem is that it is cut off from the labor market.

Starting from the lowest level of the education system, it is observed that Greece has a high proportion of the population that has completed pre-primary and primary education compared to OECD countries (Table 7.1). At the same time, however, it shows a relatively low share of the general population that has completed secondary or tertiary education.

Looking at the qualitative dimension of education in Greece through the international program for the evaluation of students, PISA 2018 (OECD, 2019), the following results are available for Greece in a total of 78 countries (OECD and non-OECD members): (A) In-text understanding, a skill focused on by the 2018 contest, Greek students gathered 457 units, while in the 2015 competition they had collected 467 units. In 2018, Greece ranked 42nd among 77 countries (the results on text understanding lack Spain, for which no data are available), while in 2015 it was 41st. The OECD average is 487 points. (B) In mathematics, Greece gained 451 points as Cyprus, and shared the 43rd position among 78 countries. In 2015, Greece gained 454 points and also ranked 43rd. The OECD average in mathematics was 489 points. (C) In natural sciences, Greece in the 2018 competition gained 452 points and ranked 44th among 78 countries. In the 2015 contest, Greeks scored 455 points, who brought Greece to the 43rd place. The OECD average for the 2018 competition was 489 points.

Figure 7.10 is indicative, showing the percentage of adults scoring at each proficiency level in literacy and numeracy for Greece and the average for OECD countries, highlighting the fact that the skills of Greeks are placed in significantly lower levels than those of OECD countries.

In addition, in terms of employment rates of higher education graduates, the employment rate (74%) for Greece is the lowest among OECD countries for 2018 (Fig. 7.11). Greece's lag is 12 percentage points from the OECD average. Moreover, there is a profound problem of linking higher education to production.

Table 7.1 The education level of individuals 25–64 (2018)

	Below upper secondary			*Upper secondary or post-secondary non-tertiary*		*Tertiary*			
	Less than primary	*Primary*	*Lower secondary*	*Upper secondary*	*Post-secondary non-tertiary*	*Short-cycle tertiary*	*Bachelor's or equivalent*	*Master's or equivalent*	*Doctoral or equivalent*
OECD	2	5	14	38	6	7	17	13	1
Greece	1	13	12	32	10	2	26	4	1

Source OECD (2020c) and authors' creation

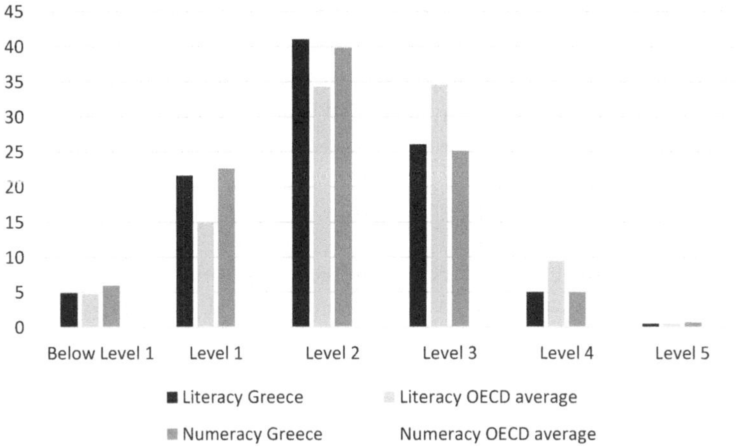

Fig. 7.10 Percentage of results scoring at each proficiency level in literature and numeracy (2018) (*Note* Level 5 indicates maximum level of proficiency. *Source* OECD [2019] and authors' creation)

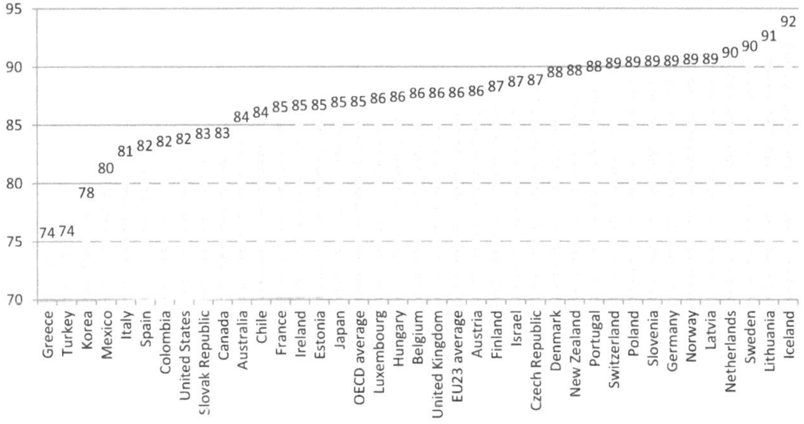

Fig. 7.11 Tertiary education graduate's employment rates (2018) (*Source* OECD [2020c] and authors' creation)

Finally, in terms of funding education, looking at total public spending in Greece, 2017 was well below the European average (EU-28 4.6% and Eurozone 4.5%) as they stood at 3.9%. In the same year, however, public spending on tertiary education was 0.9% of the GDP, higher than the EU-28 (0.7%) and the eurozone (0.7%) average (Eurostat, 2020j).

7.7 Covid-19 and Inclusivity

Major natural disasters make economic activity considerably worse. But they are usually "local" when viewed from a global perspective. Climate change is intensifying such phenomena and, while it concerns everyone, it is a long, cumulative process, whose effects on the human factor are gradually emerging. On the contrary, health disasters, hypothetically in form of a pandemic, are capable of directly and globally having a strong impact on people's lives. In eroding the existing conditions, they highlight social inequalities, or even exacerbate them. A global epidemiological crisis, such as that of Covid-19, can lead to losses of lives and income at the same time in many States around the world. Their costs and impacts, however, are differentiated at both transnational and intra-state levels, as some countries and social groups are, both in terms of health and economy, more vulnerable than others to the pandemic threat.

Each country—especially those without basic primary healthcare, public health services and infrastructure and effective infection control mechanisms—faces high costs in human and income losses. The total cost of a pandemic is the sum of the negative effects on income and the costs of premature mortality and disease. The disease leading to reduced productivity and employment, the resources allocated to the pandemic, and early deaths which reduce workforce are undoubtedly damaging the economic activity. However high the cost of the immediate impact of a pandemic on lower-income conditions (global GDP), the cost of early loss of human life is higher (Fan, Jamison, & Summers, 2016).

Rising outbreaks disrupt the whole healthcare system by reducing its capacity to respond to the crisis, leading to even greater mortality and to a further economic recession. The negative impacts are particularly deep in fragile and vulnerable environments, where poverty, poor governance, weak health systems, a lack of confidence in health services, specific cultural and religious aspects, along with armed conflicts hamper pandemic preparedness and response (Global Preparedness Monitoring Board, 2019).

In many countries, a health crisis can mean a general humanitarian crisis (UN Office for the Coordination of Humanitarian Affairs—OCHA, 2020), as the consequences for people's lives and survival can be devastating. Weak health systems are burdened, as insufficient resources or qualified professionals are not available for necessary healthcare and there are no necessary medical structures and supplies for treating patients. Addressing health crises causes the subfunction of other services, depriving human and material resources to deal with other diseases, malnutrition and provide necessary assistance to generally vulnerable groups (the elderly people, people with disabilities, etc.). In these countries, a pandemic causes millions of people to lose their jobs and income or access to resources that are essential to everyday life, with institutional insufficiency, reduced market access, and inflation phenomena reinforcing this problem. In addition, the social consequences of a health crisis include the effects of a deterioration in the quality of life and in the mental health of people staying inside and of increased domestic violence (Bergamini, 2020). It is also possible, under the pretext of protecting public health, to abuse state power or to encroach on the rights of the weakest groups, such as immigrants and refugees (UN Office for the Coordination of Humanitarian Affairs—OCHA, 2020). In the poorest countries, the non-return of many vulnerable pupils after the end of the school crisis means poor prospects for their future and a reduction in the human capital of these countries.

Pandemics and subsequent economic crises have a disproportionate impact on sections of the population, aggravate their health and social position, and increase inequality. The most aggravated groups are (International Labour Organization—ILO, 2020):

- People with underlying health situations and older people who are at a greater risk of developing serious health problems.
- Young people, who already face higher unemployment and underemployment rates, as they are more vulnerable to reduced labor demand. Older workers are also facing labor vulnerability.
- Women, as they are employed in more affected sectors (such as services) or in occupations at the forefront of the pandemic response (e.g., nurses). Women also have less access to social protection and carry a disproportionate burden in the event of school closures.
- Unprotected workers, such as the self-employed and casual workers, as they do not have access to paid or sick leave and are less protected

by contractual social protection mechanisms and other forms of income compensation.
- Migrant workers, who are particularly vulnerable to the impact of the crisis, as access to their workplaces is restricted and the possibility of returning to the countries of destination is restricted.

Other cases concern people working in sectors that are severely affected (e.g., tourism) or in enterprises that are in the black economy. This figure could be particularly significant for countries such as Greece or Italy, given the size of the informal economy and the dependence of the economy on tourism.

The rise of Covid-19 and the "freezing" of economies around the world are creating a new type of inequality between those who continue to have a stable source of income and those who have stopped. At the same time, the health of some people is more exposed to the virus. Although social welfare, which concerns governments and the state, cannot be replaced, the pandemic requires simple, daily private initiatives of solidarity and support for people vulnerable to crisis (Lustig & Birdshall, 2020).

Income and occupation are factors that can determine the likelihood of people being exposed to the virus and becoming ill. The willingness of individuals to take the risk of continuing to work by coming into contact with others, and therefore to get sick, largely depends on their income. The need to maintain the income of low-paid workers and the limited access to diagnostic tests and healthcare leaves them exposed to the pandemic, putting them even more at risk since chronic diseases appear to occur more frequently in the lower-income groups (Stabile, Apouey, & Solal, 2020). Income seems to be significantly linked to the ability of individuals to replace their physical presence at work with work from home. In the upper-income quarter, teleworking is possible for about six out of ten people, while in the lower quarter for only one out of ten (US Bureau of Labor Statistics, 2020). Of course, the very nature of the profession limits the possibility of teleworking. This is can be seen in the areas of Leisure and Hospitality (8.8%), Agriculture (11.1%) and transportation and Utilities (14%), as opposed to areas such as Financial activities (57.4%), Professional and Business Services (53.4%) and information (53.3%) (US Bureau of Labor Statistics, 2020).

The two interlinked effects of the rise of Covid-19, the health and economic crisis, put people under the double threat of their health and loss of income. People who need to continue working are considered necessary—more significantly those who fight against the pandemic and even more those in the health sector—but put their health in a risk.

The connection between income and the risk of exposure to the disease is particularly complex in precarious labor markets, with the risk of dismissal—during and after the crisis—being particularly high. The impact of the Covid-19 crisis affects more those who need to continue working, while at the same time, due to closed schools, they must take good care of their children. This means that not only their job is precarious, but also the childcare (Bergamini, 2020).

The initial estimates of the International Labour Organization (ILO) show a significant increase in unemployment for 2020 as a result of the Covid-19 crisis (International Labour Organization—ILO, 2020). Based on different scenarios for the impact of Covid-19 on global GDP growth, global unemployment is expected to increase between 5.3 million (optimistic scenario) and 24.7 million (pessimistic scenario) people, which are expected to be increased with the 188 million unemployed of 2019. Even early data show a significant increase in global unemployment. By comparison, the 2008 crisis increased unemployment worldwide by 22 million. An increase on underemployment is also expected on a large scale, as the economic consequences of the pandemic translate into reductions in working hours and wages (International Labour Organization—ILO, 2020).

At a global level, the potential impact of Covid-19 is a real challenge. A 5% decline in (per capita) income of people would result in an increase in the number of poor—compared to 2018—over 80 million for the poverty line of $1.9/day, more than 130 million for the threshold of $3.2/day and around 124 million for the higher threshold of $5.5/day. With a contraction of 10%, the number of poor people would increase by about 180, 280 and 250 million people, respectively, but if the contraction is 20%, then the increases could be about 420, 580 and 520 million people, respectively (Sumner, Hay, & Ortiz-Juarez, 2020). Covid-19 pushes to the far future the United Nations sustainable development goal of ending poverty by 2030, since both the relative and absolute size of the number of poor below the three poverty lines are expected to increase for the first time after 1990, showing a regression of a decade in poverty reduction (Sumner et al., 2020).

Notes

1. The index reflects the percentage of total income attributable to a certain percentage of the population. The lower its value, the more equal the distribution of income. The main advantage of the Gini coefficient is that it calculates the income balance taking into account not only GDP but also the way in which this percentage is distributed among the population. The Gini coefficient is independent of the personal characteristics, the units of measurement of the size of the economy, and the size of the population and is based on the principle of transfers. Its most important disadvantage is that it cannot be properly calculated by taking into account the region-by-region values it takes without taking into account the overall figures, even if all regions are included in the calculation. Moreover, it may prove to be a sub-optimal way of measuring the imbalance of income due to the fact that the Lorenz curve does not reflect the efficiency of income use. Finally, it fails to take into account the age and stage at which each individual is in society.
2. Its value ranges from 0 (or 0%), corresponding to full income equality up to 1 (or 100%) corresponding to full income inequality, and is interpreted as the statistically expected difference in the result of comparing two random incomes as a percentage of the average. If all national income was concentrated in one person, the rate would be 1. If the Gini coefficient was for example 30.0%, the income of 2 random people would differ by 30.0% of the average equivalent disposable income.
3. The above figure for Greece means that if 2 people are selected at random, we should expect their income to differ by 32.3% of the average equivalent disposable income.

References

Atkinson, A. B. (1970). On the Measurement of Inequality. *Journal of Economic Theory, 2*(3), 244–263.

Bergamini, E. (2020). *How COVID-19 Is Laying Bare Inequality*. Bruegel. Retrieved from https://www.bruegel.org/2020/03/how-covid-19-is-laying-bare-inequality/.

Cowell, F. A. (1977). *Measuring Inequality*. Oxford: Phillip Allan.

Dianeosis. (2016). *Extreme Poverty in Greece*, Dianeosis (in Greek).

European Commission. (2018). *The Gender Pay Gap in Greece*. Retrieved from https://ec.europa.eu/info/publications/gender-pay-gap-european-union_en.

Eurostat. (2020a). *Eurostat: Monthly Minimum Wages—Bi-Annual Data [earn_mw_cur]*.

Eurostat. (2020b). *Eurostat: Employment Rates by Sex, Age and Citizenship (%) [lfsa_ergan]*.

Eurostat. (2020c). *Eurostat: Unemployment Rates by Sex, Age and Citizenship (%) [lfsa_urgan]*.

Eurostat. (2020d). *Eurostat: Unemployment by Sex, Age and Duration of Unemployment (1 000) [lfsa_ugad]*.

Eurostat. (2020e). *Eurostat: Gini Coefficient of Equivalised Disposable Income—EU-SILC Survey [ilc_di12]*.

Eurostat. (2020f). *Eurostat: Income Quintile Share Ratio (S80/S20) by Sex [tessi180]*.

Eurostat. (2020g). *Eurostat: People at Risk of Poverty or Social Exclusion [t2020_50]*.

Eurostat. (2020h). *Eurostat: At-Risk-of-Poverty Rate Before Social Transfers by Age Group—EU-SILC Survey [tesov252]*.

Eurostat. (2020i). *Eurostat: At-Risk-of-Poverty Rate After Social Transfers by Sex [TPS00184]*.

Eurostat. (2020j). *Eurostat: General Government Expenditure by Function (COFOG) [gov_10a_exp]*.

Fan, V., Jamison, D., & Summers, L. (2016). *The Inclusive Cost of Pandemic Influenza Risk* (NBER Working Paper No. 22137).

Global Preparedness Monitoring Board. (2019). *A World at Risk: Annual Report on Global Preparedness for Health Emergencies*. Geneva: World Health Organization.

Hellenic Statistical Authority. (2019). *2018 Survey on Income and Living Conditions (Income Reference Period 2017): Risk of Poverty (Press Release)*. Retrieved from https://www.statistics.gr/documents/20181/13058a0c-e1cb-d2d7-dc94-f274dffb5d83.

International Labour Organization. (ILO). (2020, March 18). *ILO Monitor: COVID-19 and the World of Work* (1st Ed.) (Briefing Note). Retrieved from https://www.ilo.org/wcmsp5/groups/public/—dgreports/-dcomm/documents/briefingnote/wcms_738753.pdf.

Lustig, N., & Birdshall, N. (2020). *The New Inequalities and People-to-People Social Protection*. Vox CEPR Policy Portal. Retrieved from https://voxeu.org/article/new-inequalities-and-people-people-social-protection.

OECD. (2013). All in It Together? The Experience of Different Labour Market Groups Following the Crisis. In OECD (Ed.), *OECD Employment Outlook 2013* (pp. 19–63). Paris: OECD Publishing.

OECD. (2019). *Skills Matter: Additional Results from the Survey of Adult Skills. OECD Skills Studies*. Paris: OECD Publishing. Retrieved from https://doi.org/10.1787/1f029d8f-en.

OECD. (2020a). *Government at a Glance: Government at a Glance*. OECD National Accounts Statistics (database). Retrieved from https://doi.org/10.1787/0d31bfab-en.

OECD. (2020b). *Income Distribution*. OECD Social and Welfare Statistics (Database). Retrieved from https://doi.org/10.1787/data-00654-en.

OECD. (2020c). *Education at a Glance: Educational Attainment and Labour-Force Status*. OECD Education Statistics (Database). Retrieved from https://doi.org/10.1787/889e8641-en.

Petrakis, P. (2011). *The Greek Economy and the Crisis*. Springer Verlag.

Petrakis, P. E., Kostis, P., & Valsamis, D. G. (2013). *European Economics and Politics in the Midst of the Crisis: From the Outbreak of the Crisis to the Fragmented European Federation*. Berlin: Springer.

Sen, A. (1973). *On Economic Inequality*. Oxford: Clarendon Press.

Stabile, M., Apouey, B., & Solal, I. (2020). *COVID-19, Inequality, and Gig Economy Workers*. Vox CEPR Policy Portal. Retrieved from https://voxeu.org/article/covid-19-inequality-and-gig-economy-workers.

Sumner, A., Hoy, C., & Ortiz-Juarez, E. (2020). *Estimates of the Impact of COVID-19 on Global Poverty* (UNU-WIDER Working Paper 2020/43). Retrieved from https://doi.org/10.35188/UNU-WIDER/2020/800-9.

UN Office for the Coordination of Humanitarian Affairs (OCHA). (2020). *Global Humanitarian Response Plan Covid-19: United Nations Coordinated Appeal April–December 2020*. Geneva: OCHA.

US Bureau of Labor Statistics. (2020). *Workers Who Could Work at Home, Did Work at Home, and Were Paid for Work at Home, by Selected Characteristics, Averages for the Period 2017–2018 (Economic News Release)*. Retrieved from https://www.bls.gov/news.release/flex2.t01.htm.

CHAPTER 8

Human Behaviors

8.1 Introduction

Social psychology alters in times of crisis and change. A typical example is Covid-19. Similar crises with social psychology impacts had occurred in the past, such as the Great Depression in 1929, the Twin Towers in the United States, etc. Its effects have been detected in social trends and attitudes for many years to come. Under certain very rare conditions, a crisis and its recovery can be a starting point for a new start to a new cycle of development. But crises and recovery situations are creating trauma that accompany decision-making in the future.

The cultural dimensions and social psychological stereotypes that prevail in the Greek society measure a very long life that goes beyond the founding of the modern Greek state (Petrakis, 2011). This does not mean that they are immobilized and consolidated over time, although their systematic presence is generally observed not only in the Greek economy but in all the societies of the world, and not as defined by the national borders. Generally, these are the gnostic constructs that link the past to the present and determine the future.

However, Greek society has been particularly affected by the recession conditions in 2010 that hit the economy in the last decade and it will be hit by Covid-19 as well; however, these results require time to be

P. E. Petrakis and P. C. Kostis, *The Evolution of the Greek Economy*, The Political Economy of Greek Growth up to 2030,
https://doi.org/10.1007/978-3-030-47210-8_8

elaborated. These conditions have affected not only the Greek social environment but also the political trends in society and economic behavior, thus shaping the process of cultural evolution of the Greeks.

Thus, in this chapter the cultural evolution of the Greek society is presented, as one of the most critical factors that have affected the responses to the crisis, but not adequately enough emphasized in the economic policy that was undertaken to confront the crisis.

The structure of the chapter is the following: Sect. 8.2 presents key developments that are observed and related to the Greek social environment and related to the quality of life of Greeks. Then (Sect. 8.3) the political trends concerning Greek society are presented, as it appears that the role of ideology and non-economic realities is extremely important in the processes taking place in society. The next Sect. 8.4 presents the economic behavior of Greek society, which is mainly related to indicators such as support for the euro, trust in institutions, attitudes toward globalization, size of the public sector, taxation, etc. In Sect. 8.5 the trend toward loss-aversion behaviors in Greek society is presented, along with a presentation of different cultural dimensions. Finally, Sect. 8.6 analyzes the impact of CID-19 on human behavior.

8.2 The Social Environment

Following the onset of the 2010 crisis in the Greek economy, a number of indicators that can assess the quality of life of Greeks show either comparative (with other similar societies) or absolute deterioration or at best very slight improvement. The following developments in the Greek social environment are typical:

- Greece has been the country that has since 2010 made the largest negative dip in the Happiness Index (Helliwell, Layard, Sachs, & de Neve, 2018). Between 2010 and 2012, it was 70th among 156 countries. In the peak of the crisis it was in the 102nd position (average of 2012–2014) while it has recovered somewhat with the 2015 post-election euphoria, reaching the 87th place (average 2014–2016) and the 82nd in 2018 (average 2015–2017).
- Disposable income per capita has fallen both in absolute and relative terms compared to the European average. From 19,263 euros in 2009 it dropped to 14,768 euros in 2017 in Greece, while for the EU-28 it rose from 19,255 euros in 2009 to 22,158 euros

in 2018. This occurs along with the widening of the imbalance in income distribution (Gini coefficient) despite the slight decrease in the number of people at risk of poverty in 2018 to around 3789 thousand citizens. Greece is the country with the fourth-to-last worst performance on this index, among the EU-28 countries for 2018.
- There is also a change in life expectancy for both men and women, but not to the extent that it is observed in other economies. There is therefore a decrease in the difference in life expectancy compared with other OECD countries: While in 1960 this difference was 4 years (Greece 72 years on average, OECD 68 years), in 2015 it tends to equate (Greece 81.1, OECD average 80.6). So, as the decades pass, Europeans are increasing their life expectancy at higher rates than Greeks, who were 50 years ago among the champions of longevity.
- The age pyramid of the population is getting worse because of increased life expectancy and reduced birth-to-death ratio. Greece's population is expected to decline significantly in the future and in 2050 the country's population is estimated to be between 10 million (in the most optimistic scenario) and 8.3 million (in the worst-case scenario) (Dianeosis, 2016a). This will bring about a decrease in the population from around 800 thousands to 2.5 million people.

What is even more worrying is that the country's population is ageing. The median age, which was 26 years in 1951 and is 44 years old nowadays, is expected to increase by 5–8 years, while the population of school-age children (from 3 to 17 years) will drop from now 1.6 million to 1.4 million (optimistic scenario) to 1 million (pessimistic scenario) in 2050 (Dianeosis, 2016a). Also, the potentially economically active population (i.e., all citizens aged 20–69 who could potentially work) will be reduced from 7 million in 2015 to 4.8–5.5 million and the real economically active population will fall from 4.7 million in 2015 to 3–3.7 million (Dianeosis, 2016a).

The deterioration in the economic position of citizens during the crisis was reflected in a further negative shift in the position of the middle class (Fig. 8.1).

This figure shows that around 650,000 taxpayers from the upper middle and middle classes have been moved to lower-income brackets, while at the same time around 1,250,000 taxpayers from the middle

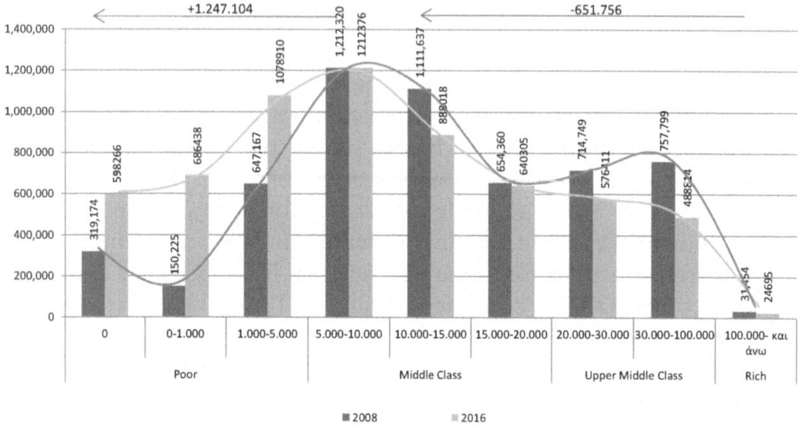

Fig. 8.1 Changes in the composition of income brackets during the crisis (*Note* The figure is based on the number of tax returns and not on the number of taxpayers. *Source* Independent Authority for Public Revenue (IAPR) of the Hellenic Republic and authors' calculations and creation)

classes have dropped to lower-income brackets. Will there be similar effects from the Covid-19 crisis? Is it something that takes a long time to capture?

8.3 Political Trends in Society

Greece has seen two major ideological currents: Neo-liberalism and liberalism, which appear to be supported by 27.4% of the population and Socialism and Social democracy, which seem to be supported by 28.6% (figures are an average for the period 2016–2017[1]).

If it is considered that Conservatism is related to neo-liberalism and liberalism, then the corresponding figure becomes 34.6%. At the same time, if we accept that Ecology in Greece is more related to social democracy and socialism, then the figure becomes 37.3% (Table 8.1).

In addition, it is interesting to estimate how the main ideologies spread to the population according to the income situation of citizens on the basis of the findings on the distribution of the population in income brackets (Table 8.2). Both political movements seem to gather with a similar manner the preferences of the electorate.

Table 8.1 Ideological designations throughout the country, by income bracket

	Total	*<€500*	*€501–1000*	*€1001–1500*	*€1501–2000*	*€2001–3000*	*<€3001*	*No reply*
Nationalism	9.1	10.9	9.8	6.5	5.7	12.8	8.3	6.9
Conservatism	7.5	8.5	6.2	8.1	5.4	7.8	8.4	5.6
Neo-liberalism	8.9	9.9	8.6	7.6	5.1	11.1	16.0	13.6
Liberalism	18.5	17.3	17.1	18.4	29.5	26.5	28.3	19.6
Social democracy	16.6	12.8	16.8	21.3	20.7	19.2	19.3	12.4
Ecology	8.9	11.6	8.5	9.3	5.5	5.6	3.4	4.3
Socialism	12.0	10.5	13.5	14.6	13.4	7.8	7.8	6.7
Communism	4.9	5.0	4.4	4.6	5.4	1.1	5.9	6.8
None of them (spontaneous)	11.0	10.7	13.3	7.8	8.2	7.2	2.8	16.9
Do not know/no reply	3.0	3.1	2.2	2.3	1.4	1.1	0.0	7.2

Note The data is an average of the data available for the period 2016–2017
Source Dianeosis: December 2016b, February 2018, and authors' creation

A second conclusion to be drawn from the above is that the role of ideology and non-economic realities is extremely important in the processes that are taking place in society because it is clear that ideological attitudes are to some extent independent of income class.

A congenital distinction with the ideologies concerns the political self-determination of citizens on the political scale from the extreme right to the extreme left. Figure 8.2 shows the dramatic change in the political scene brought about by the 2010 economic crisis with three main events (a) the appearance of extremes (but probably not previously measured), (b) the contraction of the political trend of the right and center right, with the slight increase in the center and the significant increase in the left,[2] but (c) subsequently (2017) the right, the center and the center right are the areas which increase their rates.

8.4 Economic Attitudes in Society

Citizens' behavior toward key economic and social issues is important in shaping economic policy for two main reasons:

Table 8.2 Ideologies and income brackets

	<€500	*€501–1000*	*€1001–1500*	*€1501–2000*	*€2001–3000*	*<€3001*	*No reply*	*Total*
Neo-liberalism and liberalism	326,409	426,027	294,225	85,727	37,553	22,886	134,763	1327,592
Social democracy and Socialism	350,999	444,141	312,561	92,004	40,437	24,888	126,070	1391,102

Note The data is an average of the data available for the period 2016–2017
Source Dianeosis; December 2016b, February 2018, and authors' creation

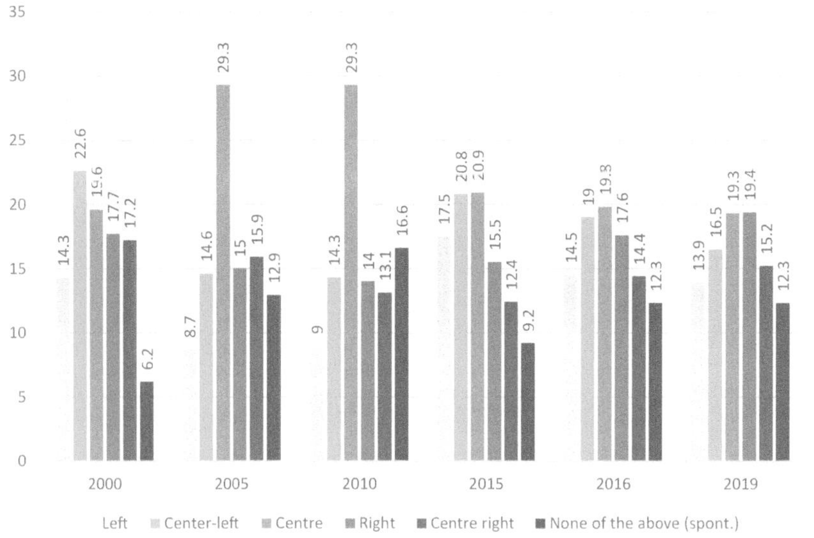

Fig. 8.2 Political self-determination of citizens (*Source* Metron Analysis [2020] and Petrakis et al. [2021] and authors' creation)

(a) Economic policy is based on policies which deal first with the efficiency of the functioning of the economy and secondly with income distribution (taxes). However, economic policy is shaped by a political party on the basis of its program obligations (pre-election commitments). Its program obligations correspond to the needs of the citizens it represents, and the objectives set by its political leadership to serve.

(b) When an economic policy is implemented, citizens adapt to it either by implementing its effects, or by adapting and possibly neutralizing it, etc. The citizens' views on economic issues are therefore of key importance.

A typical example of the economic behavior of Greeks is the tendency to support the euro. Support for the euro is a more psychological indicator of society's attitude toward the European region, the benefits, and obligations of the country's participation in the euro area. But it is the only

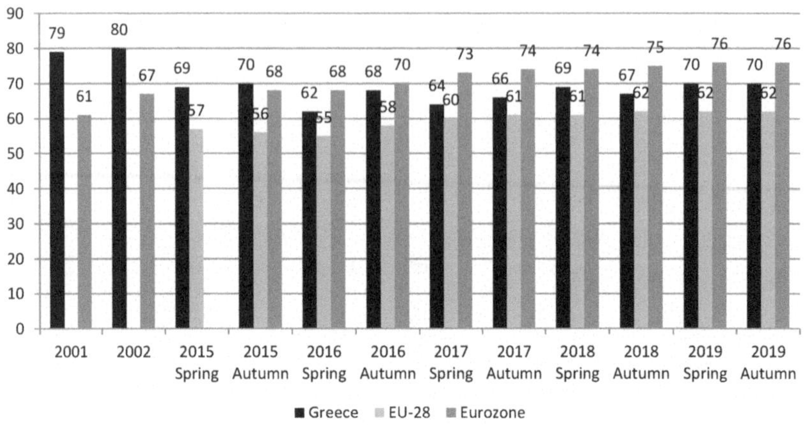

Fig. 8.3 Rate of respondents in favour of the euro (*Source* European Commission [2020] and authors' creation)

real indicator that brings together the real views of citizens on our relationship with the European area since their views around the European Union suffer from a lack of clarity (there is no European Union state).

At the same time, it is an indicator of openness and willingness for international competition. To a large extent it reflects the perception of the individual economic and social situation of citizens, whether rational or not. Of particular importance is which social groups support the use of the euro or not. Therefore, to the question: "For you personally, it would be better: Staying in the euro or returning to the drachma" 66% chose the first option and 26.3% the second option (Dianeosis, 2018). These figures are close to the ratings of the respective Eurobarometer surveys (Fig. 8.3).

The decline in trust in the euro in 2016 and the decline in trust in the European institutions and in the government that occurred in 2016 show a slight recovery in 2017 (Fig. 8.4). Moreover, the decline in trust is evolving in parallel with the increase in uncertainty.

The return to normality marked since mid-2017 has positively reestablished support for the euro. The supporters of the euro are the young, the most educated, and the most prosperous. A relative surprise is the presence of the large (65+) ages who obviously realize that they are unable to manage a major monetary turmoil that would remove them

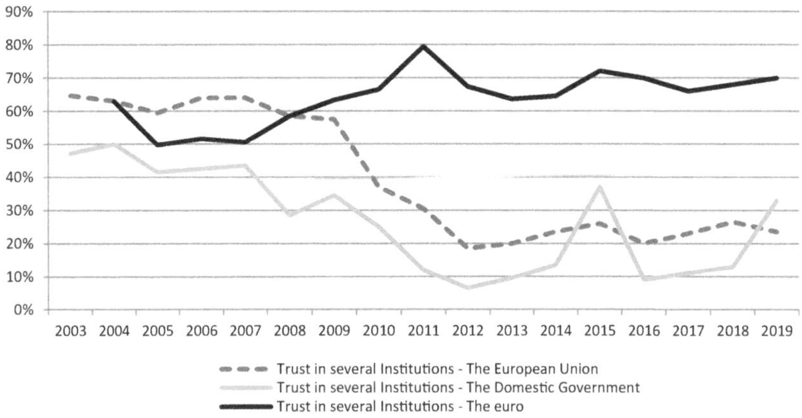

Fig. 8.4 Trust in institutions in Greece (*Note* For each year, the displayed value refers to the average of the values between Spring and Autumn. *Source* European Commission [2020]. Standard Eurobarometer [53, 55, 83–92] and authors' calculations and creation)

from the hard currency guarantee and support the euro. Further reductions in pensions may erode their trust. The advocates of the drachma are those affected by the crisis, middle ages and people with low or intermediate levels of education.

It is characteristic that those who regard globalization as a threat to Greece are a similar percentage to that of support for the euro, with the difference being the position of the more senior ones (65+) who are here in a coalition with the camp fearing of the threat from globalization. This is also reflected in the question on the "threat of globalization". 34.4% see globalization as an opportunity for Greece and 59.7% as a threat to Greece (Dianeosis—December 2016b).

To some extent, however, the trend to support the "closed economy" is in contradiction with the finding of positive support for foreign investment in Greece, although there is a slight decrease in 2017. The return to normality after 2017 is linked to an increase in trust in the domestic economy and "makes" less necessary support for foreign investment.

In fact, however, this contradiction will be removed if we realize that virtually no one denies the positive communication with the "outside world" (e.g., tourism), provided that it is (or we think it is) done under "our own terms". This seems to be guaranteed in the case of foreign investment. In the question where respondents are asked whether they are for or against foreign investment in Greece, 82.7% of respondents are in favor and 16.2% against (Dianeosis—February 2018).

The population experiencing the increased "external" threat, and in particular the "failure" of Greek society, to remain on its terms in European society, is very well aware of its weaknesses. They therefore consider that Greece has specific characteristics, not necessarily internationally competitive, but with which they have used to live. So in the question with which of the following phrases you agree most: "Greece, despite its problems, is a modern country that is not very different from other countries in Europe," and "Greece is not a modern country," 68.3% mention the first option and 29.8% the second option (Dianeosis—February 2018). Thus, the "return" to normality is clearly confirmed, as there is a spectacular improvement in the belief that Greece is a modern country.

Another key issue of economic behavior concerns the role of the state. So to the question of whether it is better for the State to put money on the market by increasing wages and pensions in order to increase consumption or to encourage increased investment and exports and the creation of new jobs, the answer is overwhelmingly in favor of the second position (73.2% against 21.8%—Dianeosis data—December 2016b).

About the same messages are given by two more questions. To the question: "In general, to address the problems of the economy, what kind of state, that is, the public sector, in your opinion is the country in need?", 10.9% says we need a larger public sector, 61% that we need a smaller public sector and 26.8% that we need the same as today's size of public sector (Dianeosis—February 2018). To the question: "Some consider that the Greek state is interfering too much in the economy, others that it is not interfering enough. With which of the two views I will read to you do you agree most?", 69.3% say that the state is intervening too much and prevents the private sector from creating wealth and jobs and 35.5% that the state is not sufficiently involved and allows the private sector to act uncontrolled (Dianeosis—February 2018). In fact, the first question, for which statistics for April 2015 are available, shows that support for the smaller role of the public sector is gradually increasing.

However, it should be pointed out that in these two questions, the younger age groups are more reluctant to support the smaller state obviously because they realize that in this way, there are less employment opportunities. On the contrary, those who suffer the negative effects of over-taxation (older ages) are much clearer in supporting against the largest state.

The same trend is maintained in a subsequent crucial question linking taxation to the welfare state. The question here becomes more difficult because it links the decision on whether there should be a strong welfare state with the result of government action that is the imposition of taxation. So, in the question "With which of the two proposals do you mostly agree?", 31% say that there must be high taxation and a strong welfare state for all and 64.2% that taxation should be low even if there is less state care (Dianeosis—February 2018).

Obviously, Greek society is tired of high taxes and is not reluctant to agree on less state care. Young people (who do not pay much tax) are more supporters of high taxation and the strong state, while older citizens are not. The fact that taxation should be low, even if there is less state concern, seems to be more evenly distributed over age and income. But the question arises whether these trends will continue to prevail after Covid-19 or will change or even intensify. A number of comments are made on this later.

8.5 Loss Aversion and the Other Cultural Dimensions in Greek Society

Loss aversion indicates that people are more sensitive to loss than gains. In other words, the absolute subjective value of a particular loss is greater than the absolute subjective value of an equivalent gain. That is, society is characterized by loss aversion in the form of support for its existing status quo.

Greek society appears to be strongly characterized by the behavior of averting damage and this may be the case following the judgment of Covid-19. The results of the study of Xie, Hwang, and Pantelous (2017) are clear, where the authors conclude that the Greek society has the lowest score of 32 countries in loss aversion (0.33 when the average of the countries is 1.74). Note that this means more loss aversion. This may justify a stronger orientation toward the acquisition of speculative opportunities and benefits contrary toward productive investment (Figs. 8.4 and 8.5).[3]

Loss aversion is combined with the existence of an idiosyncratic cultural background which does not have rationality as its main characteristic (see Petrakis et al. 2021) as we usually assume for developed societies.

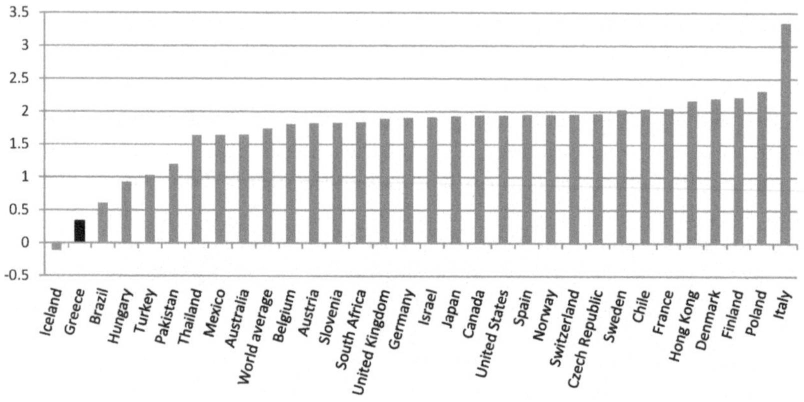

Fig. 8.5 Loss aversion behavior (*Note* The lower a country's score, the more loss aversion behaviour it shows. *Source* Xie et al. [2017] and authors' creation)

Cultural dimensions and social psychological stereotypes prevailing in Greek society count many years of existence that goes beyond the founding of the modern Greek state. This does not mean that they stay stable and consolidated over time, even though they generally have a systematic presence, not only in the Greek economy but in all societies in the world and not as these are defined by national borders. Generally speaking, it is the cognitive structures that link the past to the present and define the future (Petrakis, 2011).

In Greek society, therefore, there are essentially social-psychological stereotypes which have considerable social and economic reflections on the productive and social environment of the Greek economy and which are directly linked to its specific characteristics. These are mainly stereotypes (all data presented below are from the last available European Social Survey of 2010[4]):

- Lack of trust. 25.3% of Greek society argues that it can trust most people, while the figure for all European societies is 39.8%. Also, 53.8% of Greek society argues that most people are trying to take advantage of them, while the figure for all European societies is 30.6%. Lack of trust acts as a hindrance on investment and increases transaction costs. It also gives space to populist policies.

- The protection of in-group collectivism, and in particular the important role of the family. 52.8% of Greek society considers it particularly important that the work it chooses should enable the combination of work with care for the family, while the corresponding figure for all European societies is 35.2%. 29% of Greek society considers that it does not devote the time it should have to work because of its family responsibilities, while the corresponding figure for all European societies is 22.9%. The role of family networks in Greece is crucial. The absence of a broad social state and its services is essentially replaced by family care. In this way, social cohesion and family-based social capital are being broadened. As long as the trust and mutual service of family members increases, society is primarily driven by family entrepreneurship on the basis of independent family planning. This is the reason behind the prevailing production model of the Greek economy with the large number of small businesses. The strong family cohesion observed in Greek society (a) reduces its spatial mobility, for example where the child of a family will work, and (b) affects the mobility of career guidance over time. As a result, a significant part of the labor force is also restricted, while being in an active age group, such as that of women, which is cut off from the labor market. This condition has multiple social and economic implications.
- Uncertainty avoidance. 58.9% of Greek society considers it especially important for them to live in a safe environment, while the figure for all European societies is 30.9%. Moreover, 52.1% of Greek society feels safe in walking through the area where it lives when the darkness falls, while the figure for all European societies is 74.8%. In addition, 59.9% think it is especially important that the government of the country should show an image of security, while the corresponding figure for all European societies is 31.1%. The dominance of uncertainty leads to a reduction in investment horizons but also more generally to the avoidance of investment decisions and thus to a denial of innovation. It also leads to the acceptance of ideas about "a closed society", etc.
- The strong role of religion, namely, the Orthodox Christian concept. 91.8% of Greek society belongs to a religion, while the figure for all European societies is 64.6%. The Orthodox Christian perception of Greek society seems to be moving in the opposite direction to the

"present" property, and the process of maximizing profit, i.e., the necessary incentive to trigger the process of growth.

- Performance orientation. 29.9% of Greek society considers it particularly important to think about new ideas and be creative, while the figure for all European societies is 20.5%. Moreover, 35.9% of Greek society considers it especially important to live independently and feel free in decision-making, while the corresponding figure for all European societies is 28.6%. In addition, 23.3% of Greek society considers it important to be rich, to have money and expensive assets, while the figure for all European societies is 16.7%. There is therefore a tendency to seek performance in effort.
- Non-acceptance of inequalities. 55.5% of Greek society considers it especially important that all individuals are treated in the same way and that everyone has the same opportunities, while the corresponding figure for all European societies is 34.3%. Acceptance of inequalities, although negative in social terms, is usually found in societies which have achieved higher levels of economic performance. The impact of this cultural background extends to a number of economic activities. In general, these have an anti-developmental character. The main direction of this is to stay on anything that is familiar and the lack of competition and control, the prevalence of paralysis caused by uncertainty and hence of anxiety about taking (in their view) risky positions and finally, the lack of confidence.

The cultural background has a long-term concentric effect. In the economic prosperity phase, there are a number of "anti-growth" aspects of social values linked to lack of openness. However, in times of recession, this social model itself is giving rise to lines of defence linked to inward-looking while at the same time opposing its change. Thus, during the crisis, in-group collectivism (family) helps to reduce the negative effects of the crisis. However, the fact that in the very difficult phase of recession the cultural background works as a "life-saviour" gives it the chance to survive, possibly even stronger(!) in the development phase where it is now acting as an obstacle! (cultural anti-growth trap).

8.6 Covid-19 on Human Behaviour

Major crises may have significant effects on individual behavior. Just as an economic or natural disaster can damage people's psychology and change consumption and investment patterns, so can health disasters. A health crisis taking the form of a pandemic changes the levels of uncertainty and confidence in society, which are key drivers of economic growth. After all, the major lethal communicable diseases in the history of mankind, such as the Black Death (1348–1353) and the Spanish flu (1918), have been points of social, political and economic transformation, affecting culture and human behavior (Alfani & Murphy, 2017; Arnstein, Guido, Gandolfi, & Le Moglie, 2020).

The effects of an epidemic or pandemic on human behavior cannot be easily generalized, as they depend on its specific characteristics (mortality, transmissibility, etc.) and on the cultural and socio-economic context in which it took place. Historically, the extent of ignorance about the communicable diseases in question also identified extremities in human reactions (Cohn, 2018). The psychological mechanism developed by man against unknown risks often leads to improper assessment and widespread disruption in society.

Individuals generally form heterogeneous beliefs about the risk they face from the outbreak of a pandemic. In particular, they tend to overestimate the mortality and infectiveness of the virus, while at the same time they underestimate its transmissibility (Fetzer, Hensel, Herle, & Roth, 2020). The economic expectations generated by high levels of fear and stress create an excess of consumer behavior, placing the (already) negative outlook on economies, which is due to a decline in production and employment. Increasing employment-related uncertainty creates expectations for future lower income flows and feeds a long-term economic downturn through falling demand to lower levels. At the same time, people who overestimate risks tend to be more pessimistic about the future and the duration of the crisis (Fetzer, Hensel, et al., 2020). Thus, being informed and understanding of the risks of pandemics can play a central role in limiting and managing negative economic impacts. In addition, the unconditional cash transfers have proven to improve significantly the psychology of individuals and reduce uncertainty, with beneficial economic effects (Haushofer & Shapiro, 2016).

The common feature of pandemics is the rapid spread not only of the virus, but also of fear, which can spread panic among masses (Barry, 2005) and cause a sudden change in the behavior of individuals, such as consumer mania for specific products (Rieder, 2020). More generally, the consequences of panic may become permanent due to social unrest and widespread mistrust (Alfani & Murphy, 2017). Individuals, in response to strong shocks—for example during the Great Depression of 1929, which marked a period of major social unrest—are reacting nervous, spreading panic and causing a significant contraction in real economic activity (Mitchener & Richardson, 2020).

The main measure against the spread of the pandemic is to impose quarantine on the population, which is often an unpleasant experience. In cases of long duration, the lack of social interactions, the loss of freedom, the concerns about the evolution of the disease, the general uncertainty, and the boredom can sometimes cause serious psychological problems, even extreme reactions (Brooks et al., 2020),

In the case of Covid-19, people embrace the appropriate hygiene rules and protective measures, but at the same time they consider that their fellow citizens and governments do not correspond enough in the needs of the society (Fetzer, Witte, et al., 2020). In particular, in Greece, the situation is better regarding those measures, mainly due to the success of the fight against the epidemiological crisis, resulting in polls showing an extremely high (around 75%) confidence and approval rate of the government's management. Determined action by governments to limit the pandemic (Fetzer, Witte, et al., 2020) and accurate and timely information to the population on the nature and extent of diseases (Fan, 2003) are vital to mitigate fear and uncertainty, increase tolerance and protect mental health of citizens (Brooks et al., 2020), as well as to achieve some balance between prevention, real risks and the people's reactions. The above mentioned practices also contribute to maintaining social confidence, which is particularly important for preventing and tackling the pandemic, as it increases the people's willingness to adopt the recommended behavior (Siegrist & Zingg, 2014).

Notes

1. February 2018 data from Dianeosis "*What Greeks think*".
2. Greece is highly specific (Fig. 2.1) in that the economic crisis has strengthened the left, while the usual global political phenomenon is that the economic crisis is favorable to the far right. This may be due to the remnants of civil war. However, similar phenomena are found in Portugal, Catalonia, and to some extent in Iceland.
3. When someone averts loss, they seek "too big" gains to compensate. But here enters the concept of "easy profit" of illegal profit, etc.
4. However, it is well known that behavior does not change easily over time.

References

Alfani, G., & Murphy, T. E. (2017). Plague and Lethal Epidemics in the Pre-Industrial World. *Journal of Economic History, 77*(1), 314–343.

Arnstein, A., Guido, A., Gandolfi, F., & Le Moglie, M. (2020). *Epidemics and Trust: The Case of the Spanish Flu* (IGIER Working Paper No. 661).

Barry, J. (2005). 1918 Revisited: Lessons and Suggestions for Further Inquiry. In S. L. Knobler, A. Mack, A. Mahmoud, & S. M. Lemon (Eds.), *The Threat of Pandemic Influenza: Are We Ready?* Washington, DC: The National Academies Press.

Brooks, S. K., Webster, R. K., Smith, L. E., Woodland, L., Wessely, S., Greenberg, N., & Rubin, G. R. (2020). The Psychological Impact of Quarantine and How to Reduce It: Rapid Review of the Evidence. *The Lancet, 395*(10227), 912–920.

Cohn, S. K. (2018). *Epidemics: Hate and Compassion from the Plague of Athens to AIDS*. Oxford: Oxford University Press.

Dianeosis. (2016a). *The Demographic Development of Greece (2015–2050)*. Retrieved from https://www.dianeosis.org/research/demography/ (in Greek).

Dianeosis. (2016b). *What Do Greeks Believe? (December 2016 Research Results)*. Retrieved from https://www.dianeosis.org/research/tpe_2020/ (in Greek).

Dianeosis. (2018). *What Do Greeks Believe? (February 2018 Research Results)*. Retrieved from https://www.dianeosis.org/research/tpe_2020/ (in Greek).

European Commission. (2020). *Public Opinion Survey: Standard Eurobarometer* (53, 55, 83–92).

European Social Survey. (2010). *Round 5 Data: Data File Edition 3.4. NSD—Norwegian Centre for Research Data, Norway—Data Archive and Distributor of ESS Data for ESS ERIC*. https://doi.org/10.21338/nsd-ess5-2010.

Fan, E. X. (2003). *SARS: Economic Impacts and Implications* (Economics and Research Department Policy Brief No. 15). Retrieved from https://www.adb.org/sites/default/files/publication/28073/pb015.pdf.

Fetzer, T., Hensel, L., Hermle, J., & Roth, C. (2020). *Coronavirus Perceptions and Economic Anxiety*. Vox CEPR Policy Portal. Retrieved from: https://voxeu.org/article/coronavirus-perceptions-and-economic-anxiety.

Fetzer, T., Witte, M., Hensel, L., Jachimowicz, J., Haushofer, J., Ivchenko, A., … Yoeli, E. (2020). Global Behaviors and Perceptions in the COVID-19 Pandemic. *PsyArXiv*. Retrieved from https://doi.org/10.31234/osf.io/3kfmh.

Haushofer, J., & Shapiro, J. (2016). The Short-Term Impact of Unconditional Cash Transfers to the Poor: Experimental Evidence from Kenya. *The Quarterly Journal of Economics, 131*(4), 1973–2042.

Helliwell, J., Layard, R. Sachs, & de Neve, J. E. (2018). *World Happiness Report 2018*. New York: Sustainable Development Solutions Network.

Metron Analysis. (2020). *Studies Archive*. Retrieved from https://www.metronanalysis.gr/ (in Greek).

Mitchener, K. J., & Richardson, G. (2020). *Contagion of Fear* (NBER Working Paper No. 26859).

Petrakis, P. E. (2011). *The Greek Economy and the Crisis: Challenges and Responses*. New York and Heidelberg: Springer.

Petrakis, P., Kafka, K., Kostis, P., & Valsamis, D. (2021). *Greek Culture After the Financial Crisis: An Economic Analysis*. New York: Palgrave Macmillan.

Rieder, K. (2020). *What We May Learn from Historical Financial Crises to Understand and Mitigate COVID-19 Panic Buying*. Vox CEPR Policy Portal. Retrieved from https://voxeu.org/article/mitigating-covid-19-panic-buying-lessons-historical-financial-crises.

Siegrist, M., & Zingg, A. (2014). The Role of Public Trust During Pandemics Implications for Crisis Communication. *European Psychologist, 19*(1), 23–32.

Xie, Y., Hwang, S., & Pantelous, A. A. (2017). Loss Aversion Around the World: Empirical Evidence from Pension Funds. *Journal of Banking & Finance, 88*, 52–62. https://doi.org/10.1016/j.jbankfin.2017.11.007.

CHAPTER 9

Growth in the Greek Economy

9.1 Introduction

The economic reality in Greece appears to be the "image" of an idiosyncratic production model. It is a reality that should be judged more as a result of an evolutionary process where even the knowledge acquired itself plays an important role in shaping it.

The way the political system operates, the presence of pressure groups and elites (economic centers of concentrated economic power), political influence and alliances (diverse governments and political forces) and the external factor in various forms such as the International Monetary Fund (IMF) with the influence of the United States, the European Commission, influenced from bureaucracy in Brussels and the big players in the Eurozone (France, Germany), the European Central Bank (ECB) (which expresses monetary policy in the EZ) and the European Stability Mechanism (ESM), which is an important European institutional player, have played a significant role in shaping this economic reality.

This chapter seeks to describe the evolution of the fundamental figures of the Greek economy and, through this analysis, present a clear picture of how the Greek economy has been driven to the situation at the end of 2019.

The structure of the chapter is the following: Sect. 9.2 shows the economic development in the Greek economy by 2019, with a main reference to the GDP growth rates achieved since 2000.[1] Section 9.3 presents

P. E. Petrakis and P. C. Kostis, *The Evolution of the Greek Economy*,
The Political Economy of Greek Growth up to 2030,
https://doi.org/10.1007/978-3-030-47210-8_9

the internal and external balances of the economy, followed Sect. 9.4 with the evolution of structural reforms, Sect. 9.5 with developments in competitiveness issues, and Sect. 9.6 with developments in investment and foreign direct investment, Sect. 9.7 presents the banking system and creditless recovery, Sect. 9.8 presents issues related to the level of liquidity of the economy and the credit system, Sect. 9.9 concerns entrepreneurship and privatization, Sect. 9.10 deals with the issue of public debt and finally Sect. 9.11 presents the issue of over-taxation of the economy. Finally, Sect. 9.12 presents the transmission channels of CID-19 as well as its short- and medium-long-term effects on the economic system.

9.2 The Economic Evolution

The crisis in the Greek economy started substantially in 2006 and relates to (a) the "fall" of post-Olympic Games prosperity, (b) the entry into the EU of neighboring countries which have served as "poles of attraction" for Greek production capacity, (c) the globalization and weak position of Greece on the international curve of income elasticity of exportable goods, and (d) after 2010 the debt crisis and the "sudden stop" of international capital flows to the Greek economy (as well as to the European economy in general). The Covid-19 crisis at the beginning of 2020 created the conditions for a new depression similar to 2011. Figure 9.1 shows the phases of the evolution of the Greek economy from 2000 to 2019, through the rate of change in real GDP.

The recovery from the deep recession of 2007–2011 started in 2012 and lasted until 2014 (2012, 2013 and 2014). From 2015 (2015–2017), stagnation prevailed, with signs of recovery again after 2017, only to have again a severe recession in 2020 with Covid-19.

This long-term development freeze has resulted in Greece being further drawn away from the average economic performance of the European Union. As an example, GDP per capita in Greece was 63.7% in 2010 and 52.4% in 2020, in proportion to the GDP per capita in the euro area.

This deterioration is observed while at the same time the ratio of public debt as a percentage of GDP has also worsened (the public debt in Greece in proportion to the euro area's public debt was 174% in 2010 and 201% in 2018). At the same time, there is stagnation with signs of backward indications in the institutional sector of the operation of the economy and society (Kaufmann, Kraay, & Mastruzzi, 2010).

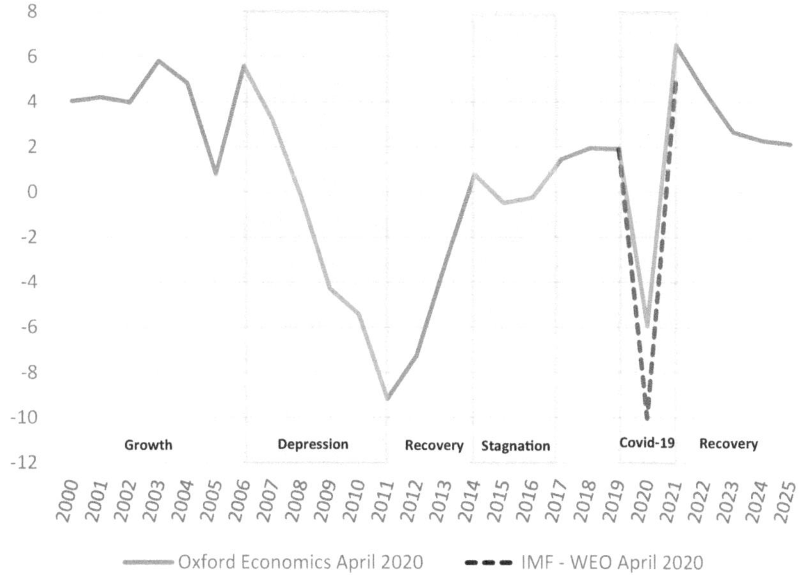

Fig. 9.1 The development phases of the Greek economy: 2000–2025: rate of change in real GDP (*Source* IMF [2020] and Oxford Economics [2020] and authors' creation)

At the same time, the three-year period of 2015–2018 was characterized by the fact that the normal process of leaving the second Memorandum of Understanding was marked by the political choices made. If we compare the forecast for GDP growth at the end of 2014 for the period 2015 2019 with the one achieved, an estimate of the GDP losses caused by the reversal of the normal end of the program could be obtained. This estimate is based on figures from the beginning of 2015 and is a reflection of the costs incurred by the government at the time (based on data at the beginning of 2015) in its decision to refuse to keep the economy evolve smoothly. If the differences that have been observed could be turned into billions of euros, it can be seen that the cost of the political turmoil in 2015 alone amounts, in terms of GDP loss for the years 2015–2017, to around EUR 10 billion.

9.3 Internal and External Balances

Greece's fiscal deficit already in 2008, before the economic crisis of 2011 reached the country, was two-digit as a percentage of GDP (10.2%) (Eurostat). In 2009, when Europe and the US plunged into recession and the signs were seen everywhere for the risks threatening Greece, the deficit was increased to 15.1% of GDP. Subsequently, in the context of the collapse of the real economy (especially in the period 2010–2012), the deficit fell each year (the 2013 figures are inflated by the one-off costs of bank recapitalization, which exceeded 10% of GDP). The primary balance became positive in 2013. Three years later, despite the renewed slippage in the recession caused by the conflict with the Eurozone and the IMF in the first half of 2015, Greece recorded a fiscal surplus (0.5% of GDP), something it continued to do in the coming years until 2018.

However, Greece's over-indebtedness is a major burden on its Net International Investment position (NIIP), which is to reflect the cumulative changes in foreign assets and liabilities and shows accurately the competitiveness levels of the Greek economy.

At the beginning of 2018, our country's net investment position was negative by EUR 250.5 billion, a level which is historically high. In particular, foreign liabilities amounted to EUR 449.4 billion, while foreign assets amounted to EUR 198.9 billion. Obviously, foreign liabilities have fallen since the beginning of 2016 when they had reached EUR 483.1 billion, mainly due to the reduction in the eurosystem's funding of domestic financial institutions. Over the same period, the private sector's net assets have fallen by around EUR 44 billion. This decrease partly reflects the gradual return of deposits to the domestic banking system, but is mainly due to the disinvestment of the banking system from South-east European countries.

It should be stressed that Greece's net investment position has been deteriorating systematically over the last 20 years and from −35.3% of GDP in 1999 it reached −140.9% of GDP at the beginning of 2018. This rate is expected to increase significantly with the Covid-19 crisis. This shows that the Greek economy has accumulated far more liabilities vis-à-vis the foreign countries than the assets it has from abroad. Reversing this situation will require a rapid repayment of public debt and a productivity growth reflected in the growth of Greek investments outside Greece.

However, NIIP is not a figure that can be used to judge the economic governance of a country. A country that has very large inflows of foreign investment would have a serious deterioration in its balance without, of course, this being a bad thing. It depends on the nature, purpose of these funds, etc. On the contrary, if it was to deteriorate due to their outflow, this could be a serious negative event because it would express a crisis of confidence in the country. Surely, in Greece, the capital controls applied have stabilized the situation because they did not allow the country to increase its liabilities significantly.

The relative stabilization (or slight deterioration) of the NIIP is also linked to the evolution of the balances of Target 2 which essentially reflects the balance of capital inflows and outflows between eurozone countries. Greece's position in the Target 2 balance has improved in relation to the major crisis of 2015. However, the emergence of capital controls has played a major role here in shaping the image, which have prevented internal Greek confidence crises from translating into capital outflows through the creation of a crisis of confidence in the euro.

9.4 The Evolution of Structural Reforms

Since 2010, the Greek economy has made a very important effort to address its fiscal problems and low competitiveness. To this end, it has implemented a very important set of structural reforms within the framework of the fiscal adjustment programs. In fact, between 2011 and 2014 the Greek economy carried out most structural reforms compared to the rest of the European Union (OECD, 2015).

The changes in tax policy (Greece belonged to the developed countries, which have further reformed its tax system as shown by the OECD report [2016] "Tax Policy reforms in the OECD") and expenditure cuts—in particular, pensions and wages of public sector—reduced the structural fiscal deficit by almost 14 percentage points of GDP. The size of the adjustment was about twice that of the other European countries facing sudden interruptions in their exit to markets. Labor market reforms were also important, with the decentralization of the wage bargaining system, the reduction of the minimum wage and the simplification of restrictions on recruitments and redundancies. In addition, reforms to reduce the regulatory burden and improve the business climate have been launched—relatively late—under the second fiscal adjustment program of 2012 and included a reduction in barriers to competition in the tourism and retail sector, facilitate the process of licensing enterprises in certain sectors and partial deregulating some restricted professions.

However, this very important effort from the Greek economy has not transformed directly into progress for the Greek economy. Some of the reasons, which illustrate the system's weakness in dealing with the crisis, for which this has happened—and which need to be addressed—are as follows (Daude, 2016):

- The mix of structural reforms was unbalanced. The emphasis on front-loaded fiscal adjustment has drastically reduced demand and contributed to a deep recession. Moreover, fiscal multipliers and the increase in government bond yields and borrowing costs have been undervalued. At the same time, the wider climate of uncertainty and delays surrounding the restructuring of public debt created significant obstacles to the image perceived by managers of international funds for the Greek economy (Daude, 2016).
- Structural reform implementation has been and remains a challenging task for the Greek economy. During the first fiscal adjustment program for 2010, structural reforms carried out were related to the fiscal aspects of the economy and the labor market and not to the product market.[2] The result of this specificity is evident when one compares the structural reforms carried out in Greece compared to Ireland and Portugal where the adjustment programs were similar to that of Greece, although much less stringent.
- The implementation of structural reforms was weak and fragmented making structural reforms less effective.
- Enrichment of the structural reform framework would offer the chance long-term success.

However, after 2015, the reform and development effort in the Greek economy has been interrupted concerning all structural competitive indicators. An interpretation of this development is that (a) significant results have been achieved over the period 2011–2015, with great social effort resulting in subsequent rest. Moreover, the reform fatigue has been an almost pan-European phenomenon during this period (but competing European countries need it less), (b) the Greek economy has faced the political resistance of established power centers and although it appeared that the reform effort has gone far, political staff have been acting in a way that has prevented competitive improvement (over-regulation, non-friendliness to entrepreneurship, public sector expansion, etc.).

9.5 Competitiveness

It has prevailed to consider the Greek crisis of 2011 as a debt crisis, but at its root is it a classic case of a competitiveness crisis (Dianeosis, 2016). One of the factors that lead to reduced competitiveness in the Greek economy was the inefficient implementation of structural reforms before the crisis, a situation which began in 2001 when, due to social reactions, the government abandoned the planned pension system reform. Since then and until Greece entered the eras of the Memorandums, few reforms have been implemented, most of which were, rather, minor (Tsakloglou, Economidis, Pagoulatos, Triantopoulos, & Apostolis Filippopoulos, 2016).

The result of this situation was a significant deterioration in the competitiveness of the Greek economy, which is evident from the observation of the evolution and of the Real Effective Exchange Rate (REER) of the economy, as well as from the evolution of real unit labor costs (Figs. 9.2 and 9.3).

Both indicators presented in Figs. 9.2 and 9.3 are linked to a reduction in competitiveness when they increase and increase in competitiveness when they decrease. Thus, there has been a significant decrease in competitiveness between 2000 and 2010, and the very serious reform actions accompanying the implementation of the fiscal adjustment programs

Fig. 9.2 Real Effective Exchange Rate, monthly data (deflator: consumer price prices—42 trading partners) (2010 = 100) (*Source* Eurostat database [2020] and authors' creation)

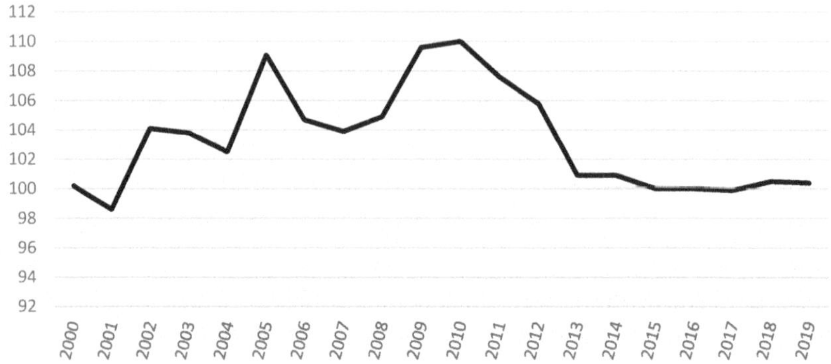

Fig. 9.3 Real unit labour costs: total economy (ratio of compensation per employee to nominal GDP per person employed) (*Source* AMECO database and authors' creation)

after 2010 (see Chapter 11) have led to a significant improvement in competitiveness.

This is also evident from the observation of the evolution of the Greek economy's score in the Global Competitiveness Index, which is being developed by the World Economic Forum (Fig. 9.4).

Greece experienced a deterioration of the index up to 2012, while at the same time there was a satisfactory improvement by 2014 and relative stability by 2017. The progress of the ranking of the Greek economy among the countries in the report is similar. However, the gap in competitiveness relative to the average of the euro area countries is particularly large. For example, for the years 2017–2018, the Greek economy ranks 87 as among 140 countries, while the average for the euro area countries is 35.

9.6 Investments and FDI

The long-term decline in investment has affected the competitiveness of the Greek economy, at a time when the money and capital markets were distinguished of high liquidity and low-interest rates. At the same time, the fiscal deficits that have accompanied the beginning of the crisis in the Greek economy have led to the need for investment in the economy. Given that the investment gap in the Greek economy exceeded 10% of the annual GDP in 2018, its cumulative dynamic was expected to lead

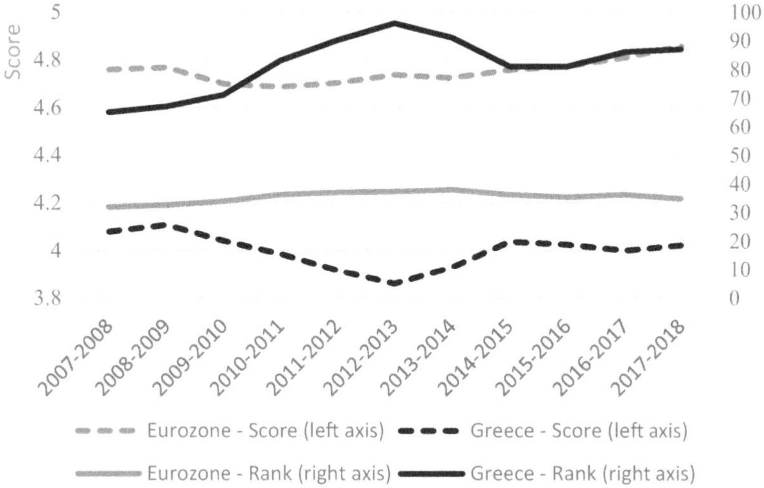

Fig. 9.4 Greece in the Global Competitiveness Index in relation to the Eurozone (*Source* World Economic Forum [2020] and authors' calculations and creation)

to an even greater reduction in the country's competitiveness, which has led, among other things, to technological backwardness in a time of rapid development and diffusion of technology.

The three potential sources of investment financing are the State, European and private resources. Of these, the State cannot finance major projects due to a lack of fiscal space. In fact, it showed an annual decrease in investment of 1.5 billion euros on average over the period 2010–2016 compared to 2000–2008 and it has been difficult to co-finance due to structural deficiencies. The state of public investment over the last two years does not change the overall picture. Net inflows of foreign direct investment (net FDI) in Greece amounted to 31 billion euros in 2002–2018 (Bank of Greece). Over the last decade, these reached 18.78 billion euros, with provisional figures showing that they have exceeded 3.6 billion euros in 2018. Net FDI in the Greek economy has been on a non-linear path since 2002, which was the year of the introduction of the euro. At the same time, FDI in Greece from 2006 to 2018 amounts to an average of not more than 7% of the total gross fixed capital formation, contributing to a lesser extent than it would have been expected in an economy belonging to a global reserve currency area.

The further analysis of net FDI in Greece for the years 2002–2018 shows that the vast majority is directed to services and single-digit rates are for the primary and secondary sectors of the economy, respectively. The secondary sector in particular accounts for 8.8% of the total, with manufacturing accounting for 2.6% of the total net FDI. In practice, this means that manufacturing in Greece is not an objective for foreign capital seeking alternative opportunities for placement in services, and very often through portfolio acquisition, without this reducing their necessity. The small contribution of FDI to the Greek economy and the even smaller one in the manufacturing sector reflect not only the problem of systemic inability to attract investments, but also the lack of confidence of foreign investors in the country's productive capacities.

According to the Hellenic Federation of Enterprises (SEV) calculations (Manifava, 2015), a minimum investment shock of 100 billion euros would be needed till 2022 to balance the economic divestment that occurred during the crisis.

Indicative of the decline in investment in Greece is Fig. 9.5 which presents the investment gap in the Greek economy. Figure 9.6 shows, respectively, the case of the euro area investment gap. The amount of the investment gap is calculated as the difference in investments made in relation to the assumption of a sustainable trend in investment growth of 20 to 22% of the GDP.

In Greece the investment gap appears to be around 16.8 billion to 20.7 billion euros for 2019, while for the Eurozone there is no investment gap.

9.7 The Banking System and the Credit-Less Recovery

It is well known that in Greece, banking intermediation (compared to a market-based economy) plays an important role even in relation to the other countries of the European Union and/or the euro area. Obviously, the structure of the Greek private sector (small and very small productive units without access to capital markets) largely justifies the very high dependence on bank financing. Thus, when the banking system is deteriorated, the Greek economy is deteriorated even more.

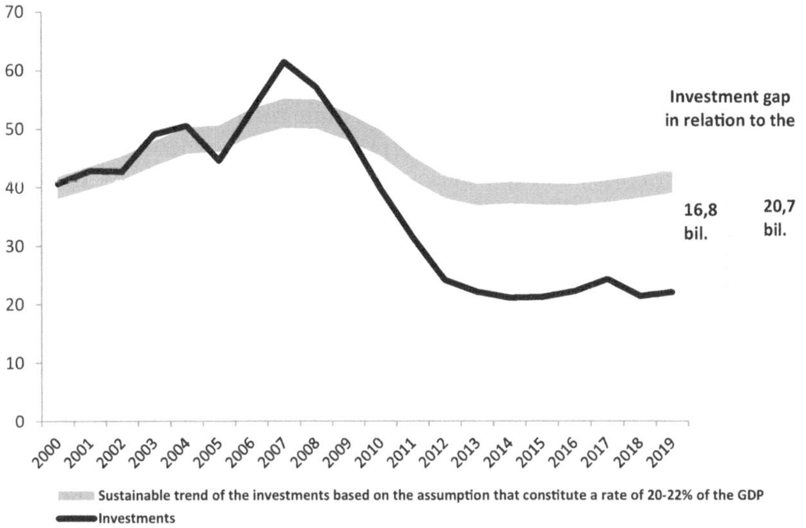

Fig. 9.5 Investment gap in Greece: Investments in billions of euros (*Source* Oxford Economics [2020] and authors' calculations and creation)

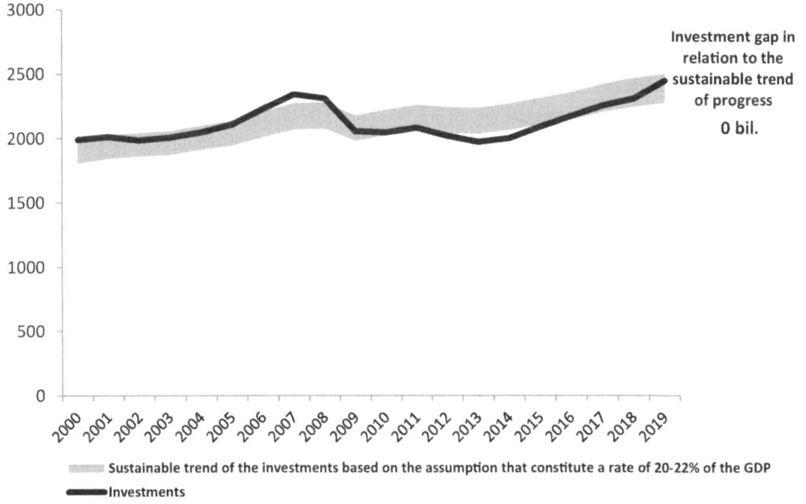

Fig. 9.6 Investment gap in the Eurozone: Investments in billions of euros (*Source* Oxford Economics [2020] and authors' calculations and creation)

However, given the disproportionate importance of bank financing for Greek companies (the ratio of loan financing to total liabilities of non-financial corporations in Greece is 85%, while for the Eurozone it is 62%), as well as the particular issues relating to the domestic banking system (outflow of deposits abroad, problem of confidence under the regime of restrictions on capital controls, non-performing loans) describe a creditless recovery.

The deleveraging process, which in the euro area appears to be completed, has not developed a corresponding dynamic in the Greek economy. To a large extent, this is due to the contraction of the Greek GDP by 25% between 2009 and 2015. If one could remove the effects of the decline in Greek production, the degree of deleveraging of the Greek economy would be a strong reminder of the corresponding path in the euro area economy.

In other words, the (in absolute terms) reduction in the debt burden of the Greek economy is accompanied by a corresponding reduction in production (and/or household income). Their relative burden therefore remains high, making it difficult to finance the private sector of the economy. This situation also defines the background of a "creditless recovery" (see Chapter 12).

International literature presents examples of creditless recoveries in economies that have returned to positive growth without the support of bank financing. More specifically, about 20% of cases of rebound of economies to positive growth after some form of crisis over the last 5 decades concern cases where bank financing did not return to pre-crisis levels (in real terms) for at least three years after the lowest point of the business activity (Darvas, 2013). However, the vast majority of creditless recoveries are characterized by lower growth rates than cases of recovery with strengthened bank financing.

In fact, when the recovery follows more severe economic activity crises and/or a banking crisis (such as the recent downturn following the global financial crisis), then the return to positive growth is much more likely not to be followed by a strengthening of bank financing (Bijsterbosch & Dahlhaus, 2011).

However, the vast majority of these cases concern developing economies. On the contrary, the developed world is rarely experiencing a recovery of economic momentum after a crisis without corresponding strengthening of bank financing.

Finally, it should be noted that in restoring positive economic growth rates without the contribution of the banking sector, the adjustment of competitiveness that should take place is much greater (Balfoussia & Malliaropoulos, 2015). It is no coincidence, therefore, that the recovery of sectors of the economy which rely more on external financing (bank lending and/or issuance of securities on the markets) is experiencing lower levels of growth in the case of creditless recoveries (Abiad, Dell'Ariccia, & Li, 2011).

Especially in the case of euro area member states, where there can be no depreciation of the domestic currency, improving competitiveness is tantamount to a greater need for the painful process of "internal devaluation" that has been applied for several years by the Greek economy as well, which as expected, but also as it was proven, is extremely painful.

9.8 Liquidity and Credit System

The Greek economy passed through the years of the crisis and at least until 2018, a period of extremely low liquidity. The only sources of liquidity after the crisis, due to the interruption of inflows from abroad, were the fiscal adjustment program and the European Central Bank with liquidity injections into the banking system. However, liquidity was drained by the Greek economy. The main source of economic liquidity reduction is the need to repay the ELA and to deleverage the private sector. The main well-known expressions of the deteriorating liquidity situation of the economy are the continuing decline in financial balances to the private sector, along with the relatively increasing difficulty of the private sector in meeting its tax obligations (see Petrakis, 2020a).

However, the liquidity of the economy has been further squeezed by two concrete actions. The first relates to the repos of public institutions in the general public sector, estimated at 14 billion euros in 2018. This operation relates to the intention to control the Local Governments, the Legal Entities of Public Law, etc., and to create a 'safety pillow' which would allow some form of access to markets.

It should also be pointed out that for about one year after summer 2012, banks' liabilities toward the ECB were reduced in parallel with the evolution in the available liquidity of the domestic private sector. Since mid-2013, however, the reduction in the liabilities of Greek banks toward the Eurosystem has become more pronounced, which have been halted only in mid-2014 (with the first signs of political uncertainty), just to be reversed by the acceleration of the election of the President of the Republic and the anticipation of political developments in December of the same year. The faster repayment of Eurosystem liabilities has made it difficult to reactivate the domestic financial system to finance the (healthy) private sector of the Greek economy.

The same development, however, appeared to be repeated in the years 2015–2017. After the peak of the Greek crisis and for about 6 months (until December 2015, when the recapitalization effort of the domestic financial sector was successfully completed), the reduction in ELA liabilities has had a full impact on the reduction of private sector liquidity. But then the repayment of bank liabilities to the ECB and the Bank of Greece became stronger, leading, cumulatively, to a reduction of around 80 billion. During the same period, the private sector's liquidity available fell by around 30 billion.

The 2015 crisis (capital controls, etc.) and the extension of the 2nd negotiation of the third Memorandum of Understanding have seriously damaged the credibility of the Greek economy. As a result, the recovery rate of deposits has been extremely slow.

If we compare the course of deposits to the first crisis of confidence 2012–2014 with its current 2015–2017 period, we see two parallel but different levels of developments in their return process. Only after the end of the second review of the MoU (June 2017) did the deposits, in particular by private individuals, started returning, aided by the proceeds of the very good tourist season. Nevertheless, the crisis of confidence has remained.

The slow evolution of deposits is linked to (a) the increase in tax obligations, (b) domestic deposits (around 12 billion euros), and (c) to consumer behavior which shows signs of recovery. The consumer recovery in turn is due to (a) a specific expectation of "better days", and (b) a "fear" of savings accounts (fear of bail in).

Figure 9.7 shows the evolution of total deposits and liabilities for the Greek economy, from January 2001 to January 2020. The significant return of deposits achieved between June 2019 and January 2020 is evident, following the huge drop in deposits in summer 2015.

Fig. 9.7 Evolution of deposits (2001–2020) (*Source* Bank of Greece [2020] and authors' creation)

9.9 Entrepreneurship Development and Privatizations

The economic crisis (2008–2018) dramatically changed the conditions of entrepreneurship. Businesses are obliged to adapt to these conditions. They are all too often forced to reduce their production costs, review their corporate strategy, change their investment strategy, and restructure their activities. Therefore, in this complex environment, which is characterized by rapid developments, as well as high uncertainty, the most important issue is how business units in the Greek economy will survive.

In Greece, the share of the population aged 18–64 in 2017 in early stages of entrepreneurial activity (including self-employment) fell to 4.8% (around 320 thousand people) from 5.7% (around 380 thousand) in 2016 and from 6.7% in 2015 (Tsakanikas, Stavraki, & Valavanioti, 2018). This performance is one of the country's lowest performance over time (2003–2017: 6.9%), while it is below the average of the countries of innovation (2017: 9.2%), i.e., of most of the developed countries in the world, to which Greece belongs. It therefore, appears that despite the stabilization of the economy, the intense uncertainties remained strong and affected business activity (Foundation for Economic and Industrial Research (IOBE), 2018).

However, the contraction of new entrepreneurship may be due to two reasons (Tsakanikas, Giotopoulos, Stavraki, & Valavanioti, 2017). One reason is that small-medium-sized business dynamism is not conducive to political control, while small-scale entrepreneurship, just like large entrepreneurship, being state-dependant, are offered for a "protection" policy. The second is that the economic policy may have a problem with small entrepreneurship due to its inability to monitor taxation. Two are considered to be the main points of this "disapproval": over-taxation of new and small entrepreneurship and its problematic relation with the production of innovation in its production sites (research centers and innovation).

Privatization in the Greek economy was low in 2015 and 2016 and increased in 2017 and 2018. For the period of 2011–2017, privatization revenues in Greece totaled 5.1 billion euros.

Thus, two key issues have emerged regarding privatization: (a) the revenue from its development was particularly low up to and including 2018, due to the political turmoil and the resulting stagnation, and (b) the restructuring of the economy, which was expected through privatization, did not proceed.

9.10 The Issue of Debt

The Greek economic crisis started as a sovereign debt crisis in 2009. However, despite the implementation of austerity and a brave "haircut", public debt stood at around 176.6% of Greek GDP in 2019 (IMF, 2019).

Figure 9.8 shows the evolution of the total debt of the Greek economy since 1980.

The total debt of the Greek economy (public and private) reached a high record of around €632 billion in 2011 (of which about 58% was public and 42% was private debt), as until then it followed a sustained increase mainly due to the large accumulation of public debt. After an attempt to drastically reduce it in 2012 (PSI), there is some stability in its evolution.

The IMF in its methodology for "Analysis of sovereign debt sustainability" addresses parameters such as average debt maturity, short-term debt ratio, creditor quality and others. The quality of creditors—in the case of Greece available to finance it with huge amounts and on exceptionally favorable terms—has perhaps been decisive in the IMF to describe the Greek debt as viable in 2014, although the majority of economists

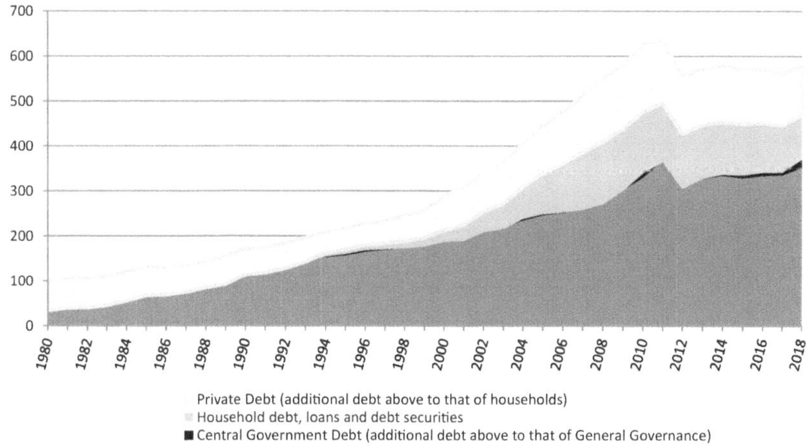

Fig. 9.8 Public and private debt in the Greek economy (bn euros) (*Source* Mbaye, Moreno-Badia, and Chae [2018] and authors' creation)

took a different view. However, it has later proved that the future sustainability of the debt is critically dependant on the future management of the economy.

What one concludes by noting the evolution and management of debt in the Greek economy up to and including 2018 is that it is not about debt sustainability, but about the sustainability of the economy. As debt sustainability is linked to high primary surpluses and a number of hypotheses/assumptions about future growth rates, debt refinancing costs, future primary surpluses, and the desired debt level target, it is the development of economic activity that is important.

9.11 The Overburden of Taxation

According to all indications, the Greeks are the most burdened tax people in the OECD in 2018. While regarding tax revenue as a percentage of GDP Greece ranks 6th among OECD economies, when the shadow economy is taken into account, tax revenues as a percentage of GDP increase from 38.56 to 49.12%. Figure 9.9 shows tax revenues as a percentage of GDP (where the tax burden is borne by the consistent

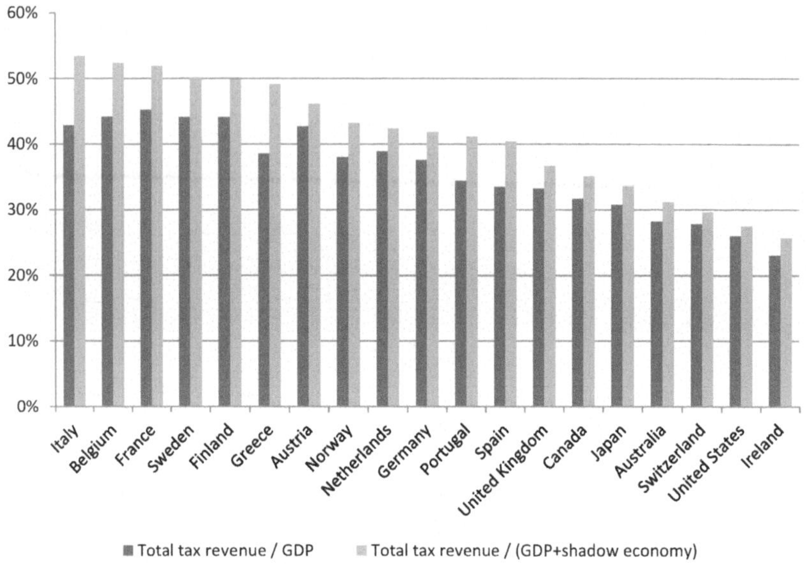

Fig. 9.9 Total tax burden as a percentage of GDP taking into account the shadow economy (2018) (*Note* It is assumed that every economy has a population of 100 citizens and that some of them [equal to the share of the shadow economy] work in the shadow economy. In order to calculate the amount of tax revenue as a percentage of GDP to take account of the shadow economy, the proportion of tax revenue is divided by the number of people employed in the formal economy. *Source* OECD [2019] and authors' calculations and creation)

taxpayer alone) in relation to tax revenues as a percentage of GDP when the shadow economy is taken into account.

Obviously, Greek society may appear to pay lower taxes as a percentage of GDP than economies such as France, Sweden, Finland, Belgium, and Italy, but one has to bear in mind that what Greek society enjoys (institutions, infrastructure, etc.) of the taxes it pays.

For this reason, Fig. 9.10 shows that tax revenues as a percentage of GDP when taking into account shadow economy and citizens' satisfaction with public services related to the health care system, the education system, schools, and the judicial system and courts (OECD, 2019). This shows the real tax burden on citizens.

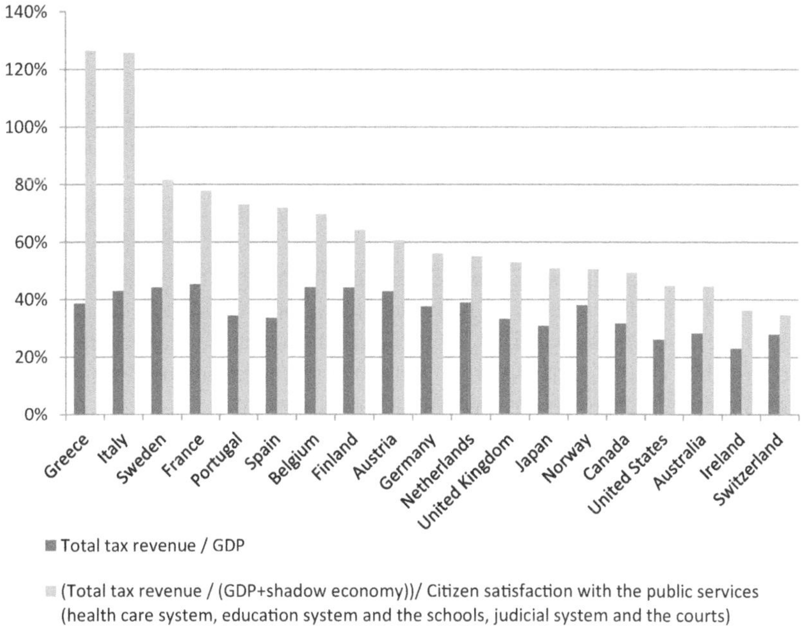

Fig. 9.10 Total real tax burden as a percentage of GDP taking into account the shadow economy and the satisfaction with services provided by public infrastructure (2018) (*Source* OECD [2019] and authors' calculations and creation)

It is noted that Greeks are the most burdened people by their tax system compared to all the countries in question.

The main feature of the two-year period 2016–2017 is over-taxation. The government has concentrated as much resources and liquidity from the private sector and the middle class as possible on public funds. In 2016 and 2017, a further €8.17 billion of primary budget surpluses were collected.

9.12 The Covid-19 Recession

The effects of Covid-19, as has happened in earlier pandemics (see Petrakis, 2020b, Chapter 20), pass through four main channels:

- Impact on the supply side. One way in which the virus damages the economy is to stop the supply of labor, goods, and services. People are sick, schools are closed, and parents stop working, staying at home to take care of their children. Thus, quarantine can force workers to work from their home or even entire factories to suspend their operations. The strict restrictive measures introduced in China and Italy have aggravated this effect through the channel of supply.

The restrictions on people's movement create a negative shock to labor supply (in fact they create an increase in unemployment). It is assumed that these conditions will last for at least one or two quarters in China and in other countries with large outbreaks (Italy, Germany, France, and Spain) depending always on the situations observed.

Thus, an additional channel for the transmission of the effects of the coronavirus spread in the Greek economy is the disruption to global value chains. Although the participation of Greek companies in global value chains is still limited, the reduction, or even interruption in some cases, of the supply of intermediate and capital goods is estimated to have a negative effect on their production capacity. In addition, the production of goods and services in particular may be adversely affected by the extensive employee abstention from their duties in the framework of preventive measures regarding the dispersal of the coronavirus.

- Impact on demand. On the demand side, people buy less goods from shops than usual, transport trips are decreased, and people do not resort to restaurants thus reducing food consumption from outside. Public health measures also limit economic activity.

An important channel is the decline in the external demand for Greek goods and services, due to the decline in world trade and the deterioration of the economic climate internationally. In fact, the effects on ocean sea shipping will probably be particularly negative, where revenue dynamics are mainly determined by the evolution of freight rates which largely reflects fluctuations in international trade. More serious, however, is estimated to be the impact on travel receipts, given the imposed travel restrictions and the generally vulnerable climate in this sector.

In addition to external demand, the spread of the coronavirus is expected to affect domestic demand as well. Private consumption is expected to decrease due to a deterioration in consumer confidence, preventive measures to prevent the dispersion of the coronavirus and the compression of household disposable income as a result of the decline in economic activity in general. In particular, transport, trade, catering and services related to tourism, the arts, entertainment and entertainment will be most affected. Also, the increase in uncertainty and the deterioration of the investment environment should have a deterrent effect on new investment projects and risk-taking.

- Uncertainty. Businesses are subject to an increased risk due to weak aggregate demand, while the pandemic is causing adverse effects. Uncertainty is likely to remain and contribute to the slowdown in productivity growth along with delayed investment decisions by companies.
- International and domestic financial markets. Another important channel for transmission is the deterioration in international and domestic financial conditions. In particular, the increase in uncertainty fuels significant turbulence in international financial markets, leading to a deterioration in the conditions for financing economies and a reconsideration of investment positions worldwide, with possible negative consequences for ongoing investment projects and the liquidity of the Greek economy in general. In addition, the increase in financing costs due to the re-pricing of risks internationally leads to a deterioration in the conditions and in increased costs for raising new financing for banks, businesses and households, as well as the Greek State.

In conclusion, the Greek economy is expected to be affected by the reduction of exports, the reduction of travel receipts, the reduction of shipping receipts, the reduction of consumer and business confidence, the reduction in the international price of oil and the reduction in production and employment as a result of the preventive measures to reduce the spread of the coronavirus.

Figure 9.11 shows the annual decrease in GDP growth in real terms in the Greek economy. This is an exceptionally large recession of −5.9%, while before the onset of the pandemic, growth of 2.26% was expected.

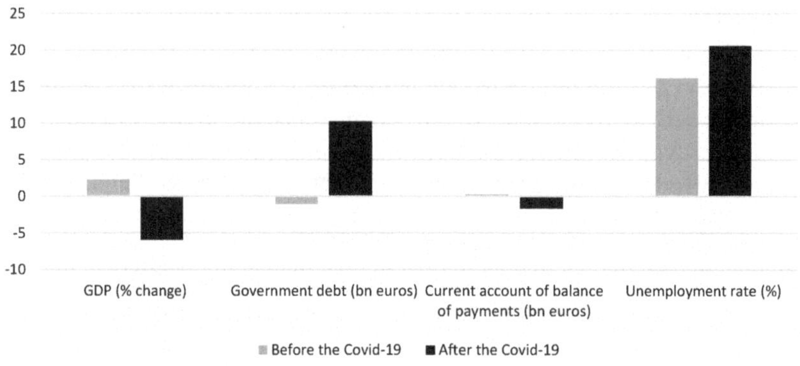

Fig. 9.11 The effects of Covid-19 on key macro-economic figures (*Notes* (1) The case "Before the Covid-19" presents estimates based on the figures of January 2020 of Oxford Economics' Global Economic Model. (2) The case "After the Covid-19" presents estimates based on the April 2020 data of the Global Economic Model of Oxford Economics. A detailed presentation of these estimates is set out in Chapters 11 and 12, where the April 2020 estimates are presented as the Normal scenario. *Source* Oxford Economics [2020] and authors' calculations and creation)

There is no doubt that such a deep recession for 2020 is extremely important for the Greek economy, which is, of course, comparable to that of 2011 for Greece.

Figure 9.11 also shows the corresponding developments concerning debt, current account balance, and unemployment rate. Due to the short- and medium-term and external nature of the crisis while the GDP reduction is very large, the effects on other figures are not on the trend of 2011.

Government debt is expected to increase by EUR 10.3 billion in 2020, while it was expected to be decreased by EUR 1.1 billion. The current account balance is expected to increase the deficit by EUR 1.63 billion in 2020, while it was expected to decrease by EUR 0.24 billion. Finally, the unemployment rate is expected after the onset of Covid-19 at 20.6% in 2020, while prior to the onset of Covid-19 it was expected at 16.2%.

Figure 9.12 shows the corresponding changes in GDP and the key factors that determine it. In absolute terms, GDP is therefore expected to fall by EUR 11.57 billion in 2020, while it was expected to increase

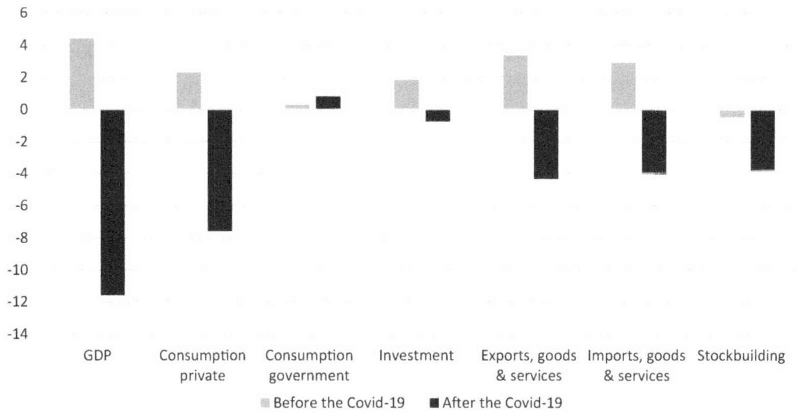

Fig. 9.12 The effects of the emergence of Covid-19 on GDP and its determinants (bn euros) (*Notes* (1) The case "Before the Covid-19" presents estimates based on the figures of January 2020 of Oxford Economics' Global Economic Model. (2) The case "After the Covid-19" presents estimates based on the April 2020 data of the Global Economic Model of Oxford Economics. A detailed presentation of these estimates is set out in Chapters 11 and 12, where the April 2020 estimates are presented as the Normal scenario. *Source* Oxford Economics [2020] and authors' calculations and creation)

by EUR 4.4 billion. Analysis of the changes in the impact of the determinants on GDP shows that the main negative effects are derived from private consumption, which is expected to decrease by EUR 7.58 billion (while expected to increase by EUR 2.3 billion), investments that are expected to decrease by EUR 0.72 billion (while expected to increase by EUR 1.81 billion), exports of goods and services expected to decrease by EUR 4.32 billion (while expected to increase by EUR 3.35 billion) and stockbuilding expected to decrease by EUR 3.76 billion (while expected to decrease by EUR 0.45 billion). Only government consumption and imports improve the situation for 2020, as government consumption is expected to increase by EUR 0.79 billion (while expected to increase by EUR 0.28 billion) and imports are expected to decrease by EUR 4.03 billion (while it was expected to increase by EUR 2.89 billion).

The implementation of an economic recovery program can be carried out in two phases: The first, covering the two years 2020–2021, where the main emphasis will be on policies addressing supply and increasing demand, and thus reducing the enlarged production gap, while the second period 2022–2030 will be a period of implementation of a broader program of structural change, enlargement and diversification of supply opportunities.

It should be noted that this will create favorable conditions for implementing a structural development program, even if there are epidemiological disturbances (albeit assumed to be of lesser importance). This point is particularly emphasized because the implementation of structural change programs is particularly facilitated when it is based on a basis of a strong recovery in demand and growth, as is expected to happen after the end of the epidemiological phenomena.

It is also stressed that the experience of ten years of implementation and economic rebalancing, together with the coordinated social response of civil society to the effects of the crisis, has created a favorable background of social behavior for a stable and systematic implementation of a structural change program which includes decisions on productive restructuring and institutional efficiency.

Notes

1. The period is approximated by the entry into the EMU and the introduction of the euro.
2. Product markets have a significant impact on hypothetical dynamic growth. Intervention on these markets usually uses measures such as easing the administrative entry restriction and reducing the administrative burden. These conditions improve the allocation of resources between product and service sectors and within these sectors. Some of the effects of these measures are immediate, but generally, their positive impact extends over time.

References

Abiad, A., Dell'Ariccia, G., & Li, B. G. (2011). *Creditless Recoveries* (IMF Working Paper No. 11/58).

Balfoussia, H., & Malliaropoulos, D. (2015). *Credit-Less Recoveries: The Role of Investment-Savings Imbalances* (Bank of Greece Working Paper No. 200).

Bank of Greece. (2020). *Statistics: Monetary and Banking Statistics*. Retrieved from https://www.bankofgreece.gr/en/statistics/monetary-and-banking-statistics.

Bijsterbosch, M., & Dahlhaus, T. (2011). *Determinants of Credit-Less Recoveries* (ECB Working Paper No. 1358).

Darvas, Z. (2013). Can Europe Recover Without Credit? *Bruegel Policy Contribution* 2013/03.

Daude, C. (2016). *Structural Reforms to Boost Inclusive Growth in Greece* (OECD Economics Department Working Paper No. 1298).

European Commission. (2020). *AMECO Database* [Online]. Retrieved from https://ec.europa.eu/economy_finance/ameco/user/serie/SelectSerie.cfm.

Eurostat. (2020). *Effective Exchange Rates Indices—Monthly Data, ei_mfef_m Database.*

IMF. (2019). *World Economic Outlook Database: October 2019 Edition.*

IMF. (2020). *World Economic Outlook Database: April 2020 Edition.*

Kaufmann, D., Kraay, A., & Mastruzzi, M. (2010). *The Worldwide Governance Indicators: Methodology and Analytical Issues* (World Bank Policy Research Working Paper No. 5430). Retrieved from www.govindicators.org.

Manifava, D. (2015). *SEV Eyes Investment Measures.* Ekathimerini.com. Retrieved from https://www.ekathimerini.com/204682/article/ekathimerini/business/sev-eyes-investment-measures.

Mbaye, S., Moreno-Badia, M., & Chae, K. (2018). *Global Debt Database: Methodology and Sources* (IMF Working Paper No. 18/111). Retrieved from https://www.imf.org/external/datamapper/datasets/GDD.

OECD. (2015). *Economic Policy Reforms 2015: Going for Growth.* Paris: OECD Publishing. Retrieved from https://doi.org/10.1787/growth-2015-en.

OECD. (2016). *Tax Policy Reforms in the OECD 2016.* Paris: OECD Publishing. Retrieved from https://doi.org/10.1787/9789264260399-en.

OECD. (2019). *Government at a Glance 2019.* Paris: OECD Publishing.

Oxford Economics. (2020). *Oxford Economics Global Economic Model.*

Petrakis, P. E. (2020a). *The New Political Economy of Greece Up to 2030.* New York: Palgrave Macmillan.

Petrakis, P. E. (2020b). *Theoretical Approaches to Economic Growth and Development—An Interdisciplinary Perspective.* New York: Palgrave Macmillan.

Tsakanikas, A., Giotopoulos, I., Stavraki, S., & Valavanioti, E. (2017). Annual Entrepreneurship Report 2016–2017: Early Stage Entrepreneurship Rates Decrease. *IOBE Foundation for Economic & Industrial Research.* Retrieved from http://iobe.gr/research_dtl_en.asp?RID=151.

Tsakanikas, A., Stavraki, S., & Valavanioti, E. (2018). Annual Entrepreneurship Report 2017–2018: Fewer Ventures, Better Employment Prospects. *IOBE Foundation for Economic & Industrial Research.* Retrieved from http://iobe.gr/research_dtl_en.asp?RID=169.

Tsakloglou, P., Economidis, G., Pagoulatos, G., Triantopoulos, Ch., & Apostolis Filippopoulos, A. (2016). A New Development Standard for the Greek Economy and the Transition to It. *Dianeosis*. Retrieved from https://www.dianeosis.org/wp-content/uploads/2016/10/teliko-arxeio-paragogikou-montelou-12-10.pdf.

World Economic Forum. (2020). *The Global Competitiveness Index Dataset 2007–2018 (Version 20180712)*. Retrieved from http://reports.weforum.org/global-competitiveness-index-2017-2018/downloads/.

CHAPTER 10

Insights of the Production Prototype Change During the Crisis (2008–2018)

10.1 Introduction

Following the outburst 2010 crisis in the Greek economy, an economic policy has been implemented which has pursued structural change in the economy to a significant extent. In particular, efforts were made for the production sector to improve its competitiveness (as outlined in the previous chapter).

This chapter attempts to investigate whether and to what extent the country's production model has changed during the period of economic crisis (2008–2017).[1] Attempts are also being made to address the issue with the productive structure of the Greek economy and the fact that there is no significant production differentiation. As a result that there is a need to change the production prototype. This fact, was highlighted by the emergence of the Covid-19 pandemic and its impact on the economic outcome.

Investigating whether and to what extent the productive model of the country has changed during the 2008 debt crisis, is attempted in two ways. The first one concerns the separation of the Greek economy into

The authors would like to thank Dr. Angelos Efstratoglou for his contribution to this chapter.

P. E. Petrakis and P. C. Kostis, *The Evolution of the Greek Economy*, The Political Economy of Greek Growth up to 2030, https://doi.org/10.1007/978-3-030-47210-8_10

two segments and the control of a number of developments within them. That is, the domestic one, which produces goods and services for the domestic market and the international and competitive segment, which produces goods and services that are tradable for international markets.

The second concerns monitoring developments in the Greek economy sectors, on the one hand, by technological specialization and on the other hand by the intensity of their work skills. This is because the process of changing the production model of the Greek economy is going through the strengthening of the internationalized and competitive segment and through the strengthening of the high and medium-technological skills sectors and through the high-intensity skill sectors. To the extent that this is the case, it could be argued with some certainty that developments in the Greek economy during the crisis have led to a process of changing its production model at the same time.

The structure of the chapter is the following: Initially (Sect. 10.2), the structural change in the Greek production system is presented, while Sect. 10.3 describes the distinction between the domestic and competitive and internationalized part of the Greek economy, and the next Sect. (10.4) shows the developments in gross value added, employment and productivity, along with imports, exports and the trade balance for the domestic and international part of the Greek economy. The next Sect. (10.5) shows the technological specialization of the Greek economy sectors and Sect. 10.6 describes the skill intensity of the Greek economy sectors. Finally, in Sect. 10.7, the impact of Covid-19 on the sectors of activity of the Greek economy is analyzed.

10.2 Structural Change in the Production System

The Greek economy has been through significant structural changes in the years of the crisis of 2011, which is evident from the observation of the Phillips curve, the Okun curve (see Chapter 12) and the Beveridge curve (see Petrakis, 2020). However, these changes are not certain that they achieved in changing significantly the productive system of the economy.

Monitoring the diversification of the country's production model, by monitoring developments in the domestic and international sectors, the technological specialization of the broader industrial sector, and the intensity of skills, does not represent the reality as it is. On the contrary, a number of developments indicate a process of diversification of the production model, while another number indicate its conservation and reproduction.

In particular, a faster recovery in employment and investment (from 2012 onwards) in the internationalized part of the economy could be seen as evidence of a trend toward diversification of the production model. However, these are annulled, at least in part, by a faster recovery in production, productivity and exports to the domestic segment. In the field of technology, limited increases in investment and productivity and lower reductions in production and employment in the highly skilled sectors are not sufficient to show a trend toward diversification, mainly due to the limited size of these sectors. The absence of a trend toward diversification can also be seen in the light of the strong reductions in production, employment, and investment in the medium-to-high technology specialization sectors, with any positive developments in the medium-to-low technology specialization sectors indicating more the reproduction of the existing model rather than its diversification. In the field of skills intensity, increasing the high-skills intensity, particularly at the expense of those with low skills, is, first and foremost, a positive development and a condition for diversification of the production model. However, this is limited by the finding that this is mainly concentrated on the domestic part of the economy, with sectors using high skills only showing positive developments in the field of employment and negative in the fields of production[2] and productivity.

10.3 The Distinction Between the Domestic and the Competitive and Internationalized Parts of the Greek Economy

The distinction of the Greek economy in a domestic and international part is usually made at the level of single-digit sectors. This is due to both the availability of statistical data and to methodological issues.[3] Such an approach, however, incorporates a significant degree of generalization as it is not mandatory for all sectors of industry to be integrated into the internationalized part of the economy or necessarily for all service sectors (except hotels—restaurants and transport—storage) to be integrated into the domestic market. The distinction between the two segments based on the breakdown (two-digit classification code) of sectors of the economy is actually closer to reality. In order to classify and integrate the breakdown into one of these sections, three criteria are used: (a) the value of their exports between 2008 and 2016 (average annual value); (b) the rate of change over the same period; and (c) the relationship between exports and gross value added.[4] On the basis of these criteria, the classification of Table 10.1 of the Appendix was obtained.

A number of issues relating to classification should be clarified. First of all, exports, which are the basic criterion of the classification, do not

Table 10.1 Changes in GVA, employment, productivity and investment in the industries in terms of their technological specialization 2008–2017

Technological specialization	*2008*	*2017*	*Change*	*% change*
Gross Value Added				
High	871	930	59	6.8
Medium-High	2729	1984	−745	−27.3
Medium-Low	12,751	8380	−4371	−34.3
Low	15,790	7273	−8517	−53.9
Agricultural products & raw materials	7610	8879	1269	16.7
Total	**39,751**	**27,446**	**−12,305**	**−31.0**
Employment				
High	22,132	20,389	−1746	−7.9
Medium-High	57,947	31,551	−26,399	−45.6
Medium-Low	178,561	123,053	−55,507	−31.1
Low	352,762	242,557	−110,215	−31.2
Agricultural products & raw materials	533,519	483,606	−49,913	−9.3
Total	**1,144,920**	**901,156**	**−243,764**	**−21.3**
Productivity				
High	39,345	47,414	8069	20.5
Medium-High	47,097	65,577	18,480	39.2
Medium-Low	71,410	70,905	−505	−0.7
Low	44,760	28,968	−15,792	−35.3
Agricultural products & raw materials	14,264	18,907	4643	32.5
Total	**65,016**	**65,484**	**468**	**0.7**
Investments				
High	242	204	−38	−15.9
Medium-High	371	319	−52	−14.0
Medium-Low	2221	2087	−135	−6.1
Low	1443	843	−600	−41.6
Agricultural products & raw materials	2780	1515	−1265	−45.5
Total	**7058**	**4968**	**2090**	**−29.6**

Source Hellenic Statistical Authority (2019a, 2019b) and authors' creation

constitute an exclusive activity of the sectors of the internationalized segment. Sectors of the domestic segment also export.[5] However, these are limited in value, but also in relation to production in the sector and are usually reduced during the crisis, which gives an important indication of their inability to respond to a highly internationalized and competitive environment.

All sectors with average annual exports of more than €500 million are included in the internationalized segment. Most of them showed an increase in their exports[6] in the crisis while their exports are high in relation to their production. Of the sectors with an export value of between €100–500 million in the internationalized segment, the paper and paper product manufacturing industries are included as they showed a high rate of growth in their exports (51.5%), and their exports were particularly high on the basis of their production, the manufacture of motor vehicles, trailers and semi-trailers sector, which showed a decrease in its exports (34.6%), but which was particularly high in relation to its production, and the computer programming, consultancy and related activities and information services activities due to the very high rate of growth in its exports (104.6%—the second highest in all sectors of the economy) but also due to its increased exports in relation to its production. Finally, the only sector with a very limited export value (below €100 million) in the internationalized segment is the repair of computers and personal and household goods, as it showed a very high rate of growth in its exports (104.6%—the second highest in all sectors), which was also relatively high in relation to its production. This classification shows that the most sectors which are integrated into the internationalized part of the economy, in addition to the primary sector, belong to the manufacturing sectors, with a limited number of service sectors, which are certainly relevant to transports, storage, hotels and restaurants and two other of smaller range, in respect of their exports.

At the same time, only two manufacturing sectors (printing and reproduction of recorded media and repair and installation of machinery and equipment) are integrated into the domestic part of the Greek economy.

10.4 Developments in the Key Figures in the Domestic and International Part of the Greek Economy

The following are developments concerning gross value added, investments, employment, productivity, imports, exports, and the trade balance for the domestic and international part of the Greek economy.

10.4.1 *Gross Value Added and Investments*

At the time of the crisis, production and investment were higher domestically than in the internationalized segment, with production showing similar reduction rates in both segments but highly diversified investments (Fig. 10.1).

The Gross Value Added GVA in 2008–2017 was decreased by 24.4% domestically and by 22.3% in the internationalized segment, with the latter showing a low (2.3%) increase from 2013 onwards and the domestic segment stabilizing its production. It therefore appears that this limited recovery in the economy is due to the internationalized segment and, in particular, to its performance since 2013.[7] This is expected to be linked to

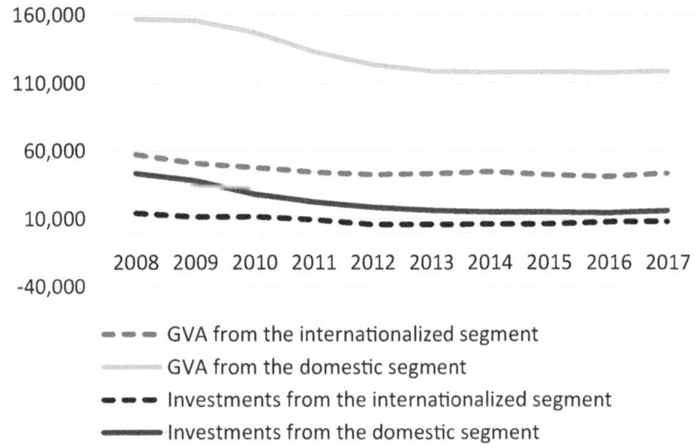

Fig. 10.1 Gross value added (GVA) and investments in the domestic and internationalised part of the Greek economy (*Source* Hellenic statistical authority [2019a] and authors' calculations and creation)

the fact that some of the leading industries (wood industry, rubber manufacture, other non-metallic mineral production, base metal production and metal manufacturing) are included in the internationalized segment, as well as the four (food and drink industry, wood industry, manufacture of rubber products and manufacture of electrical equipment) out of the five sectors with the highest direct vertical interconnections, and only the wood industry is among the five with the highest horizontal linkages.[8] At the same time, some of the leading sectors of production (film production, video production, etc., advertising and market research and other professional, scientific and technical activities) and four sectors (postal, financial, legal and accounting activities and architectural and engineering activities) are included in the domestic section of the five sectors with the highest horizontal linkages, with only the architectural and engineering sector being among the five with the highest direct vertical linkages.[9]

In the field of investment, their rapid decline in the period of crisis (57.6% between 2008 and 2017) does not allow them to act as a growth driver for the economy. Moreover, this reduction has been distributed differently between the two segments, with the internationalized segment showing a lower rate of reduction (42.0%) than domestic (63.1%), while showing a recovery of 37.2% since 2013, against a limited reduction (1.4%) in the domestic segment over the same period. This trend tends to equalize the investments of the two segments, despite the significant difference in the scale of their production, which also creates different requirements for the formation of fixed capital. Although this recovery cannot completely differentiate the picture, it is indicative of a trend toward diversification of the country's production model.

10.4.2 Employment and Productivity

Employment and productivity are significantly higher domestically than in the internationalized segment of the economy. However, developments in these two figures have been significantly differentiated.

Figure 10.2 shows employment and productivity rates in the domestic and internationalized part of the Greek economy for the period 2008 to 2017.

The decline in employment during the crisis (2008–2018) was lower in the internationalized segment (10.6%) than in the domestic segment (19.9%). In addition, the recovery in employment started earlier (2013) in the internationalized segment compared to the domestic segment (2014)

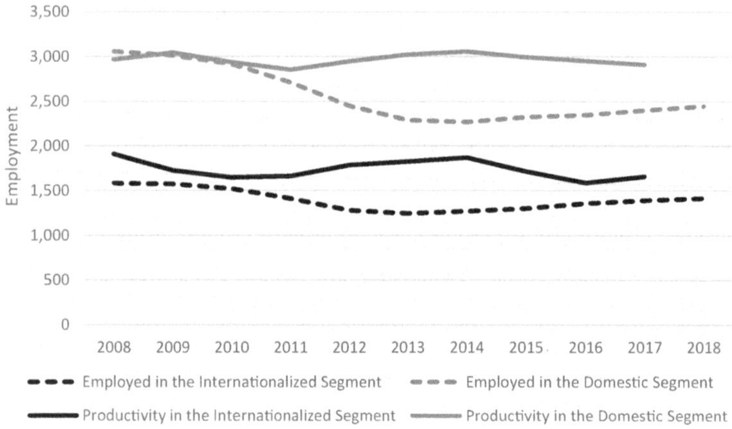

Fig. 10.2 Employment and productivity in the domestic and internationalised part of the Greek economy 2008–2017 (*Source* Hellenic statistical authority [2019b] and authors' calculations and creation)

and has expanded since then at a faster rate (13.5%), creating 168,798 new jobs, compared to the domestic segment, which showed a rate of employment growth (6.8%), creating 156,490 new jobs. However, as the majority of jobs created in the internationalized segment, mainly due to the hotel/restaurant sector, are low-skilled jobs, it appears, at least in part, to cancel one of the conditions for diversification of the production model that refers to the creation of highly skilled jobs and high added value (Efstratoglou, 2018).

In addition, the domestic section includes four (forestry, retail, architectural and engineering activities, and households as employers) of the five sectors with higher vertical and horizontal linkages to employment. Only sector 01, crop and animal production, was integrated into the internationalized part of the economy, contrary to the majority of the employment leaders in the[10] sectors of the economy (Markaki, 2018), which appears to be hampering faster employment growth in the internationalized segment.

In the field of productivity, developments have been reversed compared to employment (Fig. 10.2), with productivity in the internationalized segment showing, through more pronounced fluctuations, reductions of 13.2% (or 2.2 euros per hour of employment) and productivity in the domestic segment, through less pronounced fluctuations, reduced by 0.5% (or 0.5 euros per hour of employment). This kind of lower productivity of the internationalized segment and its further decline create potential obstacles to improving the competitiveness of the segment and its intended expansion, which is also a factor in the diversification of the production model.

10.4.3 Imports, Exports, and Trade Balance

Considering exports as the main criterion for classifying sectors in the domestic and internationalized segment of the economy, in all of their three dimensions, it is reasonable to expect that the performance of the internationalized segment related to them to be higher. However, exports should be presented separately and in relation to imports, in order to more clearly highlight the relevant procedures and opportunities or obstacles to the diversification of the country's production model.

Figure 10.3 shows the course of imports and exports and the trade balance in the domestic and international part of the economy for the period 2008 to 2017.

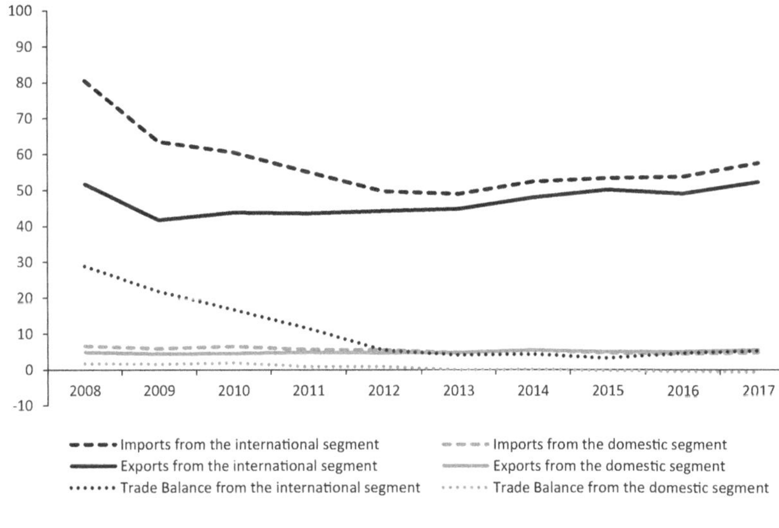

Fig. 10.3 Imports—exports and trade balance in the domestic and international part of the economy 2008–2017 (in thousands) (*Source* Hellenic statistical authority [2019a] and authors' calculations and creation)

Imports and exports of the internationalized segment are significantly higher than those of the domestic segment, throughout the period under analysis. At the beginning of the economic crisis (2008), imports in both segments were higher than exports, highlighting aspects of the country's trade deficit. During the crisis (2008–2017), in the internationalized segment imports decreased by €22.9 billion or 28.5% while exports increased by €524 million or 1.0%, improving their trade balance by 81.5%, which still remained negative until 2017. Imports reached their lowest point in 2013 (€49 billion) when their rise started again (€57.5 billion in 2017), while exports fell by €10.1 billion in 2009 when they started their slow recovery, with their intensity increasing from 2013 onwards (€52.2 billion in 2017). It is clear that the export nature of the internationalized segment is closely linked to imports, which in part cancels the process of diversification of the production model.[11] In the domestic segment imports were decreased by €1.8 billion or 27.2%, slightly below the rate of the international segment, while exports were increased by €700 million or 14.5% leading to a positive trade balance (€761 million in 2017). The internal devaluation policy imposed through the MoU in the country, with wage reductions as its main tool, did not make a significant contribution to exports, but rather to the contraction of imports, through lower domestic demand (Vagianos, Vettas, Megir, & Pissaridis, 2017).

10.5 The Technological Specialization of the Greek Economy Sectors

A second check on the diversification of the country's production model is carried out through the technological specialization of the manufacturing and wider industrial sectors. The classifications of the industry sectors based on their technological specialization are usually made in two ways. The first concerns the products produced by the sector. That is, whether the production of the products in the sector incorporates low, medium, or high technology (Yiannitsis, 2008). The second concerns direct industry classifications, mainly based on R&D expenditure,[12] which is usually a percentage of their total production (Hatzichronoglou, 1997; OECD, 2011). Under these classifications, the sectors fall into four categories of high, medium to high, medium to low and low technological specialization, while a separate category of low technological specialization is formed for agricultural products and raw materials.[13] Both of these modes of classification are of a relative nature. The first highlights issues such as the coexistence, within a sector, of different businesses and products that internalize different levels of technology. The second, despite its broad acceptance, is partially disputed, leading to different classifications, using different uses of the R&D criterion. On the basis of this classification, the primary and secondary sectors of the economy are presented in Table 10.2 of the Appendix.

10.5.1 Production, Employment, Productivity, Investment, and Technological Specialization of the Sectors

In the period of crisis, the process of restructuring manufacturing and the wider industrial sector has continued, by maintaining the leading profile of the food and drink industry, reducing the participation of traditional sectors such as textiles, clothing, leather and furniture, and strengthening capital industries, for intermediate and final goods such as machinery and equipment, base metals, repair and installation of machinery, pharmaceutical and chemical products (Koutroulis, Athanasiou, Kanellopoulos, Cotsi, & Cholezas, 2018). In the midst of this process, the country's wider industrial sector has seen a significant decline in production (19.1%), employment (22.4%) and investment (21.7%), improving only its productivity by 23.7% (Table 10.1).

These developments have been divided differently between the categories of industries in terms of their technological specialization. High-technology specialization sectors, particularly limited in size, have slightly increased their production, reduced their employment, significantly increased their productivity, while reducing their investments. The medium-high technology specialization sectors have significantly reduced their production, lost around half of their employment, which has led to productivity gains, while reducing their investments. The medium-low technology specialization sectors have seen a sharp decline in output and employment, reducing their productivity marginally and to a limited extent their investments. The low-technology specialization sectors, the most vulnerable to the effects of the crisis, have reduced their production, and have significantly reduced their employment, productivity and investments. Finally, the agricultural and raw material sectors have increased their production, decreased (12.0%) their employment, significantly improving their productivity, in an environment of reduced investments (41.9%).[14]

The extremely limited presence of high and medium-tech specialization sectors and the negative developments in most of their figures give significant indications of the absence of a strong trend toward diversification of the country's production model. Increases in production in the high-tech specialization and agricultural product sectors and improvements in their productivity (together with those of medium-high technology specialization) are not sufficient to show a strong trend toward model diversification. In addition, the long-standing strong reductions in investment up to 2013[15] in all sectors further reinforce the above findings.

10.5.2 Imports, Exports, and Technological Specialization of the Sectors

Industry in the period 2008-2017, despite a significant drop in production, increased its exports in an attempt to find a way out of the economic crisis. Overall, exports increased by 32.4% to €29.6 billion in 2017. Export increases were shown by three of the four categories of sectors, with medium-high technology specialization being the only category with a decline in exports, which in 2017 were reduced to €3.3 billion, accounting for 11.2% of all industrial exports. The main volume of exports was from the medium-low technology specialization sectors, mainly due to the oil industry,[16] with a total increase of 70.7% to €15.8 billion in 2017, accounting for 53.3% of all industrial exports. High growth (54.4%) was also seen by the highly skilled industries, but with limited contribution as they reached €2.3 billion, accounting for 7.8% of total industrial exports. Lower growth rates (18.6%) was shown by low-tech specialization sectors, with exports at €7.8 billion, accounting for 26.4% of all industrial exports.

In the same period, imports into industry decreased by 27.8% (from €60.3 billion to €45.5 billion in 2017),[17] with reductions in all four categories of the sectors. The highest (45.3%) were medium-high-tech specialization sectors (from €23.5 billion to €11.0 billion), accounting for 27.8% of total industry imports, followed by low (24.8%), high (16.7%) technology sectors, with medium-low-technology specialization sectors showing the lowest rate of decrease in their imports (5.7%). This is mainly due to the oil industry, which has seen an increase in its imports. These different developments have led to a significant diversification of their trade balance (Fig. 10.4).

A trend toward an improvement in the trade balance has emerged in all sectors, mainly due to a decrease in imports. The medium-low technology specialization sectors have succeeded in turning their negative trade balance into a positive one, with a relatively limited reduction (5.7%) in their imports and a significant increase (70.7%) in their exports. The improvement in the balance in the medium-high technology specialization sectors, which remains negative, is due to a higher decrease in imports than exports, as they are the only group of sectors with a decrease in exports. A negative but improved balance also showed low-tech specialization sectors through a combination of a reduction (24.8%) in their imports and an increase (18.6%) in their exports. Finally, a better balance has also been achieved by the high-tech specialization sectors, through a combination of limitation and reduction (16.7%) in their imports and significant increase (54.4%) in exports.

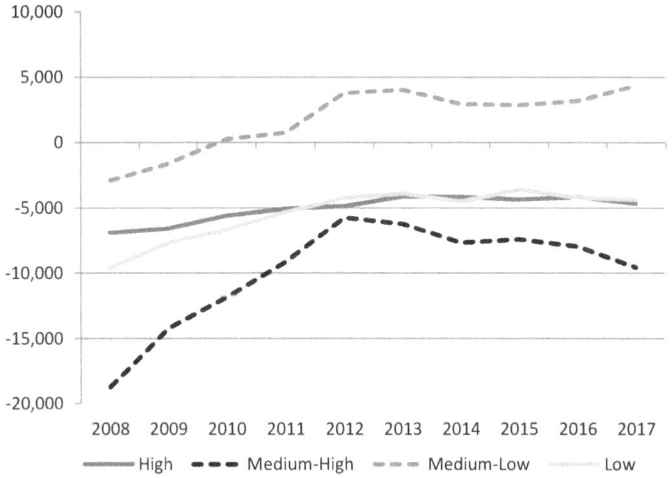

Fig. 10.4 Course of trade balance (exports minus imports) in the sectors on the basis of their technological specialization 2008–2017 (*Source* Hellenic statistical authority [2019a] and authors' calculation and creation)

If the trend toward an improvement in the trade balance of the sectors in all categories does not prove to be a one-off event, which is unlikely in view of the significant dependence of many industrial sectors on imports, its further improvement through a reduction in imports and an expansion of exports, will be an important step in the process of diversifying the country's production model and overcoming the economic crisis.

10.6 Skills Intensity in the Sectors of Greek Economy

The intensity of skills is a particularly important factor not only in the process of diversifying the production model but also in facilitating and adopting the technological changes associated with the 4th Industrial Revolution. Rapid technological change is expected to diversify the skills needed to carry out economic activities rapidly,[18] so that the capacity to adapt human skills to the specific requirements of the productive system is a particularly critical factor.

Throughout the economy, skills intensity[19] is steadily improving during the crisis period (Fig. 10.5), with high skills increasing by 16.9%, improving their participation in total employment from 24.1% in 2008 to

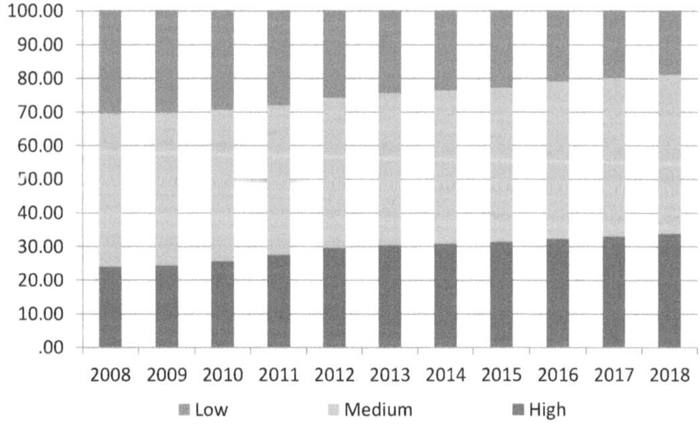

Fig. 10.5 Evolution of high, medium and low skill intensity in the Greek economy in 2008–2018 (*Source* Hellenic statistical authority [2019b] and authors' calculations and creation)

33.8% in 2018, mainly at the expense of low skills, which were decreased by 48.0%, reducing their participation from 30.4% to 18.9% in the years concerned, and medium skills, which were decreased by 13.8%, but at a rate lower than that of total employment (16.8%), slightly improving their participation from 45.6% in 2008 to 47.3% in 2018. However, it should be pointed out that this way of looking at developments in terms of skill intensity does not answer the question of whether these developments are due to (and highlight) the real needs of the productive system in terms of skills. They do not respond to whether existing jobs require these skill levels or their structure is due to oversupply leading to the use of high skills in jobs requiring medium or low skills. In other words, whether the vertical mismatch of skills occurs and prevails.[20] In addition, the positive aspects of the increase in high skills are limited if they are seen in the light of the distinction of the economy between the domestic and internationalized segments, as most of them are concentrated in the first (Efstratoglou, 2018).

At sectoral level, sectors using high skills[21] (only service sectors with just two industrial sectors among them—the oil and gas industry, and the pharmaceutical industry) experienced at the time of the crisis a relatively limited 7.0% reduction in employment with 62,362 job losses compared to the medium skills sectors, which experienced a 13.1% reduction and 263,530 job losses and the low-skilled sectors, with a 29.9% reduction and 519,697 job losses. In terms of output, between 2008 and 2016, high skill-intensive sectors lost 33.3% (€14.0 billion), medium skill-intensive sectors significantly less (in terms of percentage), by 14.3% (€17.1 billion), with low skill-intensive industries showed the highest losses both in terms of percentage (35.2%) and in absolute terms (€18.2 billion). The significant reductions in output in the high skill intensive sectors are partly due to the high presence of self-employed in them, whose activities have been significantly reduced. In terms of productivity, the highest losses by 28.3% were experienced by the highly skilled sectors (from €47,214 per person employed per year in 2008 to €33,865 in 2017), as a result of the combination of the limited reduction in their employment with a high reduction in their output, while medium skill-intensive industries almost maintained their productivity (down by 1.3%, from €59,780 to €59,012 per year over the relevant period) and low skill-intensive sectors, which also have the lowest productivity, registered losses of 7.7% (from €29,766 to €27,486 for the years concerned).

10.7 The Structural Effects of Covid-19 on the Greek Economy

In addition to the impact on the core macroeconomic figures (see Sect. 9.12), the effects of Covid-19 are also significant in specific sectors of activity of the economy.

Indeed, in an economy like the Greek one, where the production model does not offer risk diversification as the most important part of economic activity is generated by specific sectors (tourism, shipping) the risk for the Greek economy is high.

The sector with perhaps the greatest problems due to the presence of the pandemic in Greece is tourism. Greece has one of the highest dependence on tourism worldwide, as according to the OECD annual report released on 4 March 2020 (OECD, 2020), Greece is the 6th most dependent economy in terms of contribution to GDP and the 4th most dependent economy in terms of contribution to employment between the 35 Member States monitored for this sector by the Organization.

On the basis of 2018 figures, tourism contributed directly to the generation of 11.7% of Greece's GDP, while overall (directly and indirectly) tourism contributed between 25.7% (EUR 47.4 billion) and 30.9% (EUR 57.1 billion) to the GDP (INSETE, 2019).

In fact, the economy of three island regions is highly dependent on tourism, since the sector's contribution to the regional GDP is 47.2% in Crete, 71.2% in the Ionian Islands and 97.1% in the South Aegean. These regions have one of the highest GDP per capita in the Greek economy.

This very high dependence of the Greek economy on the tourism sector makes the Greek economy particularly vulnerable to any adverse situation which may affect tourism activity.

Such a situation is undoubtedly connected to the emergence of the coronavirus pandemic. One of the most important economic effects of the emergence of Covid-19 in the Greek economy is the fact that international travel receipts for the Greek economy are expected to be decreased as a result of travellers' fear, but also of the strict policies implemented by the various countries to prevent the virus from spreading.

The following shows what the effect of a EUR 1 billion reduction in tourist revenue on the GDP of the Greek economy would be. Using the Global Economic Model offered by Oxford Economics (2020), it appears that every 1 billion euros of loss of international travel revenue causes:

- A reduction in the GDP of the economy by around EUR 0.784 billion—a 0.39% reduction.
- A reduction in employment in the economy by about 5851 employees—a 0.15% reduction.
- A reduction in the balance of goods and services by around EUR 0.550 billion.

Indeed, it is not only the tourism sector that it is expected to have significant effects from the emergence of the Covid-19 pandemic in the Greek economy. A number of other sectors are expected to face a significant reduction in their added value to the economy as a result of lockdown of the Greek economy and the international and domestic uncertainty associated with the existence of the pandemic.

Figure 10.6 shows the estimate of the annual change in the real gross value added per industry of the Greek economy in 2020 compared to 2019, before and after the onset of the pandemic in Greece.

Note: (1) The case "Before Covid-19" presents estimates for the change in gross value added by sector from 2019 to 2020 based on the estimates of the Oxford Economics Global Economic Model in January 2020. The "After Covid-19" case presents estimates of the change in gross value added by sector from 2019 to 2020 based on estimates of April 2020 of Oxford Economics Global Economic Model. A detailed presentation of these estimates is set out in Chapters 11 and 12, where the April 2020 estimates are presented as the Normal scenario.

(2) Some of the sectors presented are sub-sets of others.

The biggest reduction in value added is expected for the Hotels and catering sector as before the crisis it was expected that in 2020 the added value of the sector would increase by 4.5%; after the crisis, it is ultimately expected to decrease by 16.6%. A significant reduction in value added is expected for the arts, entertainment, and recreation sector as, before the crisis, for 2020, the value added of the sector was expected to increase by 2.7%. After the pandemic, it is expected to eventually decrease by 16.1%. Significant negative (and also with a change from positive to negative) new changes in added values are expected for sectors such as trade, other services, transport and communication, manufacturing, and construction.

On the other hand, there are sectors which are presented as the winners of the crisis. This is the health sector, the extraction, the public administration, and the public services.

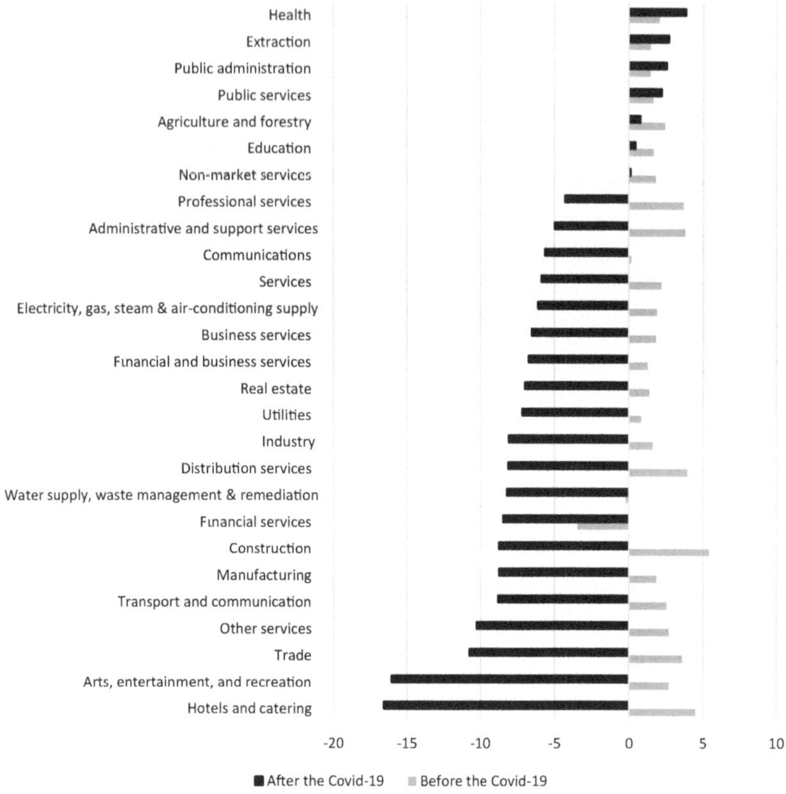

Fig. 10.6 Annual percentage change in real gross value added by sector in 2020 (%) (*Source* Oxford economics [2020] and authors' calculations and creation)

From the above, the need for a change in the production prototype arises. Production should be broken down into more economic sectors so that possible external shocks—such as the 2008 debt crisis or the Covid-19 pandemic—will be sources that will create lower imbalance for the economic activity. In order to change the production prototype, a structural reform program has to be implemented (see Chapters 11 and 12) which will focus simultaneously on the areas of sustainable development, sustainable governance, inclusivity, social behaviors that promote growth and growth and dynamic development and growth (see Petrakis & Kostis 2020).

Appendix: Classification of Sectors

See Tables 10.2 and 10.3.

Table 10.2 Classification of sectors in the domestic and internationalized segment of the Greek economy

Domestic segment	*Internationalised segment*
02 Forestry, logging	01 Crop and animal production, hunting
18 Printing & reproduction of recorded media	03 Fishing, aquacultures
33. Repair and installation of machinery and equipment	05–09 Mining and quarrying
35 Electricity, gas, steam, and air conditioning supply	10–12 Food, beverage, and tobacco industry
36 Water collection, treatment and supply	13–15 Manufacture of textiles, clothing, leather, and leather clothes
37–39 Sewerage, Waste collection, Remediation activities and other waste management services	16 Wood industry, wood, and cork products
41–43 Construction	17 Manufacture of paper and paper products
45 Wholesale and retail trade and repair of motor vehicles and motorcycles	19 Manufacture of coke and refined petroleum products
46 Wholesale trade, except of motor vehicles and motorcycles	20 Manufacture of chemicals and chemical products
47 Retail trade, except of motor vehicles and motorcycles	21 Manufacture of basic pharmaceutical products & pharmaceutical preparations
53 Postal and courier activities	22 Manufacture of rubber and plastics
58 Publishing activities	23 Manufacture of other non-metallic mineral products
59–60 Motion picture, video and television programme production, sound recording and music publishing activities, Programming and broadcasting activities	24 Manufacture of basic metals
61 Telecommunications	25 Manufacture of metal products, except machinery, and equipment
64 Financial service activities, except insurance. and pension funding	26 Manufacture of computers, electronics & optical products
65 Insurance, reinsurance and pension funds, except compulsory social security	27 Manufacture of electrical equipment
66 Other financial activities	28 Manufacture of machinery and equipment
68 Real estate activities	29 Manufacture of motor vehicles, trailers, and semi-trailers
69–70 Legal & accounting activities—activities of head offices, etc.	30 Manufacture of other transport equipment
71 Architectural and engineering activities; technical testing, and analysis	31–32 Manufacture of furniture & construction industries
72 Scientific research & development	49 Land transports and transports via pipelines
73 Advertising & market research	50 Water transports
74–75 Other professional, scientific, and technical activities	51 Air Transport

(continued)

Table 10.2 (continued)

Domestic segment	*Internationalised segment*
77 Rental & leasing activities *78 Employment activities* 79 Travel agency and tour operator activities *80–82 Other administrative & support activities* *84 Public administration, defence, compulsory social security* 85 Education 86 Medical and dental practice activities *87–88 Residential care activities & social care without accommodation* 90–92 Creative & cultural activities, such as arts, entertainment, libraries, archives, museums, gambling & betting 93 Sports activities and amusement and recreation activities orts activities, recreation, entertainment *94 Activities of membership organisations* *96 Other personal service activities* *97–98 Activities of households as employers*	52 Warehousing and support activities for transportation 55–56 Accommodation & Food and beverage service activities 62–63 Information technology and Information service activities 95 Repair of computers and personal and household goods

Source Authors' creation

Table 10.3 Classification of primary and secondary sectors for their technological specialization

Technological expertise	*Sectors of economic activity*
Agricultural products & raw materials	01 Agriculture—livestock farming 02 Forestry—logging 03 Fishing and aquaculture 05–09 Mining—quarrying
High	21 Manufacture of pharmaceutical products 26 Manufacture of computers electronic and optical products
Medium-high	20 Manufacture of chemicals and chemical products 27 Manufacture of electrical equipment 28 Manufacture of machinery and equipment 29 Manufacture of motor vehicles 30 Manufacture of other transport equipment

(continued)

Table 10.3 (continued)

Technological expertise	*Sectors of economic activity*
Medium-low	19 Manufacture of refined petroleum products 22 Manufacture of rubber and plastic products 23 Manufacture of other non-metallic products 24 Manufacture of basic metals 25 Manufacture of fabricated metal products, except machinery and equipment 33 Repair and installation of machinery & equipment 35 Electricity, gas, steam and air conditioning supply
Low	10–12 Food & beverage industry 13–15 Textiles, leather clothes 16 Wood Industry 17 Manufacture of paper and paper products 18 Printing 32 Manufacture of furniture 36 Water collection, treatment and supply 37–39 Sewerage, Waste collection, Remediation activities, and other waste management services

Source Hatzichronoglou (1997) and OECD (2011) and authors' creation

Notes

1. Employment data relate to the period 2008–2018.
2. It is clear that the presence of high skills in these sectors alone cannot create conditions for limiting the reduction of production.
3. This approach includes the primary sector, mining, quarrying, manufacturing, hotels, restaurants, and transport—storage in the internationalized and competitive segment, and all other sectors fall in the domestic and non-competitive segment.
4. This criterion does not estimate the share of production exported, as in many cases the value of exports includes the value of imports, which is not recorded in the gross value added. It provides an estimate of the value of the two figures.
5. Out of a total of 64 sectors (two-digit classification) 13 sectors do not export and are therefore included in the domestic section (in italics in the table).

6. Out of the 21 sectors with average annual exports of over €500 million, 14 increased their exports, while 7 reduced them.
7. The rate of decrease in production between 2008 and 2013 was the same (24.4%) in both segments.
8. The direct vertical linkages of a sector reflect the demand for products and services that are developing in the economy by changing demand in the sector by one unit. These are sectors which generate high demand for products and services as a result of their expansion. Overall horizontal linkages reflect the overall effect on the economy caused by an increase in the primary inputs of an industry by one unit. The sectors with high horizontal linkages are sectors with a high supply of their products and services to other sectors of the economy. Finally, key sectors or leading sectors of the economy are the most connected and therefore most important as they contribute to a greater extent to strengthening the internal dynamics of the production system (Markaki, 2018).
9. The direct vertical linkages of a sector reflect the demand for products and services that are developing in the economy by changing demand in the sector by one unit. These are sectors which generate high demand for products and services as a result of their expansion. Overall horizontal linkages reflect the overall effect on the economy caused by an increase in the primary inputs of an industry by one unit. The sectors with high horizontal linkages are sectors with a high supply of their products and services to other sectors of the economy. Finally, the key sectors or leading sectors of the economy are the most connected and therefore most important as they contribute more to strengthening the internal dynamics of the production system (Markaki, 2018; Petrakis, 2020; Petrakis & Kostis, 2020).
10. The vertical employment multiplier of an industry estimates the total number of employees created in the economy through a unit increase in the final demand of the sector. In other words, it estimates the contribution made by sectoral links to employment growth and thus the internal dynamics of the productive system for job creation. The horizontal employment multiplier estimates the total number of employees created in the economy through a unit increase in the sector's primary inputs. Finally, key sectors or employment leaders are considered to be those with high vertical and horizontal employment multipliers (Markaki, 2018).
11. For an overview of the role of exports to the Greek economy through a sectoral approach, see, inter alia, Agnantopoulos and Efstratoglou (2015).
12. For the service sectors, the criterion of research and technology is not appropriate. Indicators such as skill intensity, which are detected through the educational level of employees and the professional structure of the

sectors (i.e., the type of professional activity required by the production of the sector) are usually used in this case.

13. The absence of appropriate statistical data for our country, which would be relevant to the level of research and technology expenditure for each sector, makes the adoption of the OECD and Eurostat classifications mandatory.
14. In terms of their production, the sectors showed a hierarchical provision, whereby the higher the technological specialization the lower the output reduction and the lower the technological specialization the higher the production losses.
15. However, the recovery of investment in the wider industrial sector by 25,4% since 2013 is stronger in the medium-high (82.2%) and high (46.4%) sectors than in the low (32.7%) and medium-low (25.4%) technology specialization sectors.
16. Oil exports amounted to €10.7 billion in 2017, accounting for 36.2% of all industrial exports.
17. The country's total imports fell from €87 billion in 2008 to €62.4 billion in 2017, with the industry, without the mines, accounting for 69.5% of them.
18. For example, see the World Economic Forum (2016) and the literature presented there.
19. The intensity of skills is assessed through the educational level of employees, recommending an indirect assessment, which fails to identify their content and actual dimensions. In recent work (Grundke, Jamet, Kalamova, Keslair, & Squicciarini, 2017), it was attempted, using data on adult research (PIACC), to build six indicators based on the tasks of works. These indicators relate to ICT skills, learning potential and creative problem-solving, management and communication, self-organization, calculations and marketing, and scientific, technological, engineering and mathematical skills. Skills are perceived as a continuous one, with some of them mainly cognitive, others are more personality-related, while others combine both. It is estimated that knowledge skills such as literacy, numeracy and problem-solving are more general in nature, outside and beyond activities and tasks, closely linked to productivity and the possibility of integration into international production chains. However, other, more closely linked to economic activities and occupations, such as ICT, management and communication skills and learning capacity, contribute to productivity growth and integration into international production chains.
20. The high skills mismatch in our country is examined in Cedefop's works (2014) and (2018), which state that most of this mismatch is due to the fact that people with high educational qualifications occupy jobs requiring lower education qualifications.

21. The percentage of tertiary graduates employed in each sector was used as a criterion for classifying sectors of high, medium and low skill intensity levels. The year of 2008 served as the base year and high intensity sectors were considered to be those with more than 40.0% graduates (upper quartiles of the relevant classification), while of medium intensity sectors were those within 40.0—10.0% (intermediate quartiles) and of low intensity were those with less than 10.0% (lower quartile).

References

Agnantopoulos, A., & Efstratoglou, A. (2015). *The Role of Exports in the Greek Economy: A Sectoral Approach.* (Unpublished study) Hellenic Labour Institute of the General Confederation of Greek Workers.

Cedefop. (2014). *European Skills and Job Survey.* Luxembourg: Publications Office of the European Union.

Cedefop. (2018). *Insights into Skill Shows and Skills Mismatch: Learning from Cedefop's European Skills and Job Survey.* Luxembourg: Publications Office of the European Union.

Efstratoglou, A. (2018). *Recent Developments in Employment and the Production Model of the Greek Economy.* Hellenic Labour Institute of the General Confederation of Greek Workers.

Grundke, R., Jamet, S., Kalamova, M., Keslair, F., & Squicciarini, M. (2017). *Skills and Global Value Chains* (OECD Science, Technology and Industry Working Papers 2017/05).

Hatzichronoglou, T. (1997). *Revision of the High-Technology Sector and Product Classification* (OECD Science, Technology and Industry Working Papers 1997/2).

Hellenic Statistical Authority. (2019a). *National Accounts.*

Hellenic Statistical Authority. (2019b). *Labor Force Survey.*

INSETE. (2019). The Contribution of Tourism in Greek Economy. September (in Greek).

Koutroulis, A., Athanasiou, E., Kanellopoulos, N., Cotsi, A., & Cholezas, I. (2018). The Greek Economy and Employment. Annual Report 2018. *Greek Manufacturing: Policy Developments, Prospects and Challenges.* Athens: Centre of Planning and Economic Research.

Markaki, M. (2018). *Changes in the Social Structure of the Country as a Result of Technological Changes in the Sectors of Economic Activity, Professional Specialties and Skills: Inflow—Outflow Analysis for 2000–2016.* National Institute of Labour and Human Resources.

OECD. (2011). *ISIC REV.3. Technology Intensity Definition.* Classification of Manufacturing Industries into Categories Based on R&D Intensities Directorate for Science, Technology and Industry.

OECD. (2020). *Tourism Trends & Policies 2020*. Paris: OECD Publishing. Retrieved from: https://doi.org/10.1787/6b47b985-en.

Oxford Economics. (2020). Global Economic Model.

Petrakis, P. E. (2020). *Theoretical Approaches to Economic Growth and Development. An Interdisciplinary Perspective*. Palgrave Macmillan. ISBN 978-3-030-50067-2.

Petrakis, P. E., & Kostis, P. C. (2020). *Policies for a Stronger Greek Economy Actions for the Next Decade*. Palgrave Macmillan. ISBN 978-3-030-47078-4.

Vagianos, D., Vettas, N., Megir, K., & Pissaridis, Chr. (2017). *Beyond Austerity: For a Dynamic in the Greek Economy*. Crete: University Publications of Crete.

Yiannitsis, T. (Ed.). (2008). *In Search of the Greek Development Model: Mediterranean Studies Foundation*. Greece: Papazisis Publications.

World Economic Forum. (2016). *The Future of Jobs: Employment, Skills and Workforce Strategy for the Fourth Industrial Revolution* (Global Challenge Insight Report).

PART III

The Long-Term Evolution of the Greek Economy

CHAPTER 11

The Requirements for a Pro-growth Long-Term View

11.1 Introduction

The Greek economy in recent years has made a brave effort to bring about structural reforms, in line with the requirements of the fiscal adjustment programs implemented since 2010 in order Greek economy to recover from the effects of the recent global financial crisis. Those reforms, many of which are still on-going, are expected to a contribute in the economic activity of Greece in the future.

Of course, the crisis of the Covid-19 pandemic poses significant challenges to the Greek economy as it is expected to have significant effects on almost all sectors of economic activity. Even if these effects are short-term (recovery is expected in 2021) they are expected to change the reform strategy by creating new needs to solve new problems that emerged on the occasion of the pandemic, while at the same time there are obstacles to the effectiveness of the reforms already carried out and the achievement of goals.

The purpose of this chapter is to set the background to capture the forecasts concerning the Greek economy in the period from 2020 to 2030 and which are reflected in the next chapter (Chapter 12). For this purpose, particular emphasis is placed on the role of Total Factor Productivity (TFP), which is considered a particularly critical size for the Greek economy and is directly related to the implementation of structural reforms, but also to the strengthening of the Greek economy in

P. E. Petrakis and P. C. Kostis, *The Evolution of the Greek Economy*,
The Political Economy of Greek Growth up to 2030,
https://doi.org/10.1007/978-3-030-47210-8_11

the year 2020 through an increase in government spending to stimulate the economy in the face of the economic crisis brought by the Covid-19 pandemic. In this way, two different scenarios are presented; the Normal Scenario (business as usual) and the Optimal Pro-Growth Scenario for the Greek economy for the period from 2020 to 2030. It should be noted that the analysis presented could be regarded as a strategic foresight–a way to present multiple scenarios of possible futures to test the arsenal for strategic adaptation, while taking into using trend analysis—what to expect if the present continues, and intelligence analysis which provides adversary courses of action based on established patterns of behavior (Sotiriadis & Grove, 2020). In this way, the analysis gives the opportunity to create a virtual training ground for policy-makers and the Greek government. However, as Sotiriadis and Grove (2020) point out, in times of economic shocks, such as during a pandemic or a financial crisis, scenarios can appear imprudent. It is the capacity to develop and maintain intellectual capital for new thinking that enables research to take the high ground when a security environment is turned upside down.

The structure of the chapter is as follows: initially, Sect. 11.2 presents the need for institutional and cultural changes in order for an economy to transform an idiosyncratic, interrelated with stagnated characteristics, model into an optimal pro-growth model, with direct reference to the Greek economy. Section 11.3 presents the relationship between TFP and structural reforms in the case of the Greek economy until 2019, while Sect. 11.4 presents the Normal Scenario (business as usual) for the Greek economy for the period from 2020 to 2030. Then (Sect. 11.5) the relationship between the TFP and the reforms and the effect of the reforms on the country's GDP is described, and finally in Sect. 11.6 the Optimal Pro-Growth Scenario for the Greek economy for the period from 2020 to 2030 is presented.

11.2 The Endogenous Transformation from Idiosyncratic Stagnated to Optimal Pro-growth Model Through Institutional and Cultural Changes

The standard way to implement a pro-growth model in the long-term is to follow the Solowian or Schumpeterian growth requirements with an enlarged role of technology augmented labor and capital deepening. But what about the residual factors?

As presented in Chapter 4, when at a society predominates an idiosyncratic anti-growth model in its cultural and institutional background, then stagnated forces may prevailing. In contrast, an optimal pro-growth model is emerging when the prevail conditions that favor the long-term orientation, the investment in new technologies, and the uncertainty handling under an institutional nexus that secures the incentives and the actions of the economic agents.

In order for a transformation from an idiosyncratic stagnated model to an optimal pro-growth model to occur, this transformation must be combined with the differentiation of a series of parameters that are linked to the prevailing institutions and the cultural background.

Hence, the main question is whether a stagnated growth model can be transformed to an endogenous growth model. In other words: can an idiosyncratic stagnated growth model be transformed into a pro-growth model?

Searching for an answer we have to ask a policy oriented methodological question: Do we have to cure the sources of the generation of the SGM or we should impose policies which will directly change the existing institutions and the preferences of the society? However, this question is meaningless since no one can, in a definite manner, reverse the path-dependence evolution in order to cure the initial causes. In addition, this approach is in line with the Ng (1977) proposition of third-best policy solutions according to which if you can attend the first best conditions and since the second-order (Lipsey & Lancaster, 1956) create a risk to generate an uncertain framework of policy recommendation, then it is preferable to implement the first-order policies as much as you probably can. Therefore what we can simply do is to try to change the today's state of institutions, although we know that institutions change in the medium-term and in the long-term. But according to the coevolution principle (Kafka, Pantelis, & Petrakis, 2020; Petrakis, Kafka, Kostis, & Valsamis, 2021), the institutions should change simultaneously with the preferences status. However, we also know that preferences change with various speeds under specific circumstances as a medium to long-term process. But there are some arguments that preferences can be affected by external shocks, that they are under the influence of storming forming conditions. For that reason the initial question has a merit and it should be answered in the sense that we could form a large-scale transformation program of institutions and preferences to be applied in the medium to long-tern horizon. However, although there is a very clear idea of how—and in which direction—you can change institutions, there is no a clear proposal of how we could change preferences (during the process of changing institutions) and thus avoiding the institutions-preferences low growth trap (Petrakis, 2014). This is obviously a much more difficult task.

11.2.1 Institutional Change

While the contribution of institutions on economic development (Acemoglu & Robinson, 2012; Ostrom, 1990) is well defined, much less is known about institutional change which is limited to a theoretical level (see, for example Aoki, 2007; Greif & Laitin, 2004; Hodgson, 2004; Kingston & Caballero, 2009).

The debate about institutional change we can approach it through two points of view (Kingston & Caballero, 2009):

(a) the first category includes theories which see the institutional change as deliberate designed; and
(b) the second category refers to the case where the change can be spontaneous by following an evolutionary process.

For more information on institutional change see Kafka et al. (2020), Petrakis et al. (2021).

Institutional change is a long-lasting process that faces obstacles to any change, since in every institutional nexus there are winners and losers, so they are accompanied by the creation of opposition forces. Besides, the functioning of institutions acts in favor of the situation that exists and against the new situation that is expected to come. The main reason for changing institutions is none other than the effort of policy-makers to renew existing institutions so that they can meet pro-growth conditions.

The factors of institutional change can be classified into endogenous and exogenous determined. Exogenous factors include (Libecap, 1989):

(a) Shifts in relative prices,
(b) changes in technology of enforcing and defining property rights, and
(c) shifts in preferences and other political preferences.

Human capital, knowledge, learning, technology change may alter formal and informal rules. As Ayres (1944) points out "technological development forces change upon the institutional structure by changing the material setting in which it operates". While technology can lead to an institutional change, it alone is not a sufficient condition, since whether an exogenous shock will result to a change in an institution depends on the distribution of benefits among agents both under the existing structure and under the new structure expected to emerge.

Endogenous institutional change can be based on the Darwinian Theory. The endogenous change of institutions follows a Darwinian approach so that we can understand the process. In this context, institutional change follows a "path-dependence" process where the institutional framework at the time t is a function of both the conditions prevailing at the time t and the precedent institutions and conditions (Kingston & Caballero, 2009). Of course, it should be emphasized that as decisions are made by agents, if one sees the change of institutions as a process where participants (agents, policy-makers) have bound rationality can be led to the wrong conclusions about the changes they promote. Therefore despite the fact that the change in institutions is influenced by external factors, the overall process may follow an evolutionary pattern.

Greif and Laitin (2004) introduces the term "quasi-parameters" to describe factors which are exogenous in the short-run, but over time adopt endogenous character. Changes in these parameters have the effect of changing the range of potential equilibrium points, without this always implying that the economy is shifting to a better state. It is possible that the economy is moving away from an optimal condition.

The above factors are decisive in the development of institutions and the emergence of extractive institutions that lead to deviations from an optimal growth pattern. At the same time, however, the political power and in general the political actors influence, in turn, the distribution of the resources of the economy through the formation of the institutional background. The approach that institutional change is the result of supply and demand forces in the society (Alston, 1996) is typical. That is to say, the change of institutions is, in fact, the result of "negotiation" between the suppliers (e.g., Government) and demanders (e.g., pressure groups). On the contrary, other theories support the neutrality of political actors in determining the institutional framework. Despite the fact that politicians are under pressure from groups of the population to change the formal rules (Kantor, 1998), yet politicians, in turn, have their own motives that guide their actions, while they are also confronted by constitutional constraints.[1]

11.2.2 Cultural Changes

Cultural change should be regarded as a Darwinian evolutionary process where some cultural values prevail and others disappeart (Richerson & Boyd, 2005).

Economic growth is inextricably linked to the evolution of societies. What concerns us is whether cultural values change due to economic parameters. In general, cultural values could be regarded as stable in the long run as the parameters affecting them remain relatively unchanged (De Jong, 2009). The transformation of the prevailing cultural values is a long-lasting process that needs a great effort as it depends on a variety of factors (history legacy, geography, psychology).

The most significant sources of external influence on the formation of the cultural background are considered to be the available resources, the climate and in general the geographical characteristics (Diamond, 1999; Petrakis, 2014; Triandis, 2009). Factors that can lead to culture change may come from human psychology (as some ideas are more readily learned or remembered) or may be social and ecological (some ideas make people richer, live longer, or migrate more often, and the resulting selective processes generate culture change) (Richerson & Boyd, 2005).

Also, the changes observed in the cultural background after an external shock change are also significant. It is a fact of common observation that crisis tends to produce or accelerate cultural changes and in fact, if the changes are being accepted due to the crisis, they tend to persist. Changes of this type can cause high stress to individuals (Eschbach, Parker, & Stoeberl, 2001) by affecting their psychological adjustment to new conditions and can be—depending on the intensity of the change—a strong shock to the context of their cultural values that characterize them.

Finally, the concept of culture shock is also important. Oberg (1960) defined the term culture shock as the "anxiety that results from losing all of our familiar signs and symbols of social intercourse". Culture shock can occur due to the loss of familiar cues, the breakdown of interpersonal communications or an identity crisis (Weaver, 1994). As culture shock we could define a change that leads individuals and societies to face circumstances that are characterized by conditions different from their previous cultural context (Xia, 2009).

An individual entering in a society that is being characterized by a culture which is different from his own is an example of culture change (Kostis, Kafka, & Petrakis, 2018). For such a person, this change leads him not be able to understand the ideology and behavior of the members of the new society, thus he doesn't understand why these people behave the way they behave and how himself should behave (Xia, 2009). Under these conditions, the person will suffer—completely or partially—symptoms such as depression, anxiety. and feelings of helplessness (Mio, 1999). The more these symptoms increase, the more difficult it is to learn and adapt to the new cultural background. So the individual must adapt to the new cultural environment which is characterized by a different way of life, living conditions and business practices. However, this adjustment can only be long-term. If the individual fails to adequately adapt to his or her cultural background, this can lead to the alienation of the individual from the new society, which would lead to psychological confusion and emotional discomfort (Hess, 1994).

11.3 Total Factor Productivity and Reforms in the Greek Economy Until 2019

During the recent decades there have been notable increases in product market reforms in Greece, based mainly on the fact that competition, productivity and competitiveness should be strengthened. Recent models predict that long-term economic growth is mainly based on innovation, which in turn is strongly influenced by low market regulation (Aghion, Bloom, Blundell, Griffith, & Howitt, 2005; Alesina, Ardagna, Nicoletti, & Schiantarelli, 2005).

The key question is whether and to what extent these changes have been and are successful. While most academics agree that competitive policies increase productivity, what are the effects of lower regulation is still not widely agreed. In fact, there has been minimum effort to study whether the effects of market regulation differ between countries with different economic and institutional frameworks.

As for Greek economy, according to Malliaropoulos (2017) periods of high (low) potential growth coincide with periods of high (low) TFP growth. In addition, by examining the period from 1966 to 2015 Malliaropoulos (2017) concludes that there is a high correlation between TFP growth and capital accumulation, by 0.62. The rationale behind this relationship is that when potential growth is low, there is a large pool of unemployment which provides initial space to increase economy. However, at the same time, capital stock continues to decline due to the negative net investment. To get out of this situation, the economy needs structural reforms that will facilitate the increase in capital stock. Then the increase in capital stock combined with the fact that structural reforms are beginning to pay off, increasing TFP.

The Foundation of Economic and Industrial Research (IOBE, 2008), heaving conducted a sectoral and country analysis for the Greek economy for the period from 1970 to 2004, concludes that TFP was the main determinant of product growth (gross value added) for this period overall. However, it is noted that in contrast to the 1970s and 1980s, the TFP became negative in the 1990s and was not significantly stimulated by widespread use of information technologies, as was the case in most developed economies.

In a report conducted by the Centre of Planning and Economic Research (KEPE, 2019), Greece is being examined as a particularly interesting case study in an effort to explore the TFP growth impact of upstream regulation in all sectors of the Greek economy. As noted, although the Greek economy belongs to the group of developed economies, many of its institutional aspects are similar to those of middle-income economies, while productivity levels lag significantly behind those of the EU's leading economies.

KEPE (2019) focuses on the effect of anti-competitive regulations in the upstream areas of energy, transport, and communications whose output is used as an intermediate input in downstream industries. Upstream regulation may be harmful for the efficiency of sectors which use their services, as part of the expected efficiency gains may be captured by intermediate input providers (Bourles, Cette, Lopez, Mairesse, & Nicoletti, 2013). KEPE (2019) analyzes the TFP growth impact of entry barriers and public ownership in upstream sectors. The TFP growth impact of upstream regulation is estimated for the period 1996–2015. The empirical results illustrate that upstream regulation is not significantly associated with TFP growth of Greek industries. However, it exerts an indirect negative effect on TFP growth of less productive sectors. This indicates that the harmful effects of regulation are guaranteed in the laggard industries of the Greek economy. A strong and robust technological catch-up effect is estimated, which indicates that technological convergence plays a major role for TFP growth of Greek industries.

Finally, KEPE's (2019) analysis concludes that technology transfer could exert a beneficial impact on TFP growth of Greek sectors.

11.4 The Normal Scenario for the Greek Economy 2020–2030

But how do we expect the key figures in the Greek economy to evolve between 2020 and 2030 under normal circumstances? To answer this question we will use the Global Economic Model (GEM) model provided by Oxford Economics,[2] which is used in this book to describe the expected development in the Greek economy of the two scenarios for the period 2020–2030 that is the Normal Scenario under normal circumstances and the Optimal Scenario which is a desirable and recommended scenario. Thus, this model and its basic assumptions is firstly presented and then Normal Scenario and its relationship with the corresponding estimates of other international organizations is being presented.

11.4.1 Forecast Model

The GEM model is structured in a strict manner in order to provide consistent predictions and to proceed to effective scenario analysis. The forecasts of the model relate to the following years and are updated every month, unlike international organizations that provide forecasts, such as the IMF which renews its estimates for the next 5 years twice a year.

The GEM model is eclectic. In this sense it draws from a wide range of theory, as it is Keynesian at the short-term level and monetarist at the long-term level. Thus, increased demand is initially expected to lead to higher levels of production and employment, but this then leads into higher wages and prices. Given an inflation target, interest rates should then increase, reducing demand again. In the long run, production and employment are determined by supply-side factors. It is a structural model of general equilibrium.

Its main components are behavioral equations (which interconnect the behavior of the variables used), identities and policy rules (for example Taylor's rule[3]).

If we were to attempt an overview of the model we would say that, as its basic elements, includes consumption (function of real income, wealth and interest rates), investment, exports (which depend on global demand and labor costs), imports (which depend on final costs and competitiveness), Layard-Nickell[4] wage/price system, monetary policy (which is endogenous and the options given are related to Taylor's rule and exchange rate targets), exchange rates (as determined by uncovered interest rate parity[5] in the short-term and exchange rate equilibrium in the long term) and expectations (which may be adaptive or forward looking). However, the model also maintains a significant degree of interconnections between economies in terms of trade flows, competitiveness, trade prices, interest rates, exchange rates, commodity prices, and capital flows.

11.4.2 The Normal Scenario

Figure 11.1 presents the Normal Scenario's estimates of GDP growth in the Greek economy in contrast to the European Commission's (EC), International Monetary Fund (IMF) and Consensus Economics[6] estimates.

Normal Scenario is generally in line with the European Commission and IMF estimates for 2020 but is more optimistic than these estimates and less optimistic than Consensus Economics estimates about the depth of the Covid-19 pandemic crisis for 2020. The picture is reversed for 2021 as all estimates are expected the economy to recover and the lower

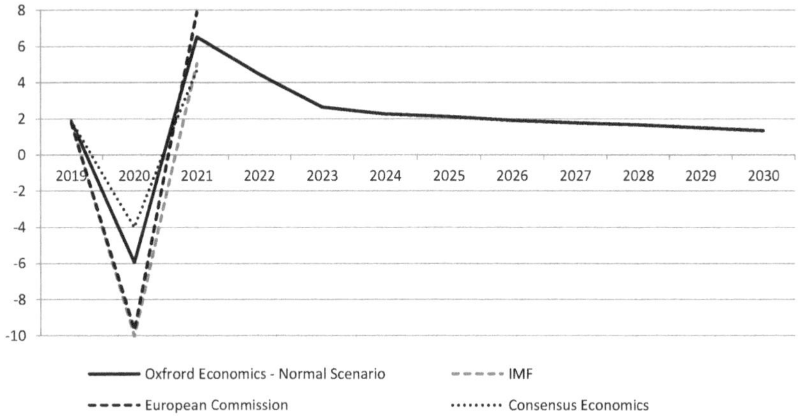

Fig. 11.1 Estimates for GDP growth rate (%) (*Sources* Consensus Economics [2020], European Commission [2020], IMF [2020], Oxford Economics [2020], and authors' creation)

the estimate for 2020, the more important this recovery is expected. After 2021 and until 2030, the growth rate of the Greek economy should be expected to be positive, although it is expected to decline over time. Oxford Economics' differentiation from the forecasts of other organizations is based on the fact that, in the long run, the importance of macroeconomic restructuring achieved during the Memorandum period and the importance of removing disruptive factors such as the balance sheet recession from which the Greek economy suffers in the medium term, increases. Normal Scenario will be the basis on which the Optimal Pro-Growth Scenario presented in the next part will be created.

Normal Scenario includes the evolution of TFP which since its inception (it is an endogenous variable of the Global Economic Model of Oxford Economics and therefore calculated through other variables of the model) does not incorporate the increased effects of structural changes that will affect the period. 2020–2030. These effects have two origins: the structural changes of the period 2010–2019 and the new structural changes of the period 2020–2030. That is why the change in TFP is essentially very small.

Essentially, the TFP is considered in the Global Economic Model, as follows: in advanced economies, where data availability permits, TFP depends on institutional quality, the R&D stock, relative energy prices, a time trend and a catch-up factor for economic growth. This is meant to make TFP partially endogenous, so that it does react within scenarios rather than being fully exogenous. In most advanced economies, Oxford Economics uses official estimates of potential GDP and things like the NAIRU (mostly from the OECD) and derive the TFP history, which is in line with Oxford Economics' equation and that data. In terms of the TFP forecasts, Oxford Economics generally assumes somewhat of a recovery from lower levels in recent years in advanced economies, but a rather moderate medium- to long-term trend. As with several key variables, Oxford Economics' forecasts can overwrite a purely model-driven output.

Based on the way TFP is calculated by Oxford Economics, for the Greek economy has prices ranging from its historic low of –7.04 in 1991 to –6.67 in 2030 in the Normal scenario (based on available data from 1980 to 2030). It is characteristic that this is a size that over time receives negative values and in which there are quite small changes over the years that, although small in number, highlight large changes in TFP.

Figure 11.2 shows the TFP growth for Greece, based on the Oxford Economics model.

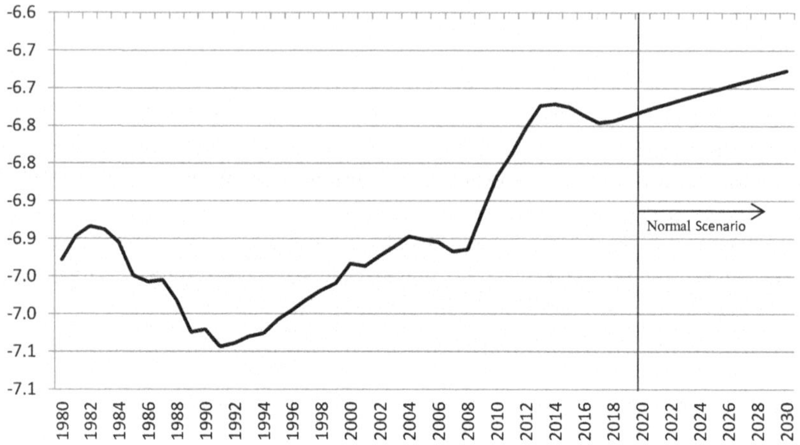

Fig. 11.2 TFP growth of Greek economy under Normal Scenario (*Source* Oxford Economics [2020] and authors' creation)

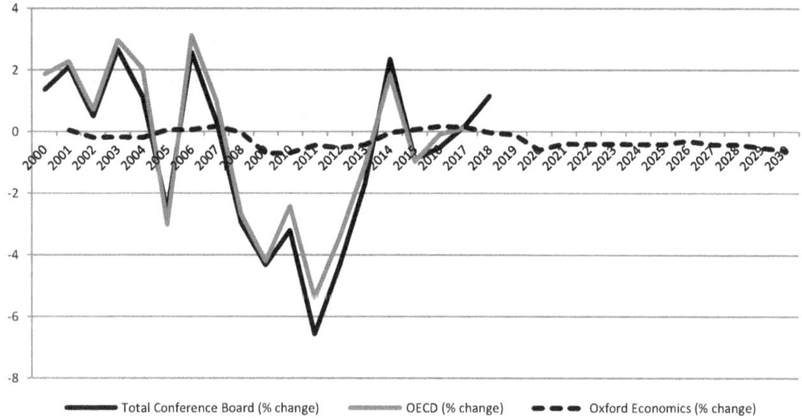

Fig. 11.3 Annual change of TFP (%) (*Source* OECD [2020], Oxford Economics [2020], The Conference Board [2020] and authors' calculations and creation)

Although the change in the Oxford Economics measure for the TFP is much smaller than the Total Conference Board and OECD measurements, the three figures show a similar trend, and the correlation between the Oxford Economics measure and that of the Total Conference Board is 0.62 and based on the OECD is 0.54 (Fig. 11.3).

11.5 Total Factor Productivity and Reforms: 2020–2030

The structural changes that took place during the period 2010–2014 in the Greek economy in combination with the structural changes that were included in the third adjustment program for the Greek economy had the effects presented in Table 11.1 on the GDP's growth rate for the Greek economy over a decade (OECD, 2016a). In the current and subsequent chapters, it is assumed that non-fiscal structural changes will continue in the period 2020–2023[7] to then pay off so as to make it possible to increase investment.

It is therefore noted that the total reforms in the Greek economy during the period 2010–2019, will have a total contribution to the GDP of the Greek economy of 13.4% over a decade. Of this change, 2.8% are expected to derive from an improvement in employment and 10.6% from an improvement in productivity due to these reforms. Also, in another distinction, it appears that product market reforms are expected to improve GDP by approximately 4.4%, labor market reforms by approximately 2.4%, tax structure reforms by approximately 0.8% and bankruptcy reforms by approximately 0.2%.

OECD estimates suggest that over the next decade, the reforms introduced since 2010 in combination with the reforms included in the third economic adjustment program will significantly boost the output of the economy, offsetting to a high degree the loss of potential production due to the crisis. Indeed, these estimates represent a threshold, in the sense that critical reforms such as reforms in the judiciary, bankruptcy regulations, and modernization of Public Administration have not been implemented. OECD's methodology also assumes that legislative reforms are implemented with the average quality of the OECD and do not take into account short-term interactions with aggregate demand or interactions derived from a combination of reforms.

Anderson, Barkbu, Lusinyan, and Muir (2014) show the effect of reforms on real GDP over the long run for the Eurozone as a whole.

Table 11.1 Effect of reforms on real GDP over a decade

Reform	*GDP*	*Via employment growth*	*Via productivity growth*
Reforms implemented 2010–2014			
Product Market Reforms	**3.4**		**3.4**
Product Market Reforms 2010–2013	*2.9*		*2.9*
Product Market Reforms 2013–2014	*0.5*		*0.5*
Labor Market Reforms	**0.9**	**0.6**	**0.3**
Employment Protection Legislation reform in 2010–2013	*0.3*		*0.3*
Pension reform	*0.6*	*0.6*	
Tax Structure Reforms	**1.3**		**1.3**
Total Implemented Reforms	**5.6**	**0.6**	**5.0**
Reforms implemented 2015–2019			
Product Market Reforms	**4.4**		
Network industries reform (electricity, gas, rail road, and transport)	*2.3*		
Other product market reforms	*2.1*		
Labor Market Reforms	**2.4**		
Pension reform	*2.2*	*2.2*	
Employment Protection Legislation	*0.2*		*0.2*
Tax Structure Reforms	**0.8**		**0.8**
Bankruptcy reforms	**0.2**		**0.2**
Total Implemented Reforms	**7.8**	**2.2**	**5.6**
Total	**13.4**	**2.8**	**10.6**

Source OECD (2016a) and authors' calculations and creation

The significant effect of the reforms on GDP seems to come, ceteris paribus, after 5 years from the time of their implementation. This means that significant benefits are expected to emerge from the overall reforms carried out in previous years in the Greek economy.

The above event, combined with the dynamics of the new non-fiscal reforms that are expected to take place in the Greek economy between 2020 and 2023, is expected to give a significant boost to the product produced by 2030 and achieve the expected excess of the observed trends.

Of course, it should be noted that the (non-fiscal) reforms expected to be carried out in the period 2020–2023 are not estimated to be of the same effectiveness as in the period 2010–2017 and therefore their effect on GDP should be expected proportionally less. This is because as we get closer to the reform frontier the reforms are getting harder and harder with smaller reform effects.

What is important, however, is not to carry out numerous structural reforms, but effective structural reforms, in the sense of reforms that significantly improve TFP and ultimately stimulate economic activity. In other words, small-scale structural reforms but in specific sectors of economic activity (such as in industry and in manufacturing and in the upstream sectors of energy, transport, and communications, which output is used as an intermediate input into downstream industries) can have the same or even higher effects on investment growth than more multidimensional structural reforms in the economy as a whole. The reason for this is the effects on TFP and thus on the productivity of the sectors of economic activity.

This is why the Optimal Scenario of this analysis differs from Normal Scenario in terms of TFP. Indeed, given that during the period 2010–2014 (5 years) the structural reforms increased the GDP of the Greek economy by 5.6% of which 5% was through increased productivity, and that the structural reforms in the period 2015–2019 (5 years) increased GDP by 7.8% of which 5,6% was due to increased productivity, one should expect that the structural reforms of the period 2020–2023 should increase GDP by an even greater extent. Table 11.2 shows these relationships and the expected benefit of structural reforms in the period 2020–2023.

Essentially, the improvement of the TFP that we expect in Optimal Scenario compared to Normal Scenario, is presented in Fig. 11.4.

Table 11.2 Effects of reforms in the Greek economy on GDP

	Number of years	*GDP growth (%)*	*Through productivity (%)*
2010–2014	5	5.6	5
2015–2019	5	7.8	5.6
2020–2023	4	8.1	8.1

Source OECD (2016a) and author's estimations

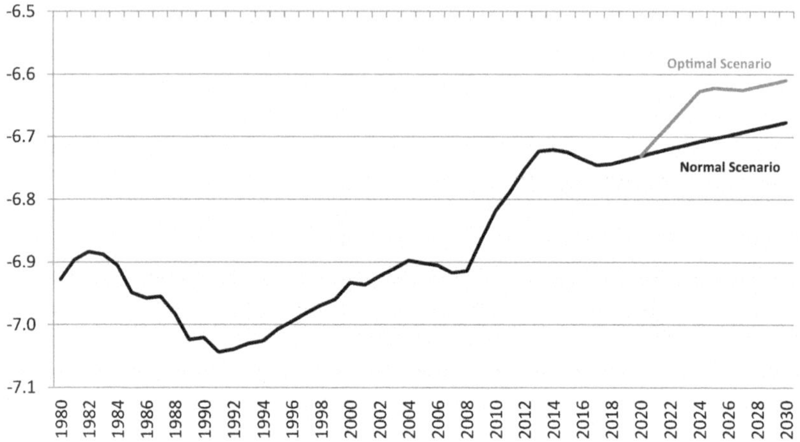

Fig. 11.4 The evolution of TFP in the Greek economy in Normal and Optimal Scenario (*Source* Oxford Economics [2020] and authors' calculations and creation)

Through this differentiation, it is sought to highlight the significant benefits of structural reforms that have already taken place and those that are expected to be realized in the Greek economy for the GDP and to highlight the benefits of structural reforms in specific sectors of economic activity.

Optimal Scenario shows improved TFP compared to Normal Scenario by 0.3% in 2020, a rate that reaches 1.2% in 2023, decreasing to 0.95% by 2028 and increasing to 1.05% until 2030.

The integration of the reforms assumes that it presents an upgrade of the TFP by 0.121 points while in the Normal Scenario it was 0.071 points. At the same time, it has effects on the key variables of the economic system as presented in Fig. 11.5 (see next chapter).

What has not been sufficiently clarified in the relevant literature is the relationship of structural reforms with TFP as well as the relationship of TFP with factors such as investment, consumption, trade balance, savings, employment, etc.

OECD in the reports of the Economic Policy Reforms (OECD, 2015, 2016b, 2017, 2018, 2019) presents the reform effort of the economies every two years. This is done by recording the percentage of OECD policy recommendations that are ultimately adopted for each economy.

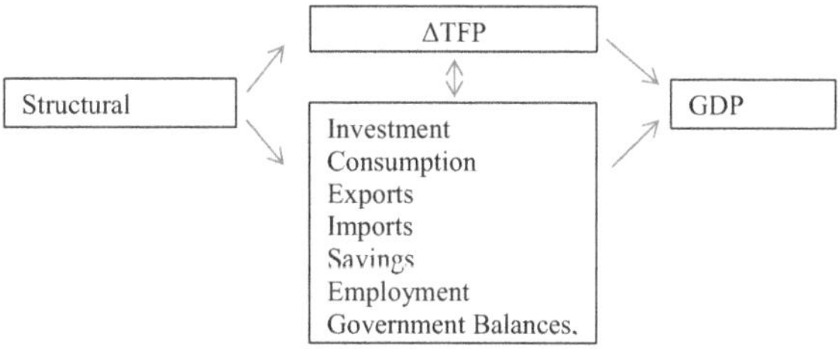

Fig. 11.5 The relationship of structural reforms and GDP growth (*Source* Authors' creation)

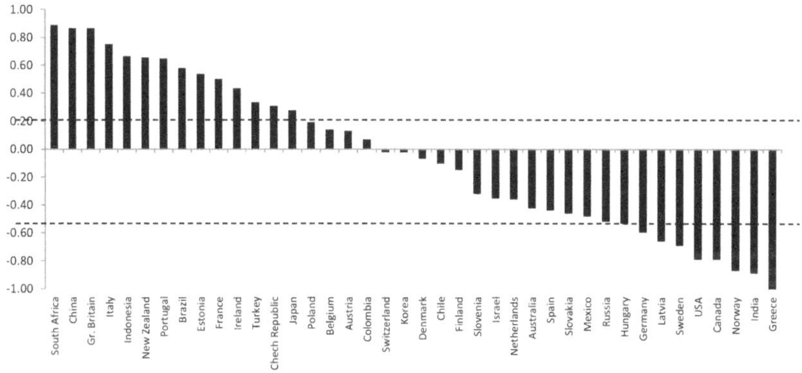

Fig. 11.6 Correlations between reform responsiveness rate and TFP change (*Source* OECD [2015, 2016a, 2017, 2018, 2019], Oxford Economics [2020], and authors' calculations and creation)

Based on the relevant data for the period from 2011 to 2018 and the corresponding development of TFP in each economy based on the Global Economic Model of Oxford Economics, Fig. 11.6 summarizes the correlations observed between the two variables.

It is noted that for 27 of the 32 OECD countries presented in Fig. 11.6 there is a strong positive or negative correlation (above 0.3 or below –0.3) which highlights the strong effect of structural reforms on TFP.

Especially for the case of the Greek economy the correlation observed is perfectly negative, having value of −1. This means that when the Reform Responsiveness Rate in Greece increases, the less the negative size of TFP decreases, the more TFP is improving. In the context of this relationship, the great importance of the reform effort to improve TFP is highlighted. More specifically, in Greece the improvement of TFP from 2010 to 2018 where there was a great reform effort was of the order of 1.09%, while in normal Scenario we should expect from 2020 to 2030 a corresponding improvement of 1.05%. At the same time, in the Optimal Scenario we should expect an improvement in TFP by 1.8%. Thus, if we take into account that the Reform Responsiveness Rate for the period 2015–2018 was about 45% for Greece, and we know that the improvement in TFP was 1.09%, a simple calculation seems to require a Reform Responsiveness Rate of about 74%, about 10 percentage points higher than the average for the period 2011–2018 which was 63%. In another book, in Palgrave Macmillan's series of books on the Greek economy under the title "The Political Economy of Greek Growth up to 2030", Petrakis and Kostis (2020) describe the reforms that are necessary to measure the appropriate Reform Responsiveness Rate that leads to the "desired" evolution of Total Factor Productivity that is "consistent" with the Optimal Scenario.

11.6 The Optimal Pro-growth Scenario for the Greek Economy: 2020–2030

The integration of the upgraded TFP into the Normal Scenario causes GDP growth so as to create an Optimal Pro-Growth path for the Greek economy in the period 2020–2030. At the same time, with the increase of TFP, the Optimal Scenario includes an increase in government spending by 3 billion euros in 2020 to stimulate the Greek economy against the crisis of the Covid-19 pandemic.

Figure 11.7 shows the comparison of Normal Scenario with Optimal Scenario in terms of the level of real GDP and is indicative of the expected benefit of the 2010–2019 reforms and those expected for 2020–2022 in GDP through the effect of TFP. Additionally, the improvement in government spending in 2020 improves the size of real GDP for that year.

Table 11.3 presents the multipliers that link TFP to GDP for the Greek economy compared to the economies of Germany, Ireland, and Portugal. More specifically, it presents GDP multipliers after a TFP increase of 0.1 units[8] each year (for 10 years), for each economy.

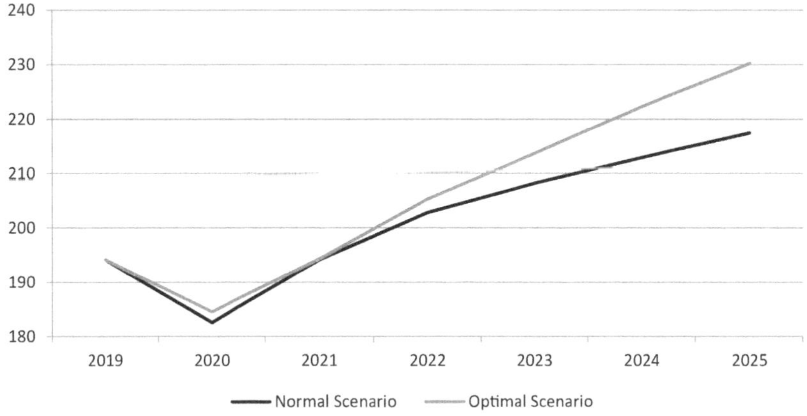

Fig. 11.7 Real GDP growth in Normal and Optimal Scenario (billion Euros) (*Source* Oxford Economics [2020] and authors' calculations and creation)

Table 11.3 GDP multipliers after TFP increase by 0.1 points

	2020	*2021*	*2022*	*2023*	*2024*	*2025*	*2026*	*2027*	*2028*	*2029*	*2030*
Greece	1.03	1.06	1.08	1.09	1.10	1.11	1.11	1.11	1.12	1.12	1.12
Germany	1.02	1.04	1.05	1.06	1.07	1.08	1.08	1.09	1.09	1.10	1.10
Ireland	1.02	1.02	1.03	1.03	1.04	1.05	1.06	1.07	1.08	1.08	1.09
Portugal	1.03	1.04	1.05	1.06	1.07	1.08	1.09	1.10	1.10	1.11	1.11

Source Oxford Economics (2020) and author's calculations and creation

For Greece, the above multiplier means that an increase in TFP by 0.1 points, is expected to increase cumulatively GDP of the economy by 3% in 2020, 6% in 2021, 8% in 2022, 9% in 2023, 10% in 2024, 11% by 2027, and 12% by 2030. The corresponding multipliers for the economies of Germany, Ireland and Portugal are slightly smaller, thus highlighting the great importance of structural changes to stimulate economic activity through the TFP channel. It is also observed that for Greece, as of course for the other economies examined, there is an increase in the multiplier over the years, reaching its maximum level after the seventh year.

Notes

1. See Chapter 4
2. The Oxford Global Economic Model (GEM) is the most widely used international macroeconomic model, with users such as the International Monetary Fund, the World Bank, the Asian Development Bank and a large number of blue-chip companies. The original specifications of the model are provided by Oxford Economics, which was founded in 1981 in collaboration with the Oxford University College of Economics. The research team of EKPA under P.E. Petrakis has been cooperating with Oxford Economics since 2016.
3. According to Taylor's rule, the real interest rate is in line with the long-term potential growth of the economy, provided that both economic activity and prices are kept close to their equilibrium. More specifically, in the event of a positive deviation from the equilibrium, the Central Bank must increase the intervention rate (i.e., decides the adoption of a restrictive monetary policy) to prevent the economy from "overheating". In contrast, in the event of a negative deviation from equilibrium, the Central Bank must decrease the intervention rate (i.e., adopts an expansionary monetary policy) to prevent a sharp recession.
4. The Layard-Nickell wage /price system includes nothing but the intersection of a total supply curve with a total demand curve in a two-axis system, where the horizontal represents the unemployment rate and the vertical represents the actual wage. The intersection point of the two curves, which have been built to incorporate all the imperfections of product and labor markets, corresponds to the state of equilibrium of the economy.
5. Uncovered interest rate parity is a strategy that aims to make a profit by taking advantage of the inequality between the interest rate difference between two currencies and the expected change in their exchange rate.
6. Consensus Economics was founded in 1989, and is the world's leading international economic survey organization and polls more than 700 economists each month to obtain their forecasts and views. Consensus Economics has cultivated a growing network of economists, drawing upon the expertise of well-established local consultants and large teams of professionals in the banks who are dedicated to particular countries and regions. These surveys cover estimates for the principal macroeconomic indicators including GDP growth, inflation, interest rates, and exchange rates in over 85 countries, as well as energy and metal prices. Consensus Economics does not use its own model for relevant predictions in the medium and long term. Instead, it uses the forecasts of a number of forecasting firms as a basis and formulates its own average estimate. Consensus Economics makes long-term estimates of a number of countries in the world. For Greece in particular, the estimates concern GDP, exports and private

consumption. Consensus Economics in general ultimately makes more conservative predictions than the OE. The way Consensus forecasts are taken into account is through GDP forecasts, imports, exports, and private consumption.

7. In the present and the next chapter, the hypothesis is made that during the period 2020–2023, the reform effort will continue intensively. Especially for 2020—and despite the crisis of the Covid-19 pandemic—the reform effort should be expected to restart in the fourth quarter of the year.
8. The improvement by 0.1 units concerns an improvement of about 1.49% for each year in Greece, by about 1.59% in Germany, by about 1.67% in Ireland and by about 1.47% in Portugal.

References

Acemoglu, D., & Robinson, J. A. (2012). *Why Nations Fail: The Origins of Power, Prosperity and Poverty*. New York: Crown Publishers.

Aghion, P., Bloom, N., Blundell, R., Griffith, R., & Howitt, P. (2005). Competition and Innovation: An Inverted-U Relationship. *The Quarterly Journal of Economics, 120*(2), 701–728.

Alesina, A., Ardagna, S., Nicoletti, G., & Schiantarelli, F. (2005). Regulation and Investment. *Journal of the European Economic Association, 3*(4), 791–825.

Alston, L. (1996). Empirical Work in Institutional Economics: An Overview. In L. Alston, T. Eggertsson, & D. North (Eds.), *Empirical Studies in Institutional Change* (pp. 25–30). Cambridge: Cambridge University Press.

Anderson, D., Barkbu, B., Lusinyan, L., & Muir, D., (2014). Assessing the Gains from Structural Reforms for Jobs and Growth, Chapter 7 in IMF, Jobs and Growth: Supporting the European Recovery.

Aoki, M. (2007). Endogenizing Institutions and Institutional Changes. *Journal of Institutional Economics, 3*(1), 131.

Ayres, C. P. (1944). *The Theory of Economic Progress*. Chapel Hill: University of North Carolina Press.

Bourles, R., Cette, G., Lopez, J., Mairesse, J., & Nicoletti, G. (2013). Do Product Market Regulations in Upstream Sectors Curb Productivity Growth? Panel Data Evidence for OECD Countries. *The Review of Economics and Statistics, 95*(5), 1750–1768.

Consensus Economics. (2020, April). Surveys of International Economic Forecasts.

De Jong, E. (2009). *Culture and Economics: On Values, Economics and International Business*. New York: Routledge.

Diamond, L. (1999). *Developing Democracy: Toward Consolidation*. Baltimore: Johns Hopkins University Press.

Eschbach, D. M., Parker, G. E., & Stoeberl, P. A. (2001). American Repatriate Employees' Retrospective Assessments of the Effects of Cross-Cultural Training on Their Adaptation to International Assignments. *International Journal of Human Resource Management, 12*(2), 270–287.

European Commission. (2020). *Spring 2020 Economic Forecast: A Deep and Uneven Recession, an Uncertain Recovery*. Retrieved from: https://ec.europa.eu/info/business-economy-euro/economic-performance-and-forecasts/economic-forecasts_en.

Greif, A., & Laitin, D. D. (2004). A Theory of Endogenous Institutional Change. *American Political Science Review, 98*(4), 633–652.

Hess, J. D. (1994). *The Whole World Guide to Culture Learning* (pp. 701–728). Yarmouth: Intercultural Press.

Hodgson, G. M. (2004). *The Evolution of Institutional Economics: Agency, Structure and Darwinism in American Institutionalism*. London and New York: Routledge.

IMF. (2020). World Economic Outlook Database: April 2020 Edition.

Kafka, K. I., Pantelis, C. K., & Petrakis, P. E. (2020). Why Coevolution of Culture and Institutions Matters for Economic Development and Growth? *Intecopen*. https://doi.org/10.5772/intechopen.90631.

Kantor, S. E. (1998). *Politics and Property Rights: The Closing of the Open Range in the Postbellum South*. Chicago: University of Chicago Press.

KEPE—Centre of Planning and Economic Research. (2019). *Structural reforms in Greece, 2010–2018* (Report prepared for European Commission). Luxembourg: Publications Office of the European Union.

Kingston, C., & Caballero, G. (2009). Comparing Theories of Institutional Change. *Journal of Institutional Economics, 5*(2), 151–180.

Kostis, P. C., Kafka, K. I., & Petrakis, P. E. (2018, July). Cultural Change and Innovation Performance. *Journal of Business Research, 88*, 306–313. https://doi.org/10.1016/j.jbusres.2017.12.010.

Libecap, G. D. (1989). *Contracting for Property Rights*. New York: Cambridge University Press.

Lipsey, R. G., & Lancaster, K. (1956). The General Theory of Second Best. *Review of Economic Studies, 24*(1), 11–32.

Malliaropoulos, D. (2017). *Greece: State of Economy, Outlook and Major Challenges*. Presentation in CRETE 2017 Conference. Bank of Greece Economic Analysis and Research Department. Retrieved from http://www2.aueb.gr/conferences/Crete2017/Papers/Malliaropulos_slides.pdf.

Mio, J. S. (1999). *Key Words in Multicultural Interventions: A Dictionary*. Westport: Greenwood Publishing Group.

Ng, Y. K. (1977). Towards a Theory of Third-Best. *Public Finance, 32*(1), 1–15.

Oberg, K. (1960). Cultural Shock: Adjustment to New Cultural Environments. *Practical Anthropology, 7*(4), 177–182.

OECD. (2015). *Economic Policy Reforms 2015: Going for Growth*. Paris: OECD Publishing. Retrieved from https://doi.org/10.1787/growth-2015-en.

OECD. (2016a). *OECD Economic Surveys: Greece 2016*. Paris: OECD Publishing. Retrieved from https://doi.org/10.1787/eco_surveys-grc-2016-en.

OECD. (2016b). *Economic Policy Reforms 2016: Going for Growth Interim Report*. Paris: OECD Publishing. Retrieved from https://doi.org/10.1787/growth-2016-en.

OECD. (2017). *Economic Policy Reforms 2017: Going for Growth*. Paris: OECD Publishing. Retrieved from https://doi.org/10.1787/growth-2017-en.

OECD. (2018). *Economic Policy Reforms 2018: Going for Growth Interim Report*. Paris: OECD Publishing. Retrieved from https://doi.org/10.1787/growth-2018-en.

OECD. (2019). *Economic Policy Reforms 2019: Going for Growth*. Paris: OECD Publishing. Retrieved from: https://doi.org/10.1787/aec5b059-en.

OECD. (2020). GDP Per Capita and Productivity Growth. *OECD Productivity Statistics* (database). Retrieved from https://doi.org/10.1787/data-00685-en.

Ostrom, E. (1990). *Governing the Commons: The Evolution of Institutions for Collective Action*. Cambridge [England] and New York: Cambridge University Press.

Oxford Economics. (2020). Oxford Economics Global Macro Model.

Petrakis, P. E. (2014). *Culture, Growth and Economic Policy*. Berlin: Springer.

Petrakis, P. E., Kafka, K. I., Kostis, P. C., & Valsamis, D. G. (2021). *Greek Culture After the Financial Crisis: An Economic Analysis*. New York: Palgrave Macmillan.

Petrakis, P. E., & Kostis, P. C. (2020). *Policies for a Stronger Greek Economy: Actions for the Next Decade*. New York: Palgrave Macmillan.

Richerson, P. J., & Boyd, R. (2005). *Not by Genes Alone: How Culture Transformed Human Evolution*. Chicago: University of Chicago Press.

Sotiriadis, C. J., & Grove, J. V. (2020). Global Futures Report. Alternative Futures of Geopolitical Competition in a Post-Covid-19 World. A Collaborative Analysis With Foresight Practitioners and Experts, Air Force Warfighting Integration Capability (AFWIC), Strategic Foresight and Futures Branch.

The Conference Board. (2020). The Conference Board Total Economy Database: April 2019.

Triandis, H. C. (2009). Ecological Determinants of Cultural Variation. In R. W. Wyer, C. Y. Chiu, & Y. Hong (Eds.), *Understanding Culture: Theory, Research and Applications* (pp. 189–210). New York: Psychology Press.

Vettas, N. (2016). *Some Thoughts on Productivity and Greece*. Retrieved from http://iobe.gr/docs/events/var/Vettas_Bank_of_Greece_%2025042016.pdf.

Weaver, G. (1994). *Culture, Communication and Conflict: Readings in Intercultural Relations*. Needham Heights: Simon & Schuster.
Xia, J. (2009). Analysis of Impact of Culture Shock on Individual Psychology. *International Journal of Psychological Studies, 1*(2), 97–101.

CHAPTER 12

The Long-Term View of the Greek Economy Under the Normal and the Optimal Pro-growth Scenario: 2020–2030

12.1 Introduction

This chapter provides an overview of the expected development for a number of macroeconomic figures by 2030. For this purpose, the relevant developments for the two scenarios described in the previous chapter are analyzed: the Normal Scenario (business as usual) and the Optimal Scenario (pro-growth scenario). The aim is, in addition to presenting the expected development of the Greek economy by 2030 based on the current picture, also to highlight the role of structural reforms in the implementation of a pro-growth scenario.

The structure of the chapter is as follows: In Sect. 12.2 the developments related to the deleveraging of Greek banks are commented, the end of Credit-Less Recovery is presented. Next (Sect. 12.3), the expected developments in the Greek economy until 2030 for the two scenarios are presented in comparison with the average of the Eurozone for variables such as GDP growth, unemployment rate, investment, and inflation. In the next Sect. (12.4), a description is being made about the way the potential output and the output gap in the Greek economy will evolve, and, in the line, there is a presentation of issues related to productivity, the Okun curve (i.e., the correlation between growth rate and the change in unemployment rate, the development of interest rates, capital stock, and depreciation). Section 12.5 presents the expected development for the public debt of the Greek economy, and its connection with the expected

P. E. Petrakis and P. C. Kostis, *The Evolution of the Greek Economy*, The Political Economy of Greek Growth up to 2030,
https://doi.org/10.1007/978-3-030-47210-8_12

development in the government balance and primary fiscal balance. Next (Sect. 12.6), presents the way in which the key factors of GDP are expected to evolve as well as the average annual contribution of the main determinants in GDP. Section 12.7 describes the issue of the competitiveness of the Greek economy until 2030 for the two scenarios, and the next Sect. (12.8) presents the expected development of investments in the Greek economy. Finally, Sect. 12.9 presents some elements that follow certain areas of inclusive growth such as how real disposable income will evolve, savings, the Gini coefficient, employment and the percentage of people at risk of poverty or social exclusion and finally an estimate about the happiness index which is a sample of the effective efficiency of the economic system.

12.2 The End of Credit-Less Recovery

The Greek economy seems to have entered the last phase of deleveraging of Greek banks from the load of non-performing loans that the almost ten-year financial crisis has brought. Of course, this is a situation that could be described as particularly difficult and demanding.

One of the most important successes of the Greek banking sector to date is that banks have successfully completed the transfer of defective consumer credit and card loans. This stock has in its vast majority moved into the hands of new investors who, as a rule, acquired it at a very low price. Of course, the problem for banks may have been closed, but obviously the management of these loans by their new owners and managers, remains and is expected to remain an open issue to be resolved since private debt remains as a burden in the real economy.

Also, so far, the activity so in the senior sales of secured loans of small and medium-sized enterprises is being considered as significant, since transactions have been completed that raise the total nominal amount transferred to investors up to 8.5 billion to 9 billion euros.

At the same time, Greek banks continue their efforts to isolate their troubled portfolios from the "good" bank in order to avoid the continued contamination of banks, which worked decisively for the formation of the market of problem loan management (NPL servicers).

The above developments are linked to a significant reduction in the exposure of Greek systemic banks to non-performing exposures, which is expected to continue in the medium term (Fig. 12.1).

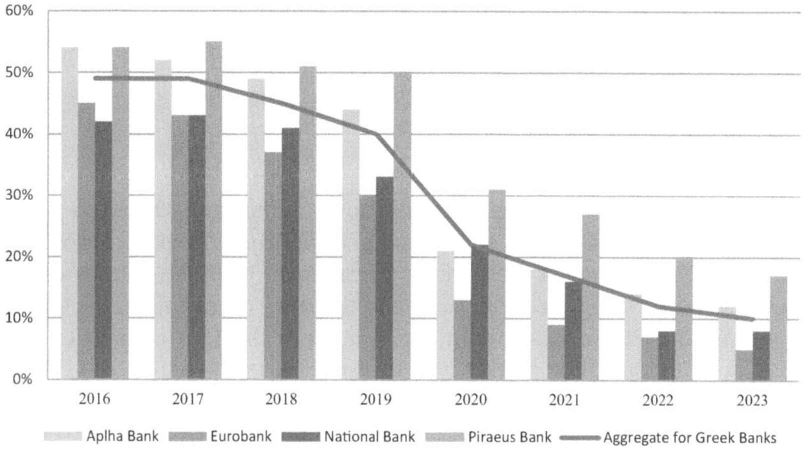

Fig. 12.1 Bank non-performing exposures to total gross loans (2016–2023) (%) (*Source* Goldman Sachs [2020] and authors' creation)

For the Greek case, an Asset Protection Scheme has been adopted, called "Hercules", which is based on the Italian model of securitization of non-performing loans. It is no coincidence that in the last financial crisis, all the countries affected by the crisis, in one way or another applied some similar schemes (USA, Great Britain, Ireland, Italy), and generally very positive results. Similar results are expected from its application in the Greek economy. With this model, Greek banks will be able to transfer part of their exposure to special purpose vehicles that will securitize the loans and make them available to investors, with the Greek state guaranteeing the transactions. It is also characteristic that already, without finalizing the draft law, the four systemic banks (Alpha Bank, Eurobank, National Bank, Piraeus Bank) have planned NPEs deleveraging transactions with a total value of 30–34 billion euros, an amount that exceeds the total reduction of NPEs that had been realized cumulatively until the end of 2019.

Therefore, in view of these actions, the four systemic banks should be expected to continue to reduce non-performing exposures both organically, supported by improving macroeconomic conditions, and non-organically, through sales and securitizations. In this sense, the period, during which the recovery of the economy could not be supported by the activation of the financial system which will gradually return to positive financing rates of the Greek economy is removed, marking the end of creditless recovery.

12.3 Eurozone and the Greek Economy 2020–2030

The Greek economy is expected to show in the next decade a fairly significant positive deviation (de-coupling) from the Eurozone, recording growth rates higher than those of the Eurozone. Of course, the structural problems of the Greek economy are such that they do not allow the Greek economy to perform better than the average of the Eurozone in critical areas, such as the labor market and investment, but progress in GDP is evident. Thus, the significant performance expected with either Normal or Optimal Scenario in the Greek economy by 2030 is expected to lead to a significant convergence of the Greek economy with the Eurozone average.

The crisis of the Covid-19 pandemic is expected to be particularly intense both in Greece and in the Eurozone. After the great recession for 2020, a significant recovery is expected for 2021 and, after that, a gradual decline in GDP growth rates. More specifically regarding the growth rate of the Greek economy, although positive in both scenarios after 2021, it is expected to decrease every year in Normal Scenario until 2030, while in Optimal Scenario it is expected to strongly increase (Fig. 12.2). On the other hand, in the case of the Eurozone, relative stability of GDP growth to rates close to 1% should be expected for the entire decade from 2021 to 2030.

More specifically, the growth rate of GDP in the Normal Scenario from −5.9% in 2020 is expected to reach 6.5% in 2021 and has since gradually decreased to 1.35% in 2030. In terms of real GDP from 194 billion euros in 2019 it is expected to reach 182.6 billion euros in 2020, to grow to 194.1 billion euros in 2021, and to approach 235.9 billion euros in 2030. With regard to the Optimal Scenario, a decrease in the rate of change in GDP of 4.93% in 2020, an increase of 5.4% in 2021 and since then a gradual decrease approaching 2030 to 1.5%. Real GDP in this scenario is expected from 184.5 billion euros in 2020 to 254.6 billion euros in 2030. For the case of the euro area, growth of −5.6% in 2020, 4.6% in 2021 and a decrease of 0.7% by 2030 should be expected.

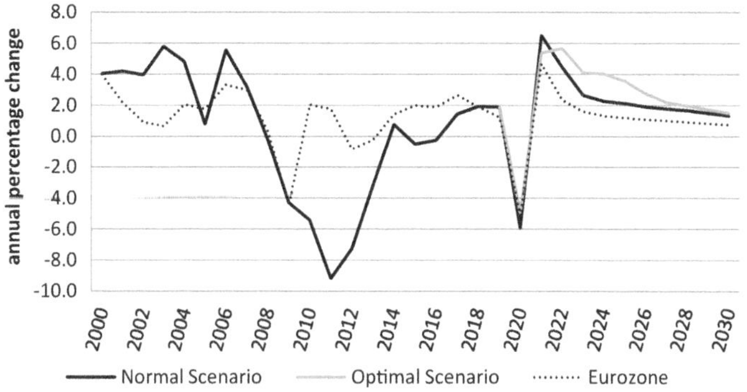

Fig. 12.2 GDP growth in the two scenarios compared to economic growth in the Eurozone (%) (*Source* Oxford Economics [2020] and authors' calculations and creation)

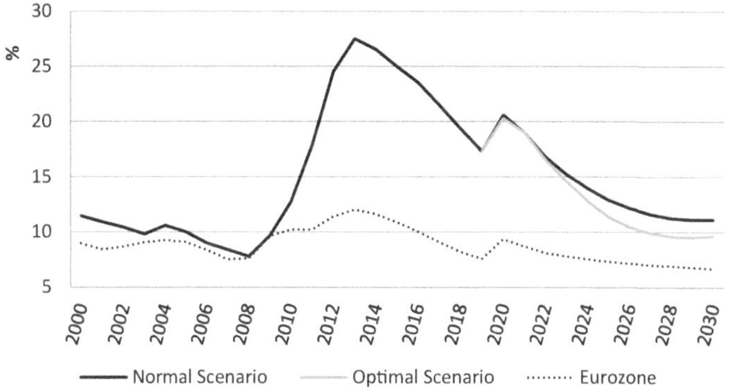

Fig. 12.3 Unemployment rate in the two scenarios compared to the unemployment rate in the Eurozone (%) (*Source* Oxford Economics [2020] and authors' calculations and creation)

Regarding labor market, the effort to recover the Greek economy by 2030 is expected to lead to a fairly significant reduction in the unemployment rate gap between Greece and the Eurozone (Fig. 12.3). Of course, the effect of the Covid-19 pandemic on the size of unemployment is estimated to be greater in Greece than in the Eurozone

The unemployment rate of the Greek economy was also higher than that of the Eurozone in the 2000s, but the high growth rates until 2007 led to the full convergence of the two rates in 2008. Of course, the crisis of 2008 opened the gap between Greece and the Eurozone and the Greek economy is expected to make a great effort to converge with the Eurozone again. This, of course, is not expected to fully occur with either scenario, although even better convergence is expected with the Optimal Scenario.

In particular, labor market conditions are expected to be much more favorable in the case of Optimal Scenario, as well as employment and the unemployment rate are expected to have a better development. As for the unemployment rate, from about 20.6% in 2020 it is expected to fall to 11.1% in Normal Scenario and in Optimal Scenario from about 20.3% in 2020 it is expected to fall to 9.6%. Respectively, in the Eurozone from 9.34% in 2020 is expected to fall to 6.67% by 2030.

One of the biggest problems brought about by the crisis in the Greek economy was the huge reduction in the size of investments. Thus, while in 2007 investments as a percentage of GDP were higher for Greece than the corresponding size in the Eurozone, the crisis reduced investment in the Greek economy by more than 50%, while the same did not happen for the entire Eurozone. Thus, while the Eurozone is expected to approach quite satisfactorily the level of investment as a percentage of GDP achieved before the crisis by 2030, this does not apply to the Greek economy, which seems to have a rather difficult road ahead, in order to achieve this (Fig. 12.4). Indeed, the impact of the Covid-19 pandemic on investments for the year 2020 has had a significant negative impact on this effort.

Finally, Fig. 12.5 presents the inflation rate in the two scenarios compared to the level of inflation rate in the Eurozone.

After the shock of the Covid-19 pandemic that is expected to lead to negative inflation in the Greek economy and to near zero in the Eurozone economy, the level of inflation is expected to be positive in the case of Normal Scenario for the entire period from 2021 to 2030, with a continued trend of growth from 2022 onwards (reaching 2.04% in 2030). However, in the Optimal Scenario the significant increase in the level of production until 2023 is expected to lead to zero levels of inflation, which from 2025 is expected to increase over time reaching 2030 to 1.81%.

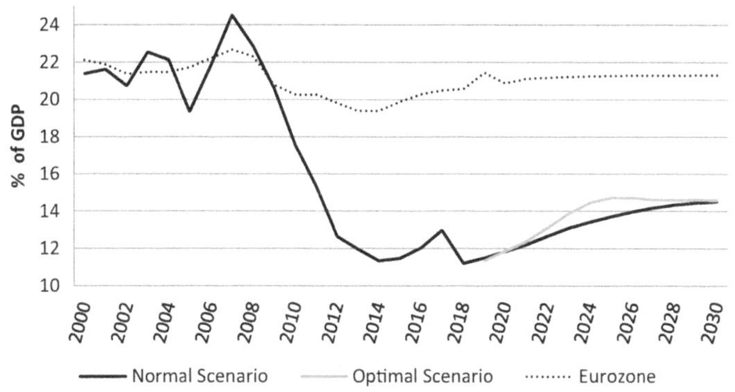

Fig. 12.4 Investments in the two scenarios compared to investments in the Eurozone (*Source* Oxford Economics [2020] and authors' calculations and creation)

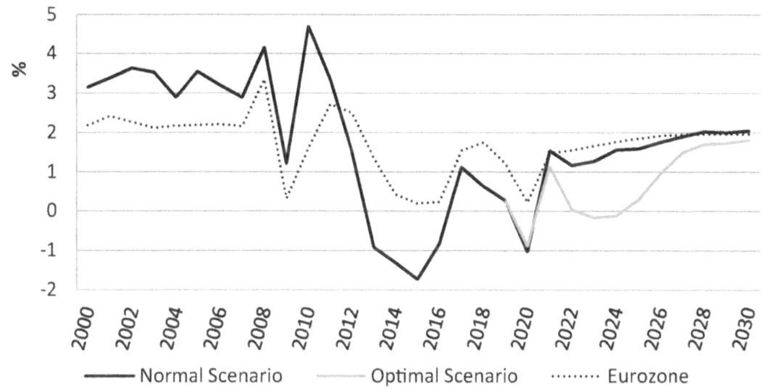

Fig. 12.5 The inflation rate in the two scenarios compared to the inflation rate in the Eurozone (%) (*Source* Oxford Economics [2020] and authors' calculations and creation)

However, it should be stressed that in Normal Scenario the rate of inflation stabilizes close to 2% after 2028, while in Optimal Scenario the rate of inflation is approaching this level.

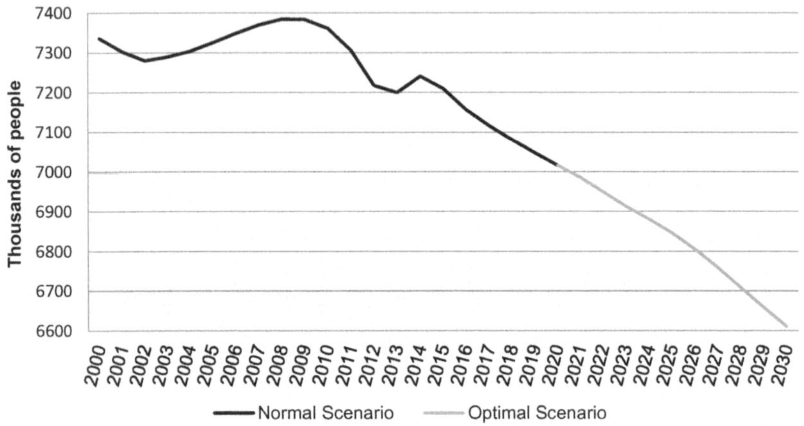

Fig. 12.6 Working age population (*Source* Oxford Economics [2020] and authors' calculations and creation)

12.4 Output Gap and Potential Output

One element that characterizes the Greek economy is the fact that since the beginning of the crisis there has been a significant decrease in the working age population, something that is significantly associated with the decline of the population in productive age due to the aging of populations in Greece and the fact that during the years of the crisis there has been a significant increase in the phenomenon of brain drain. A similar trend should also be expected in the years from 2020 to 2030, whichever scenario prevails as the size of the working age population is not affected by the improvement of the TFP in the Optimal Scenario (Fig. 12.6).

Of course, the decline in working age population is likely to be associated with the decline in potential output and therefore with the fact that labor as a productive factor is not able to deliver to its full potential. This is also one of the reasons why the potential output of the Greek economy-the product produced if all resources were employed to their maximum extent—is from the beginning of the crisis and then (until 2030) higher than the actual output of the economy (Fig. 12.7) in both scenarios.

The difference between the potential and the actual product produced is why the output gap for the Greek economy has been negative since the beginning of the crisis and is expected to remain negative whichever

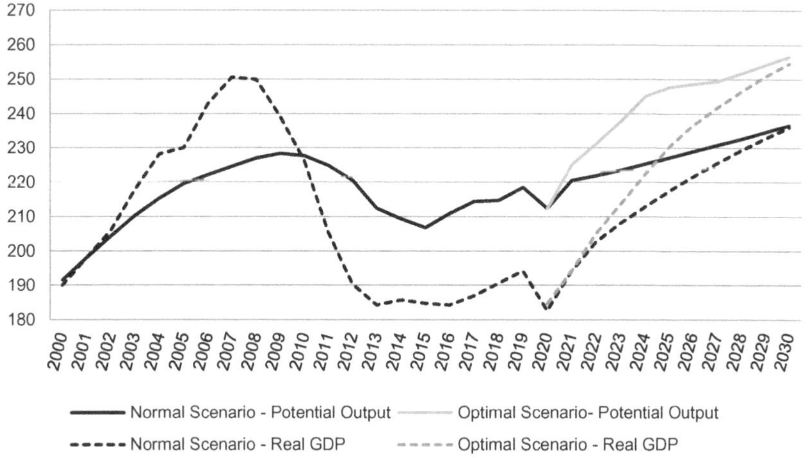

Fig. 12.7 GDP and potential output (*Source* Oxford Economics [2020] and authors' calculations and creation)

scenario prevails until 2030 (Fig. 12.8). Furthermore, the level of the output gap is crucial for understanding which are the inflationary pressures that exist. When the output gap is positive, inflationary pressures exist, while when it is negative inflation should be low since monetary policy will be lax. This is the case for the Greek economy during the period from 2000 up to 2030 (Fig. 12.8).

Of course, as presented in Fig. 12.7, an improvement in the product produced in the Greek economy should be expected despite the fact that the working age population is declining. So it seems that we should expect an increase in labor productivity from employees who remain in employment, which is evident from Fig. 12.9. In fact, as shown in the chart below, the improvement of TFP in Optimal Scenario significantly increases labor productivity.

Consistent with the negative potential output is the shift of Okun's curve for the Greek economy. Generally, Okun's Law curve shifts left when there is deterioration of potential output and right when there is improvement. More specifically, there is a shift of Okun's curve to the left, from 1991–2000 to 2008–2018, while it is expected to return again slightly to the right for the period 2020 to 2030 whichever of the two scenarios prevail (arrows show the direction) (Fig. 12.10).

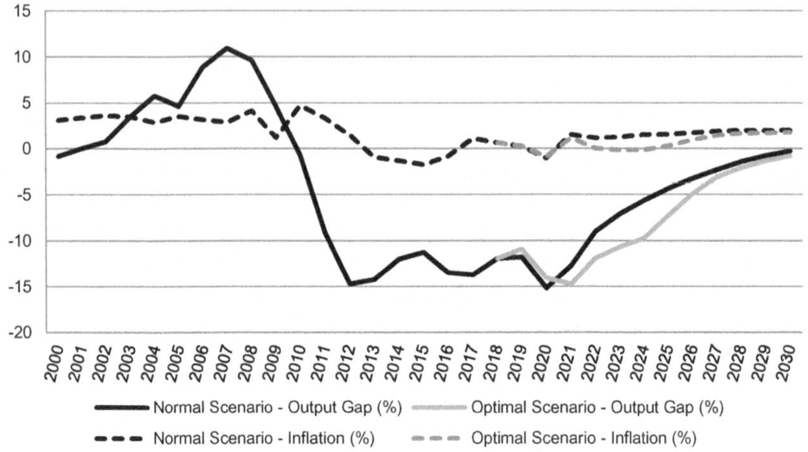

Fig. 12.8 Output gap and inflation (*Source* Oxford Economics [2020] and authors' calculations and creation)

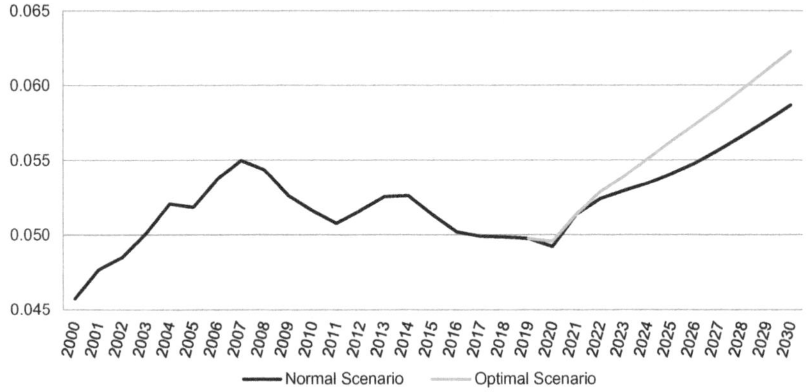

Fig. 12.9 Productivity trend (millions euro per employment) (*Source* Oxford Economics [2020] and authors' calculations and creation)

In addition, Fig. 12.11 presents the Phillips curve for the Greek economy, from 2000 to 2030 (both scenarios). We observe a shift of

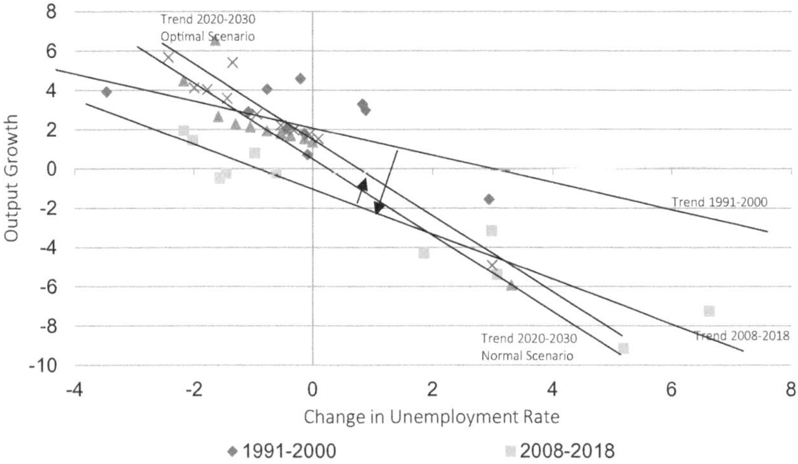

Fig. 12.10 Okun's curve for the Greek economy at various periods in both scenarios (*Source* Oxford Economics [2020] and authors' calculations and creation)

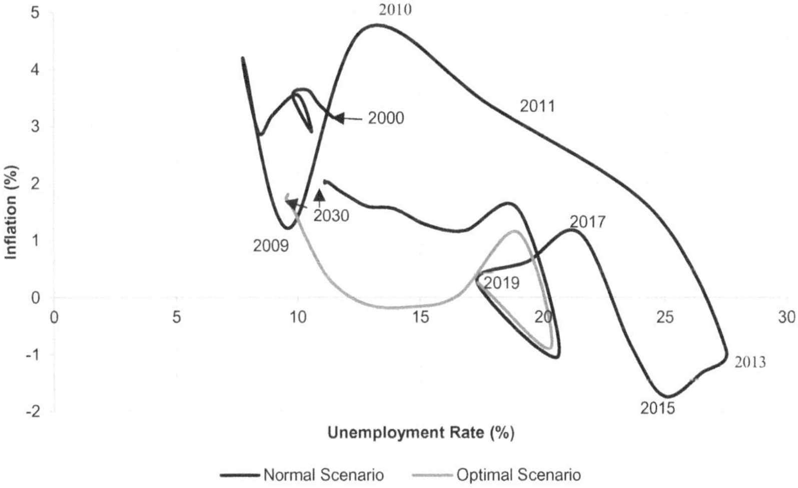

Fig. 12.11 Phillips curve for the Greek economy (*Source* Oxford Economics [2020] and authors' calculations and creation)

the Phillips curve down and right from 2010 to 2013. This is an opposite move to the desired one in order to reduce the cost of macroeconomic adjustment. Prices fell significantly, while at the same time the level of unemployment increased rather than decreased. This deterioration was happily reversed from 2014 onwards and by 2030 the Phillips curve is expected to return almost to the level it was before the crisis!

At the same time, while gross fixed capital formation and interest rates were declining during the decade of the crisis, this situation is expected to improve significantly in both Normal and Optimal Scenario (Fig. 12.12).

The high levels of unemployment that followed after the debt crisis in the Greek economy are in a phase of de-escalation without reaching pre-crisis levels until 2019. The Covid-19 pandemic significantly worsened the situation on the labor market. However, between 2021 and 2030, and especially under the conditions of the Optimal Scenario, the unemployment rate is expected to almost reach the level that existed before the crisis. The development of the unemployment rate is in the opposite direction from that of total investment in the Greek economy (Fig. 12.13).

During the crisis, companies reduced investment in order to prevent a sharp fall or in order to stabilize the return on capital, a trend which is

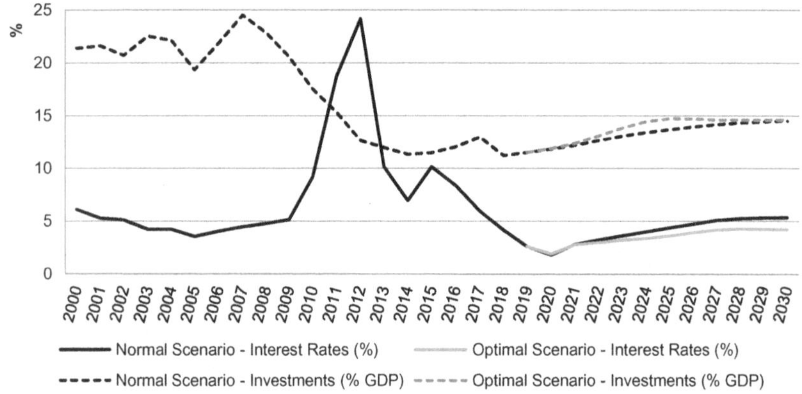

Fig. 12.12 Real investments (% GDP) and interest rates (10-Year Government Bond Yield) (%) (*Source* Oxford Economics [2020] and authors' calculations and creation)

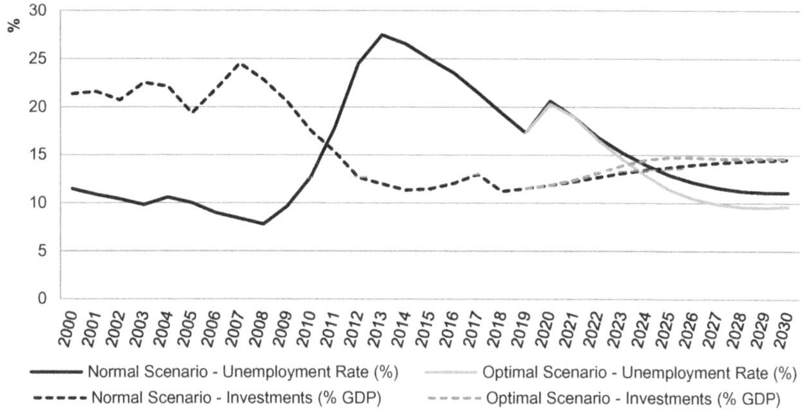

Fig. 12.13 Unemployment rate (%) and total investments (% GDP) (*Source* Oxford Economics [2020] and authors' calculations and creation)

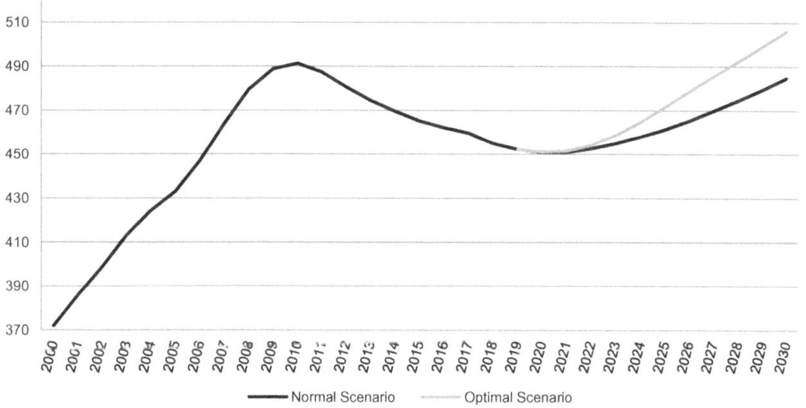

Fig. 12.14 Capital stock 2000–2030 (billion euros) (*Source* Oxford Economics [2020] and authors' calculations and creation)

expected to reverse from 2021 to 2030, resulting in a significant increase in capital stock (Fig. 12.14).

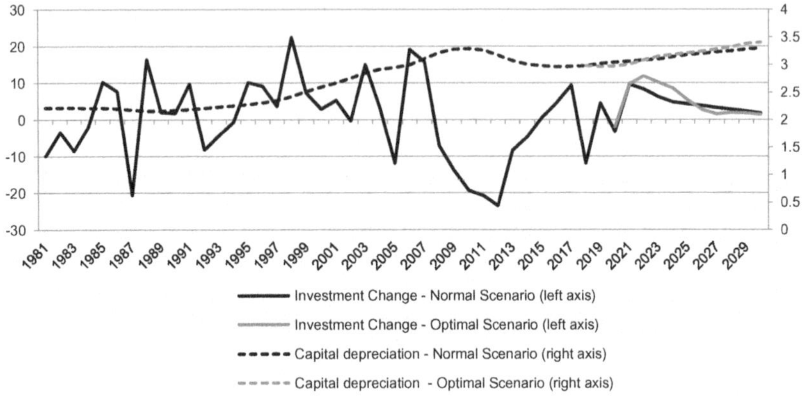

Fig. 12.15 Annual change in investment and depreciation rate of capital: 1981–2030 (*Source* Penn World Table (version 9.1), Oxford Economics [2020] and authors' calculations and creation)

At the same time, the increased capital accumulation expected by 2030, in addition to the decrease in return on capital, is expected to be responsible for the high capital consumption as companies are invited to invest to maintain the functionality of existing investments. Consequently, there is not an increase in net investments, but, instead, an increase in gross investments, due to high depreciation. This is why Fig. 12.15 shows that we should expect a significant increase in depreciation in the two scenarios.

12.5 Public Debt and Economy

The evolution of public debt during the crisis in the Greek economy is one of the most critical issues and has particularly concerned the economic policy-makers in Greece and the European institutions.

As noted by Petrakis (2020) the debt problem has two sides: the flows added to debt and the accumulated public debt (stocks). Given that the debt has to be serviced every year when a country pays interest to its creditors, the rate of change in the existing debt in the absence of new borrowing can be the same as the interest rate. Accordingly, when the rate of change in nominal GDP becomes less than the interest rate, then the government's debt-to-GDP ratio increases (the numerator grows faster than the denominator) (Petrakis, Kostis, & Valsamis, 2013). Figure 12.16 shows the expected annual change in GDP, primary balance, and structural balance.

It is of particular importance that in 2018 and 2019 debt was reduced as a percentage of GDP. However, the crisis of the Covid-19 pandemic and the Greek government's mechanism to stimulate the economy by increasing government spending despite declining government revenues are expected to significantly increase debt by 2020. But since then, debt (as a percentage of GDP) is expected to follow the course expected before the onset of the pandemic (Fig. 12.17). Under the conditions of Optimal Scenario, the assessment of the general government debt is much better, compared to those of Normal Scenario after 2021. From 178.7% of GDP for 2019 (334.2 billion euros), for in 2020 in Normal Scenario the debt as a percentage of GDP is expected at 192.03% (344.5 billion euros) while in Optimal Scenario at 190.7% (345.8 billion euros). Since then, it is expected to decrease by 150.1% (398.5 billion euros) in Normal Scenario and 132.3% (346.4 billion euros) in Optimal Scenario by 2030. Thus,

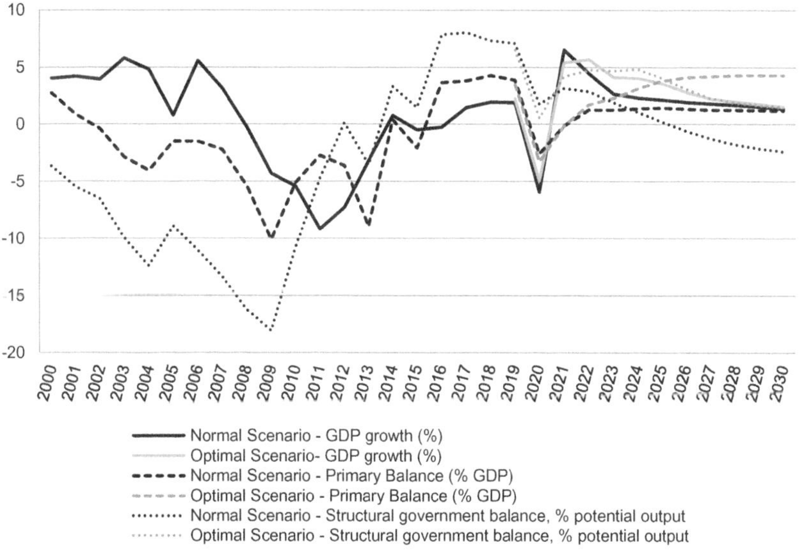

Fig. 12.16 GDP growth rate, primary balance and structural balance for Greece (*Source* Oxford Economics [2020] and authors' calculations and creation)

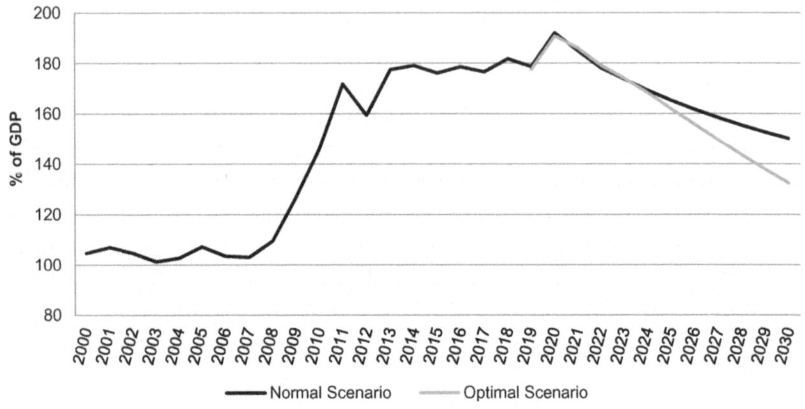

Fig. 12.17 General government debt (*Source* Oxford Economics [2020] and authors' calculations and creation)

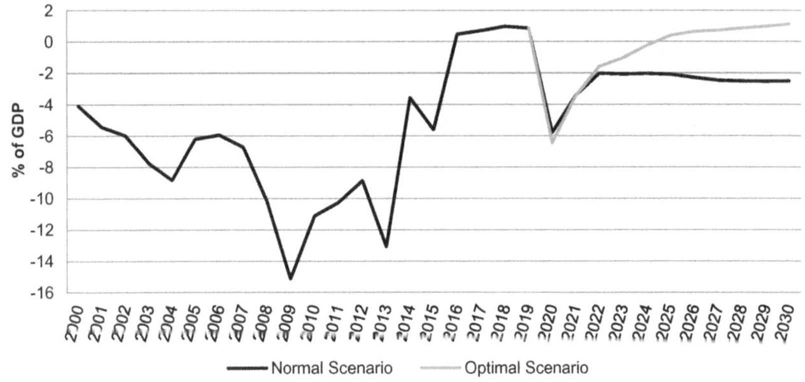

Fig. 12.18 Government balance (*Source* Oxford Economics [2020] and authors' calculations and creation)

while as a percentage of GDP the debt is expected to show a significant decrease until 2030, at levels it seems to be steadily increasing at Normal Scenario and remaining at constant levels at Optimal Scenario.

As for the government balance (Fig. 12.18) and while it had surpluses from 2016 to 2019, in Normal Scenario—after the shock of 2020—it is expected to be negative in all years until 2030. Similar picture is expected

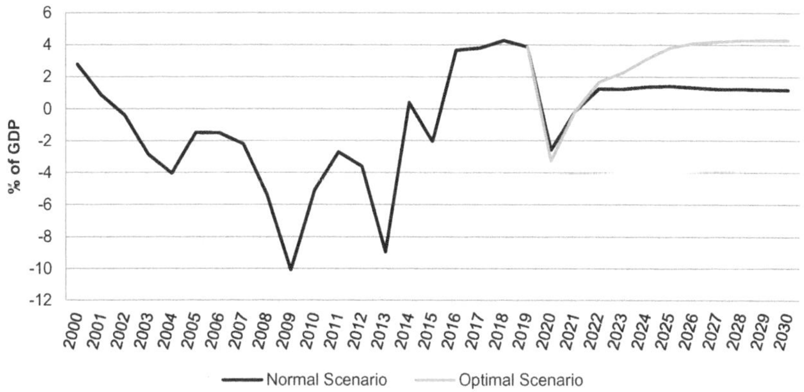

Fig. 12.19 Primary balance (*Source* Oxford Economics [2020] and authors' calculations and creation)

for the Optimal Scenario until 2022, however, after this year it is assumed to improve, with the expected result to be in surplus from 2025 onwards, reaching approximately 1.1% in 2030.

A similar picture is expected of the impact of the Covid-19 pandemic for the case of primary balance, which of course recovers and becomes surplus after 2022 in both scenarios until 2030. Figure 12.19 shows the evolution of the primary balance, by 2030, as a percentage of GDP.

Under the Normal Scenario a reduction is expected to the primary government balance by 2030, as from –4.57 billion euros (−2.6% of GDP) in 2020 is expected to approach 3.2 billion euros (1.2% of GDP) in 2030. In contrast, in the Optimal Scenario the primary result of –5.9 billion euros (−3.3% of GDP) in 2020 is expected to reach 11.25 billion euros (4.29% of GDP) in 2030.

12.6 Competitiveness

For the Greek economy there is a significant deterioration in the competitiveness of the economy up to 2010, but since then the picture of competitiveness is constantly improving. This improvement is due to the implementation of internal devaluation policies of austerity programs and the implementation of major structural reforms for the Greek economy.

In particular, the Real Effective Exchange Rate Index (REER) is a measure of the competitiveness of economies. The increase in a country's REER, related to unit labor costs, leads to a decrease in that country's competitiveness and to a deterioration in its current account balance. An increase in the unit cost index means an increased share of labor costs in the product produced. Increasing unit costs more than increasing labor productivity is a threat to the competitiveness of an economy.

The evolution of the REER index is presented in Fig. 12.20, where while in Normal Scenario the improvement in the competitiveness of the Greek economy is already significant, it should be expected even more significant in the Optimal Scenario as the additional structural reforms in the Optimal Scenario are expected to make the Greek economy considerably more competitive.

Indicative in this direction is the expected production of the manufacturing sector of the Greek economy, which is estimated to improve significantly under both scenarios after 2021 (i.e., after the negative shock of 2020) (Fig. 12.21).

Of course under the Optimal Scenario the manufacturing industry should be expected to be much more competitive as unit labor costs are estimated to move to significant lower levels (Fig. 12.22).

Respectively, Fig. 12.23 presents the evolution of the current account, until 2030, as a percentage of GDP.

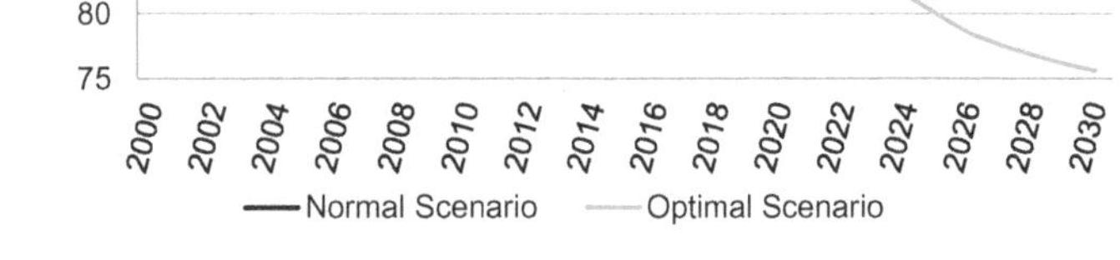

Fig. 12.20 Real Effective Exchange Rate (*Note* A decrease in REER Index indicates improved competitiveness. *Source* Oxford Economics [2020] and authors' calculations and creation)

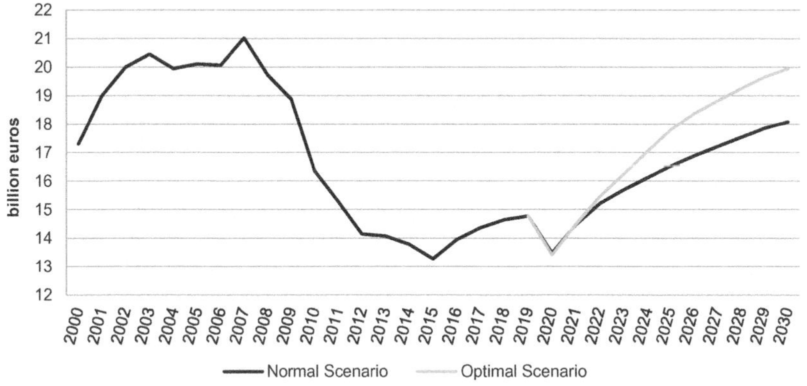

Fig. 12.21 Real GDP in manufacturing (*Source* Oxford Economics [2020] and authors' calculations and creation)

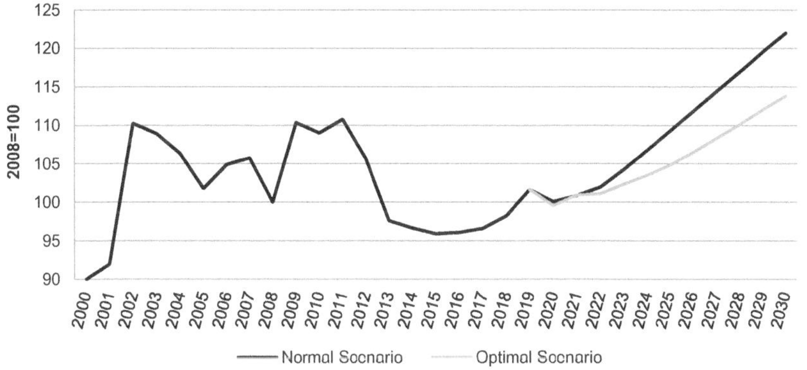

Fig. 12.22 Unit labour costs in manufacturing (nominal) (*Source* Oxford Economics [2020] and authors' calculations and creation)

The current account balance is expected to remain in deficit near 1.5% to 2% in Normal Scenario, while in Optimal Scenario after 2026 it is expected to record surplus. More specifically, from a deficit of 3.7 billion euros (approximately 2.07% of GDP) in 2020, it is expected to reach – 3.34 billion euros (deficit of 1.26% of GDP) in 2030 in Normal Scenario, and from a deficit of 4.66 billion euros (approximately 2.57% of GDP)

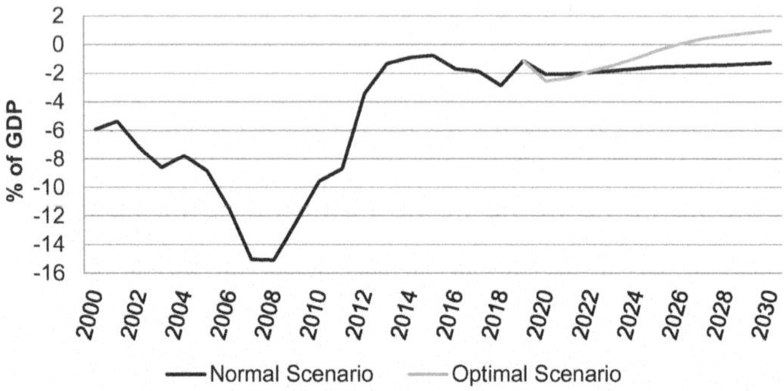

Fig. 12.23 Current account balance (*Source* Oxford Economics [2020] and authors' calculations and creation)

in 2020, it is expected to reach 2.54 billion euros (surplus of 0.97% of GDP) in Optimal Scenario.

12.7 Key Determinants of GDP

Below are the developments concerning the main determinants of GDP, namely, private consumption, public consumption, investment and exports and imports of goods and services, in the two scenarios of the analysis. As will be noted below in both scenarios a significant effort is made to recover until 2030 to the levels that were in place before the crisis, with the improvement of TFP in the Optimal Scenario pushing more in this direction, although the level of consumption, investment and public consumption that was in place before the start of the crisis is not achieved. On the contrary, an improvement in exports of goods and services is expected to almost double in the two scenarios, but this is also expected in the case of imports.

Figure 12.24 shows the evolution of real private consumption in billion euros, by 2030, for Normal and Optimal Scenario.

Private consumption in the Optimal Scenario is throughout the period of analysis higher than that of Normal Scenario, as in this scenario a significantly higher product is produced by the economy. Thus, while private consumption is expected to reach around 123.2 billion euros in 2020, it is expected to reach 154.4 billion euros in Normal Scenario and 162.6 billion euros in Optimal Scenario in 2030.

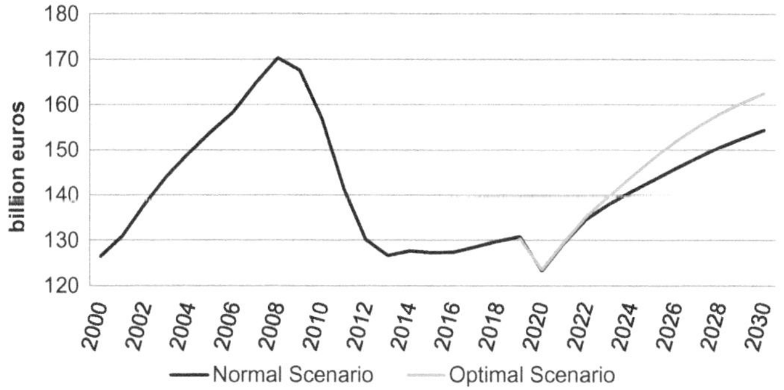

Fig. 12.24 Real private consumption (*Source* Oxford Economics [2020] and authors' calculations and creation)

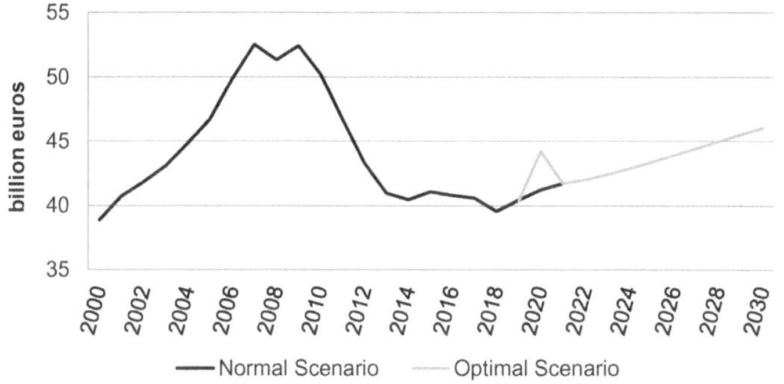

Fig. 12.25 Real public consumption (*Source* Oxford Economics [2020] and authors' calculations and creation)

Figure 12.25 shows the development of real public consumption, which is not expected to be affected by the improvement in TFP occur ring in the Optimal Scenario. However, i8t should be noted that, in both scenarios, public consumption is expected to increase every year. In 2020, a significantly higher public consumption of 3 billion euros is expected in the Optimal Scenario (this is one of the fundamental differences between the two scenarios) than in the Normal Scenario. More specifically, the Normal Scenario from 41.22 billion euros in 2020 and the Optimal Scenario from 44.22 billion euros in 2020 is expected to approach 46.04 billion euros in 2030.

Investment is one of the most important drivers of economic growth and is significantly influenced by the improvement of TFP. This is why in the Optimal Scenario investments appear higher than in the Normal Scenario for the whole period considered. Thus, in the Normal Scenario investments from 21.6 billion euros in 2020 are expected to reach 34.2 billion euros in 2030, while in the Optimal Scenario from EUR 21.9 billion in 2020 are expected to reach 37.17 billion euros in 2030 (Fig. 12.26).

Finally, Figs. 12.27 and 12.28 show the evolution of real exports and imports (respectively) of goods and services, by 2030.

In the Optimal Scenario, higher exports and at the same time lower imports of goods and services should be expected for the entire period considered, indicating a much better evolution of the trade balance. Thus, exports of goods and services from around 63.7 billion euros in 2020 should be expected to reach 95.9 billion euros in Normal Scenario and 98.3 billion euros in Optimal Scenario. Accordingly, imports of goods and services from around 64.9 billion euros in 2020 should be expected to reach 95.6 billion euros in Basic Scenario and 90.4 billion euros in Optimal Scenario.

Figure 12.29 shows the average annual contribution of the main determinants to GDP for six different cases: (a) the period of economic prosperity from 2000 to 2007, (b) the period of crisis, i.e., from 2008

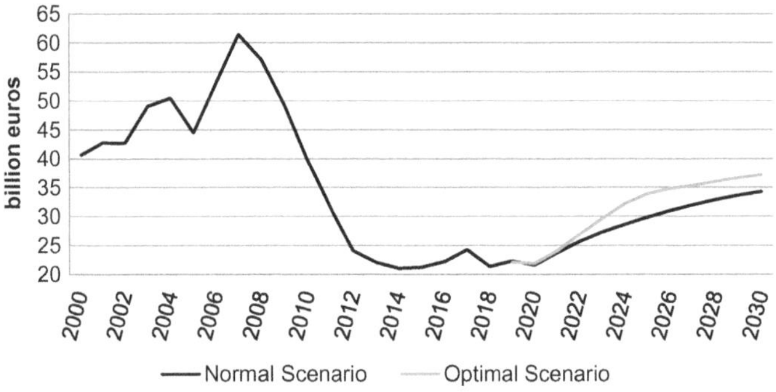

Fig. 12.26 Real investments (*Source* Oxford Economics [2020] and authors' calculations and creation)

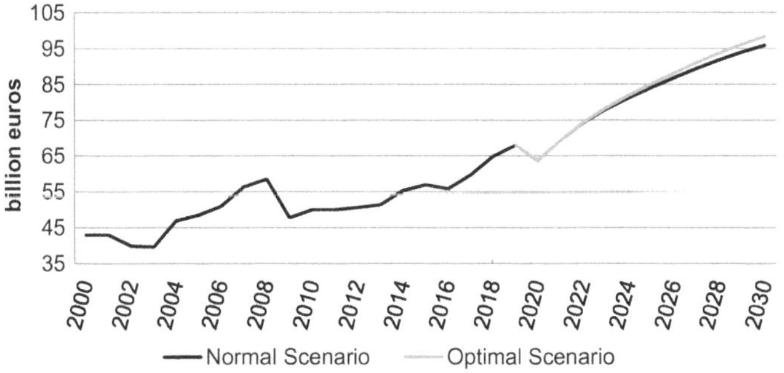

Fig. 12.27 Exports of goods and services (*Source* Oxford Economics [2020] and authors' calculations and creation)

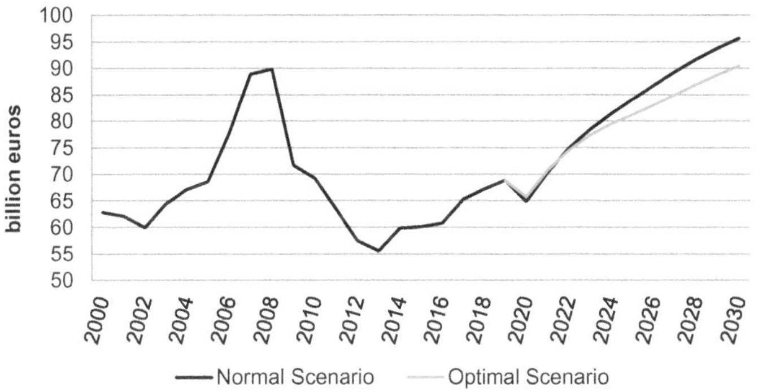

Fig. 12.28 Imports of goods and services (*Source* Oxford Economics [2020] and authors' calculations and creation)

to 2019, (c) for the period from 2020 to 2023 for Normal Scenario, (d) for the period from 2024 to 2030 for Normal Scenario, (e) for the period from 2020 to 2023 for Optimal Scenario, and (f) for the period from 2024 to 2030 for the Optimal Scenario.

It is noted that the production model of the Greek economy has in all cases similar behavior: the main growth factor is private consumption (contributes by about 64% to 68% to GDP), followed by public consumption (contributes by about 20% to GDP) and investments (contributes by

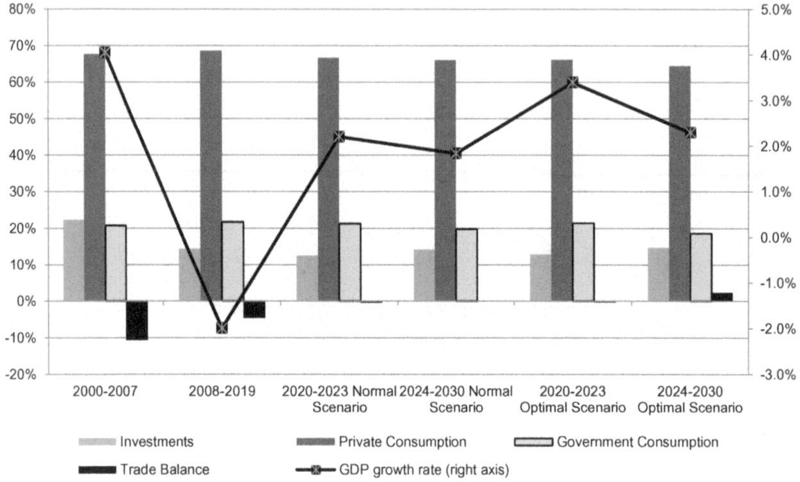

Fig. 12.29 Average annual contribution of the main determinants to GDP (%) (*Source* Oxford Economics [2020] and authors' calculations and creation)

about 15% to GDP). The role of trade balance (net exports) while negative until 2019, becomes zero until 2030 in Normal Scenario and positive during 2024–2030 in Optimal Scenario (contributes by about 2.5% to GDP).

12.8 Investments

Figure 12.30 presents a detailed picture of how investments in the Greek economy have evolved since 1999 and how they are expected to move, under normal circumstances, by 2030. In more detail, the government investments, private investments by business and private investment for dwellings and FDIs (in billion euros) for Normal Scenario are presented.

What is interesting is that, over time, the size and role of the investments of private business remains stable (although declined immediately after the crisis occurred), while at the same time the huge decline suffered by private investment in dwellings from 2008 onwards is evident. Significant, as well, was the shock of the austerity programs to government investment, which declined quite a lot after 2009. It is also evident that the attraction of FDIs to the Greek economy is very low over time and that during the years of the great crisis it was almost zero.

In addition, Fig. 12.31 shows the differences between Normal and Optimal Scenario in terms of investments.

The large differentiation between Normal and Optimal Scenario concerns private business investment. This is a difference that goes from 0.3 billion euros in 2020 to 3.9 billion euros in 2025 and then decreases to 2.8 billion euros by 2030. It thus becomes clear that the improvement of TFP has a direct and greater impact on private business investment. In addition, the inward of Foreign Direct Investments (FDIs) in the Greek economy and private investment in dwellings should be expected to be slightly higher in the Optimal Scenario. Finally, it should be noted that government investments are not affected by the improvement of TFP in the Greek economy.

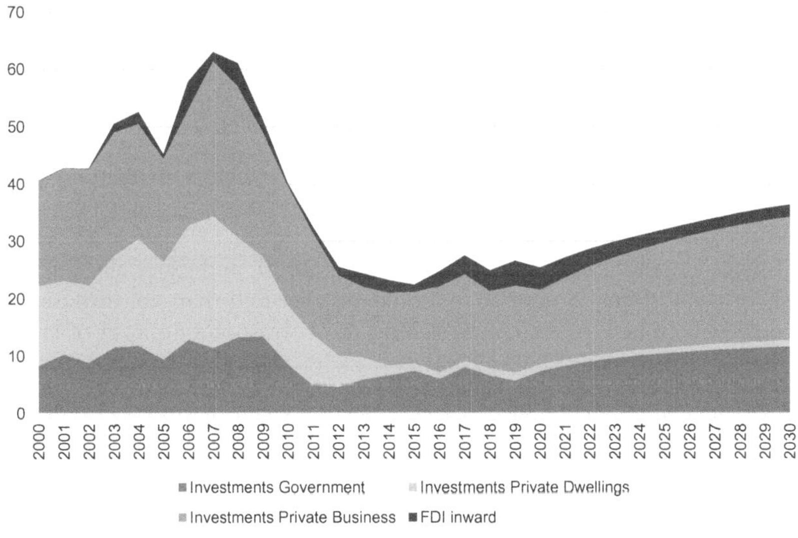

Fig. 12.30 GDP and types of investments (EUR billion, fixed prices 2010) (*Source* Oxford Economics [2020] and authors' calculations and creation)

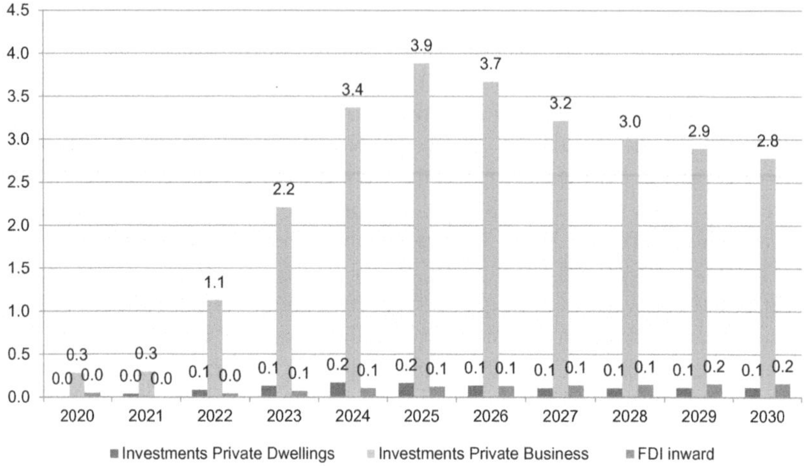

Fig. 12.31 Difference in investments between Optimal and Normal Scenario (*Source* Oxford Economics [2020] and authors' calculations and creation)

12.9 Inclusive Growth

In recent years there have been several improvements in inclusiveness issues in the Greek economy and society. Nevertheless, there are still several challenges that need to be addressed.

Initially, it should be highlighted that by 2030, and especially on the basis of the Optimal Scenario, it should be expected that real disposable income will come closer to approaching the corresponding level of crisis in the Greek economy (Fig. 12.32).

The real disposable income in the case of Optimal Scenario is over time higher than Normal Scenario and by about 123.6 billion euros in 2020 is expected to reach 159.5 billion euros in Normal Scenario and 167.7 billion euros in Optimal Scenario. As a percentage of GDP the real disposable income picture is reversed as GDP in the case of Optimal Scenario increases significantly.

Both the overall savings level of the economy and the savings level of the personal sector are significantly higher in the case of the Optimal Scenario (Figs. 12.33 and 12.34). More specifically, national savings from 21.2 billion euros in 2020 are expected to reach 34.7 billion euros in

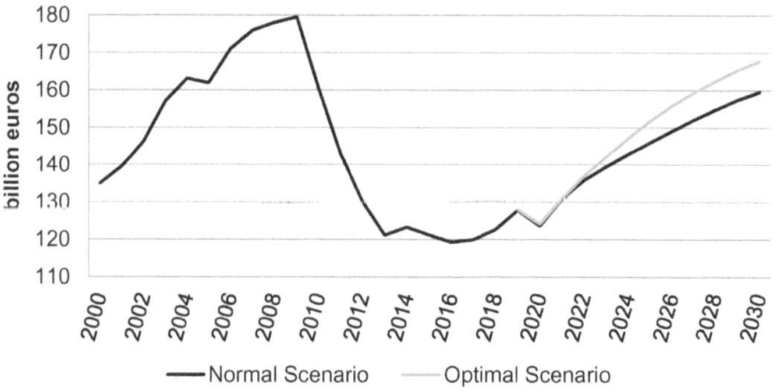

Fig. 12.32 Real disposable income (*Source* Oxford Economics [2020] and authors' calculations and creation)

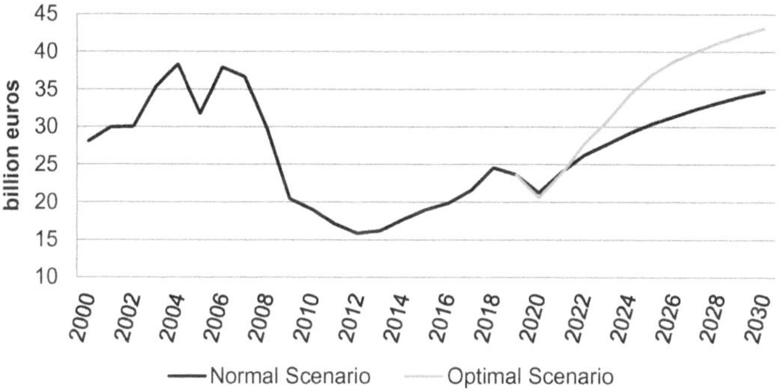

Fig. 12.33 Real national savings (*Source* Oxford Economics [2020] and authors' calculations and creation)

2030 in the Normal Scenario. Similarly, in the Optimal Scenario the national savings from 20.6 billion euros in 2020 are expected to reach 43.1 billion euros in 2030.

This significant improvement in both real income and savings of the Greek economy is expected to have a significant impact on how the Gini index for the Greek economy will evolve (Fig. 12.35).

Of course, the situation in the labor market is expected to significantly improve by 2030, which was also shown in Fig. 12.3 where the expected development for the unemployment rate was presented, but is

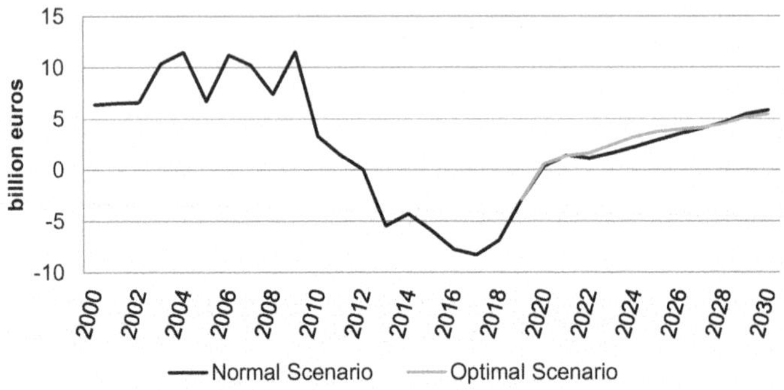

Fig. 12.34 Savings of personal sector (*Source* Oxford Economics [2020] and authors' calculations and creation)

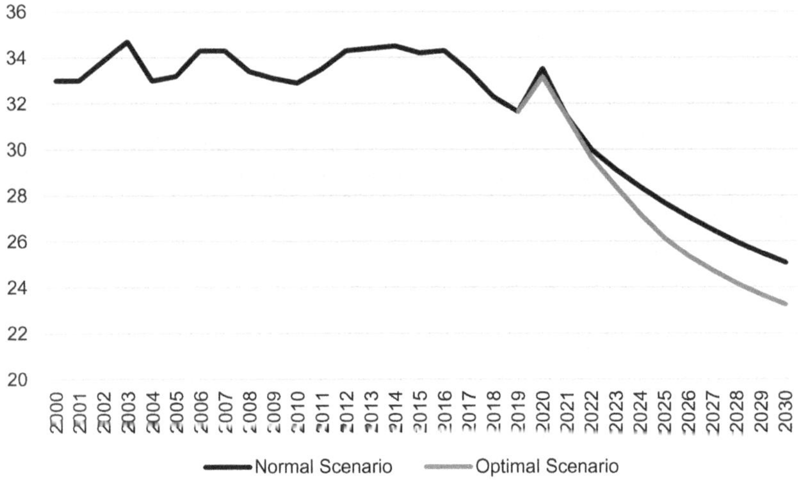

Fig. 12.35 Gini coefficient (scale from 0 to 100) (*Note* The estimates for the evolution of Gini Coefficient after 2020 in the two scenarios are based on the estimates for the change in GDP per capita in the two scenarios, since the relevant literature highlights a high correlation between GDP per capita and Gini Coefficient, above −0.7 [Moatsos et al. 2014]. *Source* Eurostat [2020a], Oxford Economics [2020] and authors' calculations and creation)

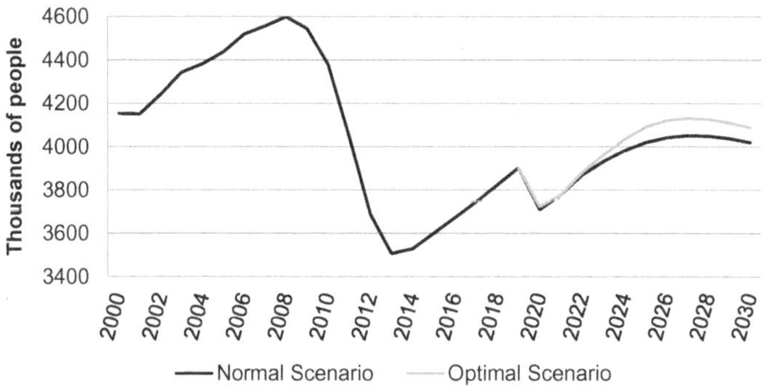

Fig. 12.36 Employment (*Source* Oxford Economics [2020] and authors' calculations and creation)

also shown in Fig. 12.36 where the corresponding expected development for employment is presented.

More specifically, the number of people employed, by about 3.7 million in 2020 is expected to reach 4.05 million in 2027, declining to 4.03 million in 2030 in Normal Scenario. Respectively, in Optimal Scenario the number of employees is expected to reach 4.13 million people in 2027 and to decrease to 4.08 million people in 2030.

This significant increase in the number of employees is expected to be accompanied by a significant decrease in the number of people at risk of poverty or social exclusion (Fig. 12.37), where especially under the Optimal Scenario it should be expected to approach the rate which had before the crisis of the Greek economy.

Finally, Fig. 12.38 indicates the higher level of happiness which should be expected on the basis of Optimal Scenario, in comparison to the Normal Scenario, given that Optimal Scenario expects higher per capita income and better living conditions.

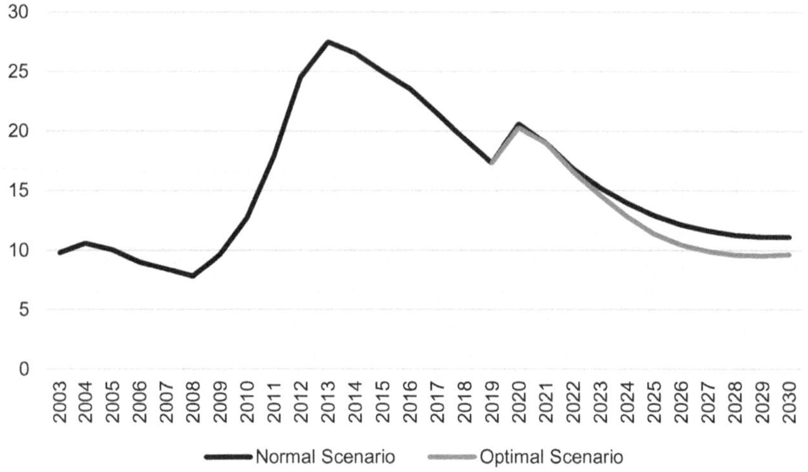

Fig. 12.37 Percentage of people at risk of poverty or social exclusion (*Note* The estimates for the rate of people at risk of poverty or social exclusion after 2020 in the two scenarios are based on the estimates for the change in the unemployment rate in the two scenarios, since there is a high correlation between the rate of unemployment and the rate of people at risk of poverty or social exclusion, of 0.89 for the Greek economy from 2003 to 2018. *Source* Eurostat [2020b], Oxford Economics [2020] and authors' calculations and creation)

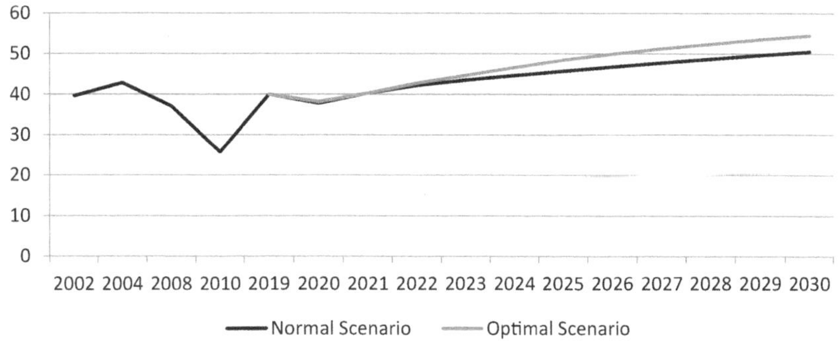

Fig. 12.38 Percentage of population declaring extremely happy (%) (*Note* The estimates of the evolution of the percentage of the population declaring extremely happy [responses from 8 to 10 on the scale from 1 to 10] after 2020 in the two scenarios are based on the estimates of the change in GDP per capita in the two scenarios, since there is a high correlation of 0.77 between happiness and GDP per capita based on World Happiness Report 2019 data [2008–2018 data for 156 countries]. *Source* European Social Survey [2018], Petrakis, Kafka, Kostis, and Valsamis [2021], Oxford Economics [2020] and authors' calculations and creation)

References

European Social Survey. (2018). European Social Survey Cumulative File, ESS 1-8. Data file edition 1.0. NSD—Norwegian Centre for Research Data, Norway—Data Archive and Distributor of ESS Data for ESS ERIC. https://doi.org/10.21338/nsd-ess-cumulative.

Eurostat. (2020a). Gini Coefficient of Equivalised Disposable Income—EU-SILC Survey, ilc_di12 Database.

Eurostat. (2020b). People at Risk of Poverty or Social Exclusion by Age and Sex, ilc_peps01 Database.

Goldman Sachs. (2020). *Banking Union: Risk Reduction Targets, a Meaningful Challenge for Greece* (Equity Report).

Moatsos, M., et al. (2014). Income Inequality Since 1820. In J. van Zanden et al. (Eds.), *How Was Life? Global Well-Being Since 1820*. Paris: OECD Publishing. https://doi.org/10.1787/9789264214262-15-en.

Oxford Economics. (2020). Oxford Economics Global Macro Model.

Petrakis, P. E. (2020). *The New Political Economy of Greece Up to 2030*. New York: Palgrave Macmillan.

Petrakis, P. E., Kafka, K. I., Kostis, P.C., & Valsamis, D. G. (2021). *Greek Culture after the Financial Crisis: An Economic Analysis*. New York: Palgrave Macmillan.

Petrakis, P. E., Kostis, P. C., & Valsamis, D. G. (2013). *European Economics and Politics in the Midst of the Crisis: From the Outbreak of the Crisis to the Fragmented European Federation* (p. 274). New York and Heidelberg: Springer. ISBN 978-3-642-41343-8.

Index

P. E. Petrakis and P. C. Kostis, *The Evolution of the Greek Economy*, The Political Economy of Greek Growth up to 2030,
https://doi.org/10.1007/978-3-030-47210-8

U

W

The manufacturer's authorised representative in the EU is Springer Nature Customer Service Centre GmbH, Europaplatz 3, 69115 Heidelberg, Germany. If you have any concerns regarding our products, please contact ProductSafety@springernature.com

Printed and bound by CPI Group (UK) Ltd, Croydon, CR0 4YY

30/09/2026

02225645-0009